Thorstein Veblen and the Revival of
Free Market Capitalism

Thorstein Veblen and the Revival of Free Market Capitalism

Edited by

Janet T. Knoedler

Bucknell University, USA

Robert E. Prasch

Middlebury College, USA

Dell P. Champlin

Western Washington University, USA

Edward Elgar

Cheltenham, UK • Northampton, MA, USA

Published by
Edward Elgar Publishing Limited
Glensanda House
Montpellier Parade
Cheltenham
Glos GL50 1UA
UK

Edward Elgar Publishing, Inc.
William Pratt House
9 Dewey Court
Northampton
Massachusetts 01060
USA

A catalogue record for this book
is available from the British Library

Library of Congress Cataloguing-in-Publication Data
Thorstein Veblen and the revival of free market capitalism / edited by Janet T. Knoedler, Robert E. Prasch, and Dell P. Champlin.
   p. cm.
   Includes bibliographical references and index.
   1. Free enterprise. 2. Capitalism. 3. Right of property. 4. Democracy. 5. Veblen, Thorstein, 1857–1929. I. Knoedler, Janet T. II. Prasch, Robert E., 1958– III. Champlin, Dell P., 1947–
   HB95.T53 2007
   330.12'2092—dc22

2006035017

ISBN 978 1 84542 540 1

Printed and bound in Great Britain by MPG Books Ltd, Bodmin, Cornwall

Contents

Contributors

Glen Atkinson is Foundation Professor Emeritus in the Department of Economics at the University of Nevada, Reno. He received his Ph. D. in 1968 from the University of Oklahoma. At Nevada, he has served as Chair of the Department of Economics and Associate Dean of the College of Business Administration. He has served as President of the Association for Institutional Thought and the Western Social Science Association. He served as Editor of the *Journal of Economic Issues* from June 2000 until June 2006. In addition to numerous chapters in books, his articles have been published in the *Journal of Economic Issues, American Journal of Economics and Sociology, Inter-American Economic Affairs, Southwestern Journal of Economics, System Dynamics Review, Western Tax Review, The Proceedings of the National Tax Association,* and *The Social Science Journal.* He has directed research projects and written numerous reports for state and local government in Nevada. His main research interest is currently intergovernmental relations, or the effects of political boundaries on economic performance. These regions range from northern Nevada, the member countries of the North American Free Trade Agreement to the European Union. He is currently working to found a Center for Regional Studies at the University of Nevada, Reno, which will focus on northern Nevada.

Dell P. Champlin is Visiting Professor of Economics at Western Washington University in Bellingham. She was formerly Professor of Economics at Eastern Illinois University. Professor Champlin currently teaches Labor Economics, the History of Economic Thought, the Economics of Immigration and Principles of Macroeconomics. She writes frequently with Janet T. Knoedler and has published articles in the *Journal of Economic Issues*, the *Review of Social Economy*, and the *International Journal of Social Economy*. She has served as President of the Association for Institutional Thought and on the Board of Directors for the Association for Evolutionary Economics.

Eric R. Hake began teaching at Eastern Illinois University in 1999. His teaching interests include Economic History, Comparative Economics, and History of Economic Thought. Without much deviation, Hake's research has focused on proof and application of Veblen's theory of the credit economy. His most recent papers address the relevance of Veblen's analysis to the corporate scandal and stock market manipulations of recent years ('Financial Illusion: Accounting for Profits in an Enron World', 2005). He has also applied the credit economy thesis to the consolidation and merger activity in the meatpacking industry ('The Veblenian Credit Economy and the Corporatization of American Meatpacking', 2002, 'Immigration as Industrial Strategy in Meatpacking', 2006). Currently, he is interested in exploring the overlap between the traditional insights of economic anthropology and institutional economics with recent developments in mainstream economic methodology.

David Hamilton is Professor Emeritus at the University of New Mexico, where he still teaches History of Economic Thought. He received his initial training in Economics at the University of Pittsburgh; after service in the Pacific in World War II, he received his Ph. D. from the University of Texas where he studied with Clarence E. Ayres. He is author of many important works in institutional economics, including the classic *Evolutionary Economics* and numerous articles in the *Journal of Economic Issues*. He is a recipient of the Veblen-Commons award from the Association for Evolutionary Economics.

Geoffrey M. Hodgson is Research Professor in Business at the University of Hertfordshire, England. His books include *Economics in the Shadows of Darwin and Marx* (2006), *The Evolution of Institutional Economics* (2004), *How Economics Forgot History* (2001), *Economics and Utopia* (1999), *Economics and Evolution* (1993) and *Economics and Institutions* (1988). He has published over 100 articles in academic journals, as detailed on his website www.geoffrey-hodgson.info

Janet T. Knoedler is Associate Professor of Economics and Chair, Department of Economics, Bucknell University, Lewisburg, Pennsylvania. Professor Knoedler teaches Industrial Organization, Intermediate Political Economy, Economics and Technology, and Principles of Economics. She has written extensively on institutional economics, frequently with the co-editor of this volume, Dell P. Champlin, and her articles have appeared in the *Journal of Economic Issues*, *History of Political Economy*, and *Business History*. She also serves as Secretary–Treasurer for the Association for Evolutionary Economics.

Anne Mayhew is Professor Emerita at the University of Tennessee where she was a member of the faculty in Economics and in History and also served in a variety of administrative roles, most recently as Vice Chancellor for Academic Affairs. She was editor of the *Journal of Economic Issues* from 1991 to 2000. She has published on a variety of topics in US Economic History and the History of Economic Thought, with particular emphasis on Institutional Economics and the work of Thorstein Veblen. Her work has appeared in a number of journals, including the *Journal of Economic History*, *History of Political Economy*, *Business and Economic History*, *Cambridge Journal of Economics*, and the *Journal of Economic Issues*. Two recent articles, 'All Consumption is Conspicuous' and 'Where do Economies Come From?' have appeared in collections of essays edited by Edward Fullbrook.

Sidney Plotkin is Professor of Political Science at Vassar College, where he teaches courses on American Politics, Political Power, Public Policy, and Urban Politics. His research and writing interests currently center on the political ideas of Thorstein Veblen. Mr. Plotkin's books include *Keep Out: The Struggle for Land Use Reform* (California) and *Private Interest, Public Spending* (South End). Professor Plotkin has served as President of the International Thorstein Veblen Association since 2004.

Robert E. Prasch is Associate Professor of Economics at Middlebury College where he has taught since 2000. Previously he was on the faculties of Vassar College, the University of Maine, and San Francisco State University. His areas of research and teaching include the History of Economic Thought, American Economic History and Monetary Economics. He is the author of approximately 80 articles, book chapters and reviews in the *Journal of Economic Issues*, the *Journal of the History of Economic Thought*, the *Review of Political Economy*, the *Review of Social Economy*, the *Journal of Economic Perspectives*, and elsewhere. He is also co-editor, with David Colander and Falguni A. Sheth, of *Race, Liberalism, and Economics* (University of Michigan Press, 2004).

William T. Waller is Professor of Economics and Director of Wine Studies at Hobart and William Smith Colleges where he has taught since 1982. He received his B.S. (1978) and M.A. (1979) in economics from Western Michigan University. He received his Ph. D. in economics from the University of New Mexico (1984). He is past-president of the Association for Evolutionary Economics and the Association for Institutional Thought. He has served as a trustee of the Association for Social Economics, a member of the editorial board of the *Journal of Economic Issues*, and member of the board of directors of the Association for Evolutionary Economics; where he served for a year as acting Secretary–Treasurer. He is currently a trustee of the Association for Evolutionary Economics. He has co-edited two books: *Alternatives to Economic Orthodoxy* (M.E. Sharpe, 1987) and *The Stratified State* (M.E. Sharpe, 1992). His articles on institutionalist methodology, feminist economics, public policy and the work of Thorstein Veblen have been published in *Journal of Economic Issues*, *Review of Social Economy*, *History of Political Economy*, *Review of Institutional Thought* as well as a number of edited collections. He is active in the Association for Evolutionary Economics, the Association for Institutional Thought, the Association for Social Economics and the International Association for Feminist Economics.

Introduction

In the view of the editors and contributors to this volume, and indeed to many modern scholars in a number of disciplines, Thorstein Veblen was a most fascinating and unique American economist. To him also belongs the almost singular distinction of being the author of a classic book that is actually read – albeit, by few of today's economists. Indeed, this lack of influence over today's economics profession is an important anomaly, given his importance in related social sciences such as sociology or marketing. Of course there are intelligible, if indefensible, reasons for this oversight. While the absence of Veblen in today's economics is not the sole subject of the following essays, it may be stated without equivocation that, to the editors and contributors to this book, the neglect of Veblen's work has been to the detriment of American intellectual life, the economics profession, and ultimately to informed discussions of public policy.

The facts of Veblen's early life have often been recounted and for that reason will not be treated here in any detail. Often mentioned is the influence of his upbringing on his later career as a 'non-conformist' scholar and what would today be termed a 'public intellectual'. While each of us undoubtedly has our own personal history that underlies our later outlook and motives in life, in the case of Veblen these speculations too often convey the impression that his life (and thereby) work were simply idiosyncratic to the point that they do not need to be taken seriously. As a consequence the collective, if inadvertent, effect may be to contribute to and indirectly affirm the marginalization of his work both within and without the academy.

Nevertheless for completeness, and in keeping with long-standing practice, let us begin this introduction with a few words concerning Veblen's family background and early education. He was born on 30 July 1857 on a farm in a recently settled area in Wisconsin. His family, like much of his community, was constituted of recent Norwegian immigrants who brought from that nation a strong attachment to the family farm as both a means of earning a living and as the foundation to a broader claim for social status within the community. Veblen, like his older brother Andrew, eschewed the nearby Lutheran college, St Olaf's, in favour of Carleton College, which was further both from home and from the more eastern seaboard in its overall ethos and orientation. At Carleton, in addition to meticulous instruction in the then theologically approved and virtually mandatory Common Sense school of philosophy, Veblen was also exposed to a broadly 'liberal' education that included several courses by a most able and broadly educated young scholar, John Bates Clark. However, according to his most authoritative biographer, Joseph Dorfman, Veblen also had additional, and substantial, intellectual influences. One was his older brother Andrew, with whom he engaged in a study of Old Norse along with some of the sagas and myths written in that language. Additionally, he had the benefit of friendship with a German exile named Pentz who shared his ideas, along with books from his excellent private library. It included, besides Immanuel Kant, some of the greatest social philosophers of the late eighteenth and mid-nineteenth century, including Herbert Spencer, John Stuart Mill, David Hume, Jean-Jacques Rousseau, Thomas Huxley and others (Dorfman, 1934, p. 30).

But these facts of personal biography are inadequate to a full understanding of Veblen. True, most biographers report that he alienated a fair number of the people in his otherwise close-knit immigrant community. The cause appears to be his quick wit, sarcastic manner of speech and lack of religious orthodoxy. These were supplemented by his apparent indifference to the mores and work ethic of the immigrant Norwegian farmer, but there was more to it.[1]

Veblen came of age in the northern Midwest. This fact is not only indicative of some elements of his personality and his apparent reluctance to ingratiate himself with American intellectuals – most of whom were drawn from eastern protestant families with middle class or professional backgrounds. Rather Veblen was raised in the Midwest at a very particular and interesting time in the history of that region and of the nation as a whole. As a young person from a family that valued intellectual and social engagement Veblen was exposed to the discussions and debates surrounding the political and social movements of the nineteenth century that we now call the Grange movement, and its transformation into the broader political movement that we think of as Populism. But this movement had largely peaked and even begun to subside by the time Veblen came of age as a scholar (Veblen published his first scholarly essay in 1891 and his first book in 1899). With hindsight it is now evident that Populism's political energy had largely dissipated with the end of the deep depression of the mid-1890s, and the end of the long deflation of the post-Civil War era.

Veblen's most productive and important years were those during what we now call the Progressive Era, a period that runs from about 1900 to America's entry into World War I in 1917. By contrast to the most influential speakers and leaders of the Populist movement, Progressives were non-radicals in their politics, middle-class in origin, well-educated, and often members of established professions such as law, medicine, engineering and university teaching. To the extent that this fractured movement shared some broad principles, they were that society and social institutions, such as government, business trusts, or urban housing or labour markets, could and should be restructured along the lines that applied science could reveal, and that experts – that is to say, well-educated and civic-minded middle-class professionals such as themselves – should devise, monitor and manage. In short, these principles were anything but the intellectual foundation of a mass political movement. Not surprisingly, even at the height of Progressivism's political influence, the 1912 election, they did not constitute a mass movement. What did exist was a general and widely held outlook or point of view that even an avowed conservative such as Robert Taft felt obliged to adopt.

Thus, to understand Veblen, it must be appreciated that as a youth he came of age in a time and place influenced by the Populist movement, but, intellectually, he came of age during the Progressive era. As a consequence, his thinking shares elements of both, but cannot be located in either. He attended Johns Hopkins, Yale, Cornell and Chicago universities with graduate students and younger faculty who were imbued, or on the cusp of becoming imbued, with the ideals and ethos of Progressivism. But one of Progressivism's attributes was that it was a movement dominated by the young, and many of its leaders and most important figures were a half-generation younger than Veblen. Indeed, he was an important intellectual mentor and inspiration to several of them (Fitzpatrick, 1990, ch. 3; Mitchell, 1936 [1964]; White, 1957, ch. 15). By the early 1900s, on the campuses and in the settlement houses of several major cities, this youthful generation of reformers was beginning to devise ideas and social theories that questioned and at times overturned the *laissez faire* liberalism of the older generation. As an additional influence, many of the leading intellectual figures and activists of the Progressive movement (these were often the same people) looked to Europe, and in particular to Germany for answers. The list of prominent figures who studied political economy in Germany or Zurich is long and includes Florence Kelley, Katharine Davis, Samuel Lindsay, Richard Ely, John Bates Clark, Henry Rogers Seager and W.E.B. DuBois. The exposure of these young and engaged scholars to the intellectual and social milieu of German and Swiss universities was both formative and lasting (Rodgers, 1998, ch. 3; Rutherford, 2000). At a minimum these were places where political economy in the Ricardian tradition, then so dominant in England, was being subjected to severe criticism. The above-named scholars and numerous others returned from Germany confirmed in their belief that society needed its economists to deploy the inductive and empirical methods of science to identify problems and devise solutions to the myriad of problems confronting modern life. Specifically, it was believed that the legal and political institutions that may have been adequate to a largely homogeneous, rural and entrepreneurial economy might be unsuited to one that was modern, multi-ethnic and increasingly urban. This was especially the case for an economy that was becoming increasingly monopolized as a consequence of the tendency of modern manufacturing and transportation technologies to favour large-scale production.

Veblen fits into neither of the above moulds. His writing clearly affirms his disdain for the mass politics of the Populists, especially as they became increasingly nativist and imbued with religious fundamentalism over the first decade of the twentieth century. It is equally evident that he did not subscribe to the ideal of American agrarian life as a fading utopia that had to be recovered and restored. At the same time Veblen did not share the optimism, elitism and eastern Yankee–Protestant outlook that were the undercurrents of so much of Progressive thought and politics (Hofstadter, 1955a).

Yet Veblen's ideas did not appear *ex nihilo.* Intellectually, it is evident that he drew some inspiration and perspective from the ideas, arguments and moral stances of each of these movements. To restate the assertion made above, Veblen belongs to neither and to both of the most important reformist intellectual and political movements of his lifetime. On the one hand, one can find in Veblen the deep distrust of the motivations of big business – the Captains of Industry, as he called them. One can also find a deep distrust of government, and the view that the courts, legislature and several government agencies were, as a matter of course, beholden to these same Captains of Industry (Veblen, 1904 [1978], 1923 [1997]). In sum, Veblen displayed the tendency to nihilism that was a characteristic theme of Populism. But while this tendency is evident, his politics were also much richer than has previously been supposed, as is evident in the important essay by Sidney Plotkin that appears in this volume.

Yet it is clear that it would be an error to characterize Veblen as a Populist. His last book, *Absentee Ownership,* makes it plainly evident that he does not share one of the foundational myths of the Populists: that at some point in its recent past America could be characterized as a wonderful, but now eclipsed, agrarian utopia. He finds the English agricultural tradition, as transferred to the United States, to be rife with land speculation, poor husbandry, sharp trading practices and small-time hustling (Veblen, 1923 [1997]). Certainly this disdain for American farming practices was a perspective that was consistent with the views of the Norwegian immigrant farmers of the community within which he was raised. Moreover, a careful sifting of his views on money suggests that they were, for his time, rather orthodox (that one cannot say the same for his views on credit and capital is evident from Eric Hake's essay below). Moreover, his writings clearly drew upon the attitude of scientific argument, empiricism, and close analytic methods characteristic of the Progressive thinkers. We also see the footprint of the Progressives in his belief that, if society was ever to be reconstituted upon a workable and non-predatory basis, it would have to be accomplished by a group of more or less disinterested experts imbued with a producerist ethic, such as the engineers.

In short, while Veblen clearly was an American thinker in his methods, outlook, perspectives and examples, he also was and remains unique in the sense that his writings defy classification. One unfortunate consequence was a lack of a school of followers, although over the longer run his work inspired, and continues to inspire, many scholars (Mitchell, 1936 [1964]).

VEBLEN'S CONTRIBUTION

The economist Joseph Schumpeter once remarked that intellectuals spend their lifetimes working out the prejudices that they developed over their first 25 years. This was, as so many of his greatest pronouncements were, somewhat overstated, but as a generalization it has an important insight. The most obvious explanation is that, as must be admitted, most intellectuals simply do not change their minds as they age. But, for many of our most original thinkers, there is another reason. Of necessity the most daring and original thinkers must begin their work with a hunch, an intuition or a notion. This is almost obvious in the sense that no genuinely original idea can be born, as was alleged of the goddess Venus, in a completely perfected form. It follows that when an idea is indeed original it will often take a great deal of time to work out the many implications, insights and understandings embedded within it, many of which may not be evident at the moment that the new idea is born. This gestation may take an even longer period of time if there is lack of support, or even resistance, to the new ideas or insights in question – which is typically the case in the history of economic thought, art and music.

Such was also the case for the ideas of Thorstein Veblen whose academic career was notoriously unstable. As will be sketched below, it is evident that he developed many of his more important insights fairly early in his scholarly career. This claim can be confirmed by rereading his (in hindsight poorly titled) first published essay on economics 'Some neglected points in the theory of socialism' (1891). That Veblen considered this to be an important essay is evident from the fact that he included it when he gathered together a collection of a few of his many essays and reviews in *The Place of Science in Modern Civilisation and Other Essays*. In this essay, Veblen presents several criticisms of the theory of socialism, but his arguments had much broader implications. It was these broader themes, and not his criticisms of socialism, that were to become substantially developed in the course of his later writings.

Veblen begins this essay with a criticism of the famous nineteenth century social philosopher Herbert Spencer. In a paper entitled 'From Freedom to Bondage' (1891), Spencer had reiterated his long-standing argument that the modern legal framework of private property and free contract had made the overwhelming majority of people better off, and for that reason socialists and other critics of capitalist arrangements had no grounds for complaint. Veblen accepted the empirical claim, but disputed the conclusion Spencer drew by making a point that would become a signature of his later work: that people conventionally measure their standard of living and thereby their well-being in relative, not absolute, terms. 'The existing system has not made, and does not tend to make, the industrious poor poorer as measured absolutely in means of livelihood; but it does tend to make them relatively poorer, in their own eyes, as measured in terms of comparative economic importance, and, curious as it may seem at first sight, that is what seems to count' (Veblen, 1891, p. 61).

But determining that it was relative, not absolute, levels of wealth that mattered was only the first step in this refutation. Veblen pointed out that our relative standing was important because our primary concern was for our social status. But this could only be assured through a particular process of tasteful display. Here, then, is another suggestive quotation from this early essay:

> It is not enough to possess the talisman of industrial success. In order that it may mend one's good fame efficiently, it is necessary to display it. One does not 'make much of a showing' in the eyes of the large majority of the people whom one meets with, except by unremitting demonstration of ability to pay. That is practically the only means which the average of us have of impressing our respect-ability on the many to whom we are personally unknown, but whose transient good opinion we would so gladly enjoy. (Veblen, 1891, pp. 62–3).

What, to Veblen, was novel about the 'modern system of industry' was not that it had created the human desire for status or the consequent motive to emulation. Rather it was that 'the system of free competition has accentuated this form of emulation, both by exalting the industrial activity of man above the rank which it held under more primitive forms of social organization, and by in great measure cutting off other forms of emulation from the chance of efficiently ministering to the craving for a good fame' (Veblen, 1891, p. 64).

Another fundamental and, with hindsight, prescient issue that Veblen raised in his early critique of Spencer concerned the latter's willingness to reduce the extensive range of all known social systems into his simple duality of systems of 'status' or 'contract'. Spencer simply ignored the possibility of a myriad of in-between points, along with the extensive possibilities for overlap and interchange between these two (to Spencer exclusive) categories. That Veblen was not exaggerating Spencer's position is clearly evident in the following:

> For as fast as the *regime* of contract is discarded the *regime* of status is of necessity adopted. As fast as voluntary co-operation is abandoned compulsory co-operation must be substituted. Some kind of organization labour must have; and if it is not that which arises by agreement under free competition, it must be that which is imposed by authority. (Spencer, 1891, p. 13)

To demonstrate the opposing point, that the economic system is always evolving even after competitive markets are the norm, Veblen pointed to the rise of 'natural monopolies'. Here was a well known and, during this era, troubling example of competitive markets demonstrating a tendency to evolve into another form of economic system, one that would certainly bring about a new social form (Veblen, 1891, pp. 69–70). However, this evolution did not imply that a return to a system of 'status' (in Spencer's terminology) was the only logical consequence. Rather, a new manner of social organization, one that Veblen did not attempt to describe, could be a consequence. In sum, Veblen believed that if one took the idea of evolution seriously, then one also had to reject the notion that the then-current system of 'contract' was the end of history.

EVOLUTIONARY ECONOMICS AND INSTITUTIONS

The theory of evolution, and the multiple efforts that were made to apply it to the social sciences, were important developments in nineteenth and early twentieth century social theory. None of this is to suggest, as innumerable scholars have, that such theorizing had no pernicious effects on ideas and social policy. Some evolutionary ideas, as is well known, were applied in highly irresponsible and often racist ways. But such disastrous applications should not be taken to imply that the notion that societies evolve was simply a false statement. Anyone who reads a history book is struck by both the similarities and the differences between our era and that earlier time. When this occurs, one cannot help but speculate on how things have come to change, or not change, over time. If one begins to think this way, one is soon involved in evolutionary social science.

In its basic, and perhaps most popular formulations, Social Darwinism held that social life was a struggle between and amongst persons (and sometimes races) from which, on average, only the 'fittest' (or most advanced race) would emerge to take the leading positions in society. In this guise, the political economy of Spencer and William Graham Sumner was not only acceptable, but was rather flattering to the newly rich, their retainers, and their kept intellectuals and apologists. It could now be maintained that the rich held their exalted positions as a consequence of their innate superiority. Moreover failure, while undeniably difficult or even devastating to an individual and those persons dependent upon them, was socially beneficial over the longer term. A presumed consequence of individual failure was that society, on average, would be strengthened as people made of 'better stuff' rose to their 'natural positions' of leadership. This theory did have several weaknesses, however. One cause of tremendous consternation at that time was the observation that immigrants, the poor, and racial minorities all had larger families than their presumptive 'betters': established and prominent families of Anglo-Saxon heritage. Anxious public discussions on the subject of 'race-suicide' were often heard at the turn of the century and these were often the voices of elites. Theodore Roosevelt and Charles Francis Adams were among the many prominent citizens who were publicly voicing their concern for the 'future of the race' (Degler, 1991; Hofstadter, 1955b; O'Flaherty and Shapiro, 2004).

By contrast to the Social Darwinists, Veblen proposed a very different conception of evolutionary social science. He was not particularly interested in the evolution of people as a species – indeed, he often stated that many virtual constants could be found, including our need for self-esteem and the tendency to emulation discussed above – rather, he took the position that an evolutionary economics should take as its primary subject the evolution of institutions (Hodgson, 1998). That this interest was established early on is evident in the subtitle of his first book, *The Theory of the Leisure Class: An Economic Study of the Evolution of Institutions* (1899a). By 'institutions' Veblen meant much more than the formal or legal institutions of society such as banks, clubs or corporations – rather, he wished to broaden the understanding of institutions by thinking of them as the 'habits of thought' or 'common sense of the community' that constituted the norms and conventions of society.

> The evolution of social structure has been a process of natural selection of institutions. The progress which has been and is being made in human institutions and in human character may be set down, broadly, to a natural selection of the fittest habits of thought and to a process of enforced adaptation of individuals to an environment which has progressively changed with the growth of the

community and with the changing institutions under which men have lived. (Veblen, 1899a, ch. 8; see also Daugert, 1950, ch. 2)

In light of Veblen's understanding that the proper subject of evolution was a study of the evolution of institutions, it is now evident why he thought that Spencer had made a fundamental error when he attempted to build an evolutionary theory of social science while simultaneously presuming that the conventional Anglo-Saxon understanding of property and contract was somehow eternally fixed. It was Veblen's intention to address this error while retaining Spencer's core insight: that social science needed to escape its static conceptions. This latter tendency was an error that Veblen associated with almost the entirety of economic thought from the Physiocrats to the Classical economists, the Marxists and the marginalists, whom he was the first to give the name 'Neoclassical Economists'. That this latter school included his former undergraduate professor, John Bates Clark, was not a consideration that induced him to restrain his criticism (Veblen, 1899b, 1899c, 1900, 1906a, 1906b, 1907).

To Veblen, then, the proper subject of an evolutionary economics was to be institutions. He wished to know what they were, how they functioned, and how they evolved over time. He was interested in how institutions and culture evolved in ways that enabled different groups of persons, Americans of English heritage, the German nation or the Jews of Europe, to succeed or not. His answers were based upon an examination of the economic and social institutions and structures of their societies, and the effects of day-to-day lived experiences on these institutions and the consequences for society. By contrast to the Social Darwinists, he remained substantially less interested in evolutionary theories that theorized about hereditary or genetic effects on the aptitudes or dispositions of different individuals or races.

CONCLUSION

The essays that follow will review, re-examine and comment upon the subjects that Veblen examined, and consider how his evolutionary theory of the economy and society can continue to inform our understanding of the modern world. Consumption, the legal system, finance and capital, the operations of markets, neoclassical economics, private property, business enterprise, cultural and economic change, the place of science, the good society, and higher education will each and severally be subjects of study. We hope that these essays will shed light on our present system and its likely trends, through a re-examination of a similar system as it was interpreted by an astute and highly capable observer.

NOTE

1. Of course, when recounting the impressions of Veblen's neighbours we must be conscious of the tendency of most people, then and today, to consider reading and study to be leisure activities (unless they are pursued for the express and limited purpose of obtaining a specific certification such as a degree). Hence the general impression that Veblen was 'lazy' is consistent with the fact that he devoted a tremendous amount of time to his studies.

REFERENCES

Daugert, Stanley Matthew (1950), *The Philosophy of Thorstein Veblen*, New York: King's Crown Press.

Degler, Carl (1991), *In Search of Human Nature: The Decline and Revival of Darwinism in American Social Thought*, New York: Oxford University Press.

Dorfman, Joseph (1934), *Thorstein Veblen and His America*, New York: Viking Press.

Fitzpatrick, Ellen (1990), *Endless Crusade: Women Social Scientists and Progressive Reform*, New York: Oxford University Press.

Hodgson, Geoffrey, M. (1998), 'On the evolution of Thorstein Veblen's evolutionary economics', *Cambridge Journal of Economics*, **22**, 415–31.

Hofstadter, Richard (1955a), *The Age of Reform: From Bryan to F.D.R.*, New York: Vintage.

Hofstadter, Richard (1955b), *Social Darwinism in American Thought*, rev. edn, Boston: Beacon.

Mitchell, Wesley Clair (1936), 'Introduction', in W.C. Mitchell (ed.) (1964), *What Veblen Taught: Selected Writings of Thorstein Veblen*, New York: A.M. Kelley.

O'Flaherty, Brendan and Jill Shapiro (2004), 'Apes, essences, and races: what natural scientists believed about human variation, 1700–1900', in David Colander, Robert E. Prasch and Falguni A. Sheth (eds), *Race, Liberalism and Economics*, Ann Arbor, MI: University of Michigan Press.

Rodgers, Daniel T. (1998), *Atlantic Crossings: Social Politics in a Progressive Age*, Cambridge, MA: Harvard University Press.

Rutherford, Malcolm (2000), 'Understanding institutional economics, 1918–1929', *Journal of the History of Economic Thought*, **22**(3) (September), 277–308.

Spencer, Herbert (1891), 'From freedom to bondage', Introduction to Thomas MacKay, *A Plea for Liberty: An Argument Against Socialism and Socialistic Legislation*, New York: D. Appleton and Company.

Veblen, Thorstein (1891), 'Some neglected points in the theory of socialism', *Annals of the American Academy of Political and Social Science*, **2** (November), 57–74.

Veblen, Thorstein (1899a), *The Theory of the Leisure Class: An Economic Study of the Evolution of Institutions*, New York: Macmillan.

Veblen, Thorstein (1899b), 'The preconceptions of economic science I', *Quarterly Journal of Economics* (January), 121–50.

Veblen, Thorstein (1899c), 'The preconceptions of economic science II', *Quarterly Journal of Economics* (July), 396–426.

Veblen, Thorstein (1900), 'The preconceptions of economic science III', *Quarterly Journal of Economics* (January), 240–69.

Veblen, Thorstein (1904 [1978]), *The Theory of Business Enterprise*, New Brunswick, NJ: Transaction Publishers.

Veblen, Thorstein (1906a), 'Professor Clark's economics', *Quarterly Journal of Economics* (February), 147–95.

Veblen, Thorstein (1906b), 'Socialist economics of Karl Marx and his followers I'. *Quarterly Journal of Economics* (August), 578–95.

Veblen, Thorstein (1907), 'Socialist economics of Karl Marx and his followers II', *Quarterly Journal of Economics* (February), 299–322.

Veblen, Thorstein (1923 [1997]), *Absentee Ownership: Business Enterprise in Recent Times: The Case of America*, New Brunswick, NJ: Transaction Publishers.

White, Morton (1957), *Social Thought in America: The Revolt Against Formalism,* Boston: Beacon Press.

1. The place of science in society: progress, pragmatism, pluralism

Anne Mayhew

Science has been the source of massive improvement in the lives of a significant portion of mankind over the past 200 years. It is indisputable that science-based medicine, machines and knowledge of the natural world have made it possible to feed more people who survive longer, travel further and know more about the world they inhabit. And yet numerous polls show that, even in the US, where scientific endeavor has been well supported and where its benefits have been widely shared for decades, science is not held in high esteem by a large portion of the population. As long ago as 1980, Philip Handler wrote in *Science* on 'Public Doubts about Science', and over the quarter century since, public attacks on science have become more common. Throughout the world, and no less so in the US, even in those regions of the country widely thought to be the most secular, there has been an apparent turn to religious belief as a substitute for or an antidote to secular science. The possibility of peaceful coexistence between science and religion seems less certain today than it did half a century ago, and political attack on scientific evidence has become more acceptable. The place of science in society is in doubt.

In 1906, Thorstein Veblen published an essay entitled 'The place of science in modern civilisation', in the *American Journal of Sociology*, and in 1908 he followed this with the closely related 'The evolution of the scientific point of view', a paper delivered to the Kosmos Club at Berkeley and published in the *University of California Chronicle* (Veblen, 1906 [1990]; 1908 [1990]). Joseph Dorfman tells us that Veblen regarded the first of these articles as his best (Dorfman, 1934 [1972], p. 260). Both repay attention today, and especially so as events of the second half of the twentieth century and the early years of the twenty-first century have heightened the importance of the issues about which Veblen wrote.

TWENTY-FIRST CENTURY MULTICULTURALISM AND SCIENCE

Over the course of the twentieth century the idea that all people should be accorded, not only equality of opportunity, but also respect for their biological and cultural heritages, has come into increasing conflict with a growing intolerance for the traditions of others. Somewhat ironically, this intolerance has accompanied, and perhaps been at least partially caused, by the growing economic and political integration that has also characterized this period. As people of quite different ethnic and racial backgrounds have come to be in close and continuing contact, what were once academic issues of cultural relativism have become real and difficult. It is also the case that discussion and action in the troubled arena of multicultural contact have been made even more difficult by the reality that the technology and science that offer solutions to basic human problems throughout the planet have, to date, reached their highest levels of development in the nations of Europe or of European heritage. Even in the Asian nations that are now seen as economic and scientific threats to Western supremacy, scientific pursuit and 'Westernization' are most often seen as synonymous.

Readers with a knowledge of the history of science will be quick to point out that many of the basic concepts of mathematics and early scientific and technological achievement came originally out of India and China, but over the last century and a half modern science has in large measure been an accomplishment of the West. Further, the apparent superiority of Western science has often been used to assert a superiority of other aspects of Western societies as well, thereby directly challenging the ideals of pluralism.[1] Even among those Westerners who have been reticent to claim general superiority, the obvious advantages of science and technology closely associated with Western nations have produced difficult dilemmas, dilemmas that have practical as well as intellectual consequences. How far should a US physician, practicing medicine in a highly patriarchal country, go in insisting on care for women and children when such care may necessarily trespass concepts of appropriate modesty of women and of male rights over both women and children? What happens in a situation where the technological requirements of a complex construction job contravene local concepts of on-the-job authority and control? To what extent and how should religious authority be challenged by health care officials when religious prohibitions against, let us say inoculations, threaten the health of a large group? Do the representatives of nations donating food to displaced or otherwise threatened populations have the right or responsibility to override, perhaps by force, local authorities in food distribution. These, and many similar dilemmas, arise not only across national boundaries but within diverse nations as well.

Perhaps there was a time in the middle of the twentieth century when confidence in science and technology, and in our ability to derive and deliver their benefits in a largely acultural way, made the moral dilemmas inherent in interactions of people of different cultures and unequal technological achievements seem easily manageable. Perhaps. But as concern about the cultural embeddedness of science, and the loss of faith in the benign effects of technological change, have grown, it has become harder to deal confidently with these dilemmas.

We now recognize that scientific investigation is driven, at least in part, by differential power among human groups and by cultural bias. The diseases of rich nations receive more attention than the diseases of the poor. The nature and maintenance of soils of rich nations are more likely to be investigated than are those of poorer areas. We have also become aware of the dangers of new technologies. Dams designed to provide irrigation water and prevent floods can harm the biosphere of adjacent regions in devastating ways. Pharmaceuticals that prevent diseases in animals, or increase their output for human consumption, may affect human health and reproduction. Genetic modification of plants may have both good effects and unintended and harmful consequences.

Even as we have become wary of science and technology, and suspicious of the inevitability of progress, the moral and political dilemmas that have resulted from the increased availability of their fruits have also multiplied and have done so in a world in which many more people seem driven to find solutions to human problems in the non-scientific (but equally human and real) arenas of religion and mysticism. The turn to religious fundamentalism that is apparent in many parts of the world has come as a shocking surprise to many social scientists who, over the twentieth century, came to believe that the scientific method could and would replace supernatural accounts of human interaction and change.

What, then, did Veblen say about the place of science in society? Are his early twentieth-century essays still relevant today?

VEBLEN ON THE PLACE OF SCIENCE IN SOCIETY

The essence of Veblen's argument was that modern science, meaning in Veblen's terms the search for a non-animistic and impersonal cause and affect in nature, had become, by the first decade of the twentieth century and in many Western societies, the final arbiter of truth. As the development of modern science was hastened by the technological changes of the Industrial

Revolution, and with the ascension of science to being the best and final test of validity, the effect was to create feedback upon the technological processes themselves, thereby elevating science to even greater importance, and speeding further development of technology. In Veblen's view there had been nothing inevitable about this process but it was a process that could be accounted for in a scientific manner, and this is what he attempted.

Veblen begins 'The place of science' with the statement: 'It is commonly held that modern Christendom is superior to any and all other systems of civilised life' (Veblen, 1906 [1990], p. 1).[2] He immediately notes that this is 'not an all-around superiority', but one 'within a closely limited range of intellectual activities, while outside this range many other civilisations surpass that of the modern occidental peoples'. But the advantage, says Veblen, of the 'modern occidental peoples' is a practical advantage which means that '[Christendom] has proved itself fit to survive in a struggle for existence as against those civilisations which differ from it in respect of its distinctive traits' (Veblen, 1906 [1990], p. 1).

The most distinctive trait of 'Christendom' is that 'modern, civilised peoples are in a peculiar degree capable of an impersonal, dispassionate insight into the material facts with which mankind has to deal' (Veblen, 1906 [1990], p. 1). Unfortunately, this sentence may appear to grant a superior intelligence to 'modern civilised people' but it becomes clear that this is not what Veblen means. He says that, in other areas, such as 'creative art, handicraft, folklore, occult symbolism, metaphysical insight, dialectical versatility, unsparing faith, and political finesse, other peoples surpass their modern occidental brethren'.[3] It is only in science and technology that 'modern civilised people' have an advantage, but a powerful advantage it is. And how did this advantage come to exist?

Veblen's account, put simply, is this. All humankind has a proclivity to manipulate nature and to use the natural world for its own purposes. The dominance of science emerged in one biological/cultural context because of an evolutionary process based on nothing more than the development of that proclivity in an accidentally conducive climate. Veblen was at pains to base his conclusions on the then most current biological and psychological understanding, an understanding that attributed this proclivity to the biological/psychological character of the human animal. During Veblen's lifetime as a scholar there was a revolution in the way that psychologists and other social scientists, as well as many philosophers, conceived human action and knowledge.[4] 'Knowledge,' Veblen noted, had come to be perceived by then current psychologists, including John Dewey and the other pragmatists, to be 'functional'. This, says Veblen, is 'a corollary under the main postulate of the latter-day psychologists, whose catchword is that The Idea is essentially active' (Veblen, 1906 [1990], p. 5).

For Veblen the individual human was an 'agent' who responds to stimuli in a way that has 'teleological character' (Veblen, 1906 [1990], p. 6). That is, humans take action in a purposeful manner to achieve specified ends. It was at this point in his argument that Veblen added a new and very important element to his list of fundamental human characteristics or instincts, an element that he called 'idle curiosity'. In what he called an 'outlying chain' of manipulation and reasoning, humans, even as they were manipulating nature to achieve specific goals, were also idly seeing what would happen if they did something different. It was this idle curiosity that formed the driver of the 'unteleological natural selection' that has changed human societies through time. To put it simply, as humans manipulate their world to achieve goals (pragmatic ends in Veblen's words), they also, to use a currently colloquial phrase, 'mess around,' and they make up stories to explain why what happens happens.

> This idle curiosity formulates its response to stimulus, not in terms of an expedient line of conduct, nor even necessarily in a chain of motor activity, but in terms of the sequence of activities going on in the observed phenomena. The 'interpretation' of the facts under the guidance of this idle curiosity may take the form of anthropomorphic or animistic explanations of the 'conduct' of the objects observed. (Veblen, 1906 [1990], p. 7)

What kind of stories serve to satisfy the idle curiosity that runs alongside the manipulation of the material world? For 'savage and barbarian peoples'[5] the explanations formed the myths and legends that we still read as classics of human literature. The life-stories of gods, giants and other special beings explain the natural world in this domain.

As pragmatic and everyday knowledge accumulated and the means of livelihood changed from hunting and gathering to settled agricultural and pastoral ways of life, the stories also changed. Drawing on the accepted accounts of unilinear human evolution of his day, Veblen described a transformation from 'peaceable life with sporadic predation to a settled scheme of predaceous life' and a 'higher barbarian culture' in which the 'tests of theoretical validity' that would serve idle curiosity were 'those of graded dignity, authenticity, and dependence'. 'The laws of nature were perceived to be those imposed by an all-powerful Providence, with a view to the maintenance of his own prestige' (1906 [1990], p. 11). What is important in this account is not the details of Veblen's understanding of how ancient myth and legend gave way to alchemy and astrology in the latter stage, and to newer 'dramatizations' more consistent with the socioeconomic structure that evolved with changing technology. What is important is to understand that Veblen saw the adequacy of the stories that people made for themselves as always judged against precepts that derived from their ways of dealing with the natural environment.[6] As these ways changed, so did the standards for judging their stories. And, for Veblen, modern science is simply another set of stories, though a set with a powerful difference.

> The changes in the cultural situation which seem to have had the most serious consequences for the methods and animus of scientific inquiry are those changes that took place in the field of industry. [(Note: Veblen had attributed earlier changes to evolving agriculture and pastoral practices which he contrasts with 'industry' or what we today might call craft and industrial manufacturing.) 'Industry] is the characteristic trait of the modern culture, very much as exploit and fealty were the characteristic traits of the earlier time'. (Veblen, 1906 [1990], p. 13)

Early modern industry was, as Veblen notes, about workmanship and 'Workmanship gradually supplanted differential dignity as the authoritative canon of scientific truth, even on the higher levels of speculation and research' (Veblen, 1906 [1990], p. 14).

> The deity, from having been in medieval times primarily a suzerain concerned with the maintenance of his own prestige, becomes primarily a creator engaged in the workmanlike occupation of making things useful for man. His relation to man and the natural universe is no longer primarily that of a progenitor, as it is in the lower barbarian culture, but rather that of a talented mechanic. The 'natural laws' which the scientists of that era make so much of are no longer decrees of a preternatural legislative authority, but rather details of the workshop specifications handed down by the master-craftsman for the guidance of handicraftsmen working out his design. (Veblen, 1906 [1990], pp. 14–15)

But the craftsmen were gradually replaced by machines and with that came another shift in the tests of validity that could satisfy the idle curiosity that for mankind runs alongside purposeful manipulation of nature. As this has happened, says Veblen, 'latter-day theories of the scientists appear highly opaque, impersonal, and matter-of-fact' and 'the run of causation unfolds itself in an unbroken sequence of cumulative change' (Veblen, 1906 [1990], p. 16). Although the impetus, the idle curiosity that leads to new events and their explanation, remains the same for the modern scientist as for the story teller of old, the two processes, the pragmatic manipulation of nature and the story telling, converge and with often dramatic results. To use Veblen's words again:

> In so far as touches the aims and the animus of scientific inquiry, as seen from the point of view of the scientist, it is a wholly fortuitous and insubstantial coincidence that much of the knowledge gained under machine-made canons of research can be turned to practical account. Much of this knowledge is useful, or may be made so, by applying it to the control of the processes in which natural forces are engaged. This employment of scientific knowledge for useful ends is technology, in the broad sense in which the term includes, besides the machine

industry proper, such branches of practice as engineering, agriculture, medicine, sanitation, and economic reforms. The reason why scientific theories can be turned to account for these practical ends is not that these ends are included in the scope of scientific inquiry. These useful purposes lie outside the scientist's interest. It is not that he aims, or can aim, at technological improvements. His inquiry is as 'idle' as that of the Pueblo myth-maker. But the canons of validity under whose guidance he works are those imposed by the modern technology, through habituation to its requirements, and therefore his results are available for the technological purpose. (Veblen, 1906 [1990], pp. 16–17)

It may be useful to step back at this point in our argument and remember that, when Veblen wrote these words, sponsored science, whether paid for by private business or by governments, was in its infancy. There had been earlier and important government subvention of particular projects but the regular employment of scientists and engineers in laboratories designed to produce new products or new ways of producing products was still quite new. What Veblen saw, therefore, was a convergence of science and technology that was still in its early stages.

In the early twenty-first century it seems odd and wrongheaded to say, as Veblen did, that 'useful purposes lie outside the scientist's interest'. Today's scientists are most often at pains to persuade government agencies, universities and firms of the practicality of their work. Indeed, without the grants and other forms of patronage, few scientists would remain employed. For better or worse, much of this support comes from institutions or organizations run by committees or private investors that have to 'account' for their expenses; this is most readily accomplished if tangible results are the product, or at least the proximate target, of research. Happily, young scientists are often drawn to their work by a desire to find a cure for cancer, or develop lightweight and strong materials for safer automobiles, or any number of other highly pragmatic ends. Do the obviously pragmatic quests of modern science undermine the validity of Veblen's claim that the inquiries of the scientist are as idle as those of the Pueblo myth-maker? Can we possibly entertain seriously the notion that the scientific theories that result are on a par with the stories of the myth-maker?

There are other reasons as well why Veblen's account in 'The place of science' and in 'The evolution of the scientific point of view' seems misguided. His history of mankind is drawn in overly broad terms that now seem antiquated. His focus is Eurocentric. He was, as he himself said in 'The scientific point of view', putting forth a circular argument, for he was attempting to explain the rise of science and its place in modern science in scientific terms. And, even if we use time and place to soften criticism of Veblen, and even if his arguments are reasonably correct, how do they help us respond to the dilemmas posed at the beginning of this chapter?

MOKYR ON SCIENCE AND TECHNOLOGY

Before turning to this last question I propose comparing Veblen's analysis to recent work on the place of science in society. It will be particularly useful to do so using work of the late twentieth and early twenty-first centuries that is not 'Veblenian' in intent or by attribution. Some, such as Clarence Ayres, and several of his followers, have written works that follow Veblen and argue quite passionately for the correctness and relevance of his vision. But, critics will rightly say, this body of work shows little other than that Veblen's ideas, or variations on them, can be used to build satisfying accounts. What we need for a good test are works that do not begin in tribute to Veblen.

The work of Joel Mokyr, an economic historian who has written two important books on science and modern society, *The Lever of Riches* (1990) and *The Gifts of Athena* (2002), provides material for such a test. There is a brief reference to Veblen in a footnote in *The Lever of Riches* and Veblen's *The Instinct of Workmanship* is cited in the bibliography, but these are clearly not works written to validate Veblen's assertions about science and technology. In that sense they provide a test (and a rigorous one), for Mokyr's work is of the highest standards.

Mokyr's works are also among the very few that deal with a substantial range of human history in order to examine the role that science and technology have played over time in economic change. There are many accounts of technological change and scientific advance in specific industries and many more that provide theoretical investigations of innovation. But there are few that deal in any detailed way with the growth over a long period of time of what Mokyr calls 'useful knowledge'.[7]

In *The Gifts of Athena*, Mokyr posits two kinds of knowledge that come together to provide this 'useful knowledge' where useful knowledge is that which can be translated into economic production. The first type, 'propositional knowledge', forms an epistemic base for 'prescriptive knowledge' which can be used for 'production'. It does no harm to Mokyr's definitions to say that 'propositional knowledge' is what Veblen called 'science' and 'prescriptive knowledge' is what he called 'technology'.

In both *The Lever of Riches* and *The Gifts of Athena*, Mokyr's main task is to account for economic growth and, in both books, technological change, which is to say technological creativity, is accorded the place of honor in this search. Both books contain detailed accounts of technological change, accounts that often have 'no famous inventors, just an endless succession of anonymous improvements on the margin' (Mokyr, 2002, p. 63). But simply telling the story of technological change does not answer the question that Mokyr wants to answer, which is how to account for the differential rates of technological change in various parts of the world at various times, and particularly how to account for the speed and spread of technological change in the West over the last two centuries.

It is this quest that takes Mokyr directly to the analysis that parallels Veblen's efforts. What Mokyr focuses on in *The Lever of Riches* (Mokyr, 1990, pp. 167–86) is the relationship of scientific ideas and knowledge to the creation of new technology. His description of the relationship is equivocal, in part because he finds it difficult to draw the line between the two realms, but also because, as often as not, technology aided science rather than scientific discovery leading to technological change. This confounds the common expectation and certainly makes it more difficult to argue that *mentalities*, or attitudes of mind and ideas, are the leading factor in long-term growth.[8] What Mokyr does find evidence for is the proposition that, after around 1850, in the United Kingdom, the US and many parts of Western Europe, science became more important than it had previously been in leading technological change. This thesis is central to his later book, *The Gifts of Athena.*

Here, briefly stated, is Mokyr's thesis in this later work. Before around 1800 much technological progress was what he calls a change in 'singleton techniques' that emerged as the result of 'serendipitous discoveries'.

> Although new techniques appeared before the Industrial Revolution, they had narrow epistemic bases and thus rarely if ever led to continued and sustained improvements. At times these inventions had enormous practical significance, but progress usually fizzled out after promising beginnings. (Mokyr, 2002, p. 19)

As he would have to, given the rich documentation that he provides in *The Lever of Riches,* Mokyr does acknowledge that 'pure singleton techniques were rare' in the more distant past and serendipity still works (Mokyr, 2002, p. 19). However it does appear that there was a change in the middle of the nineteenth century, with 'singleton techniques' increasingly rare and serendipity less important.

What makes Mokyr's argument that the relationship between science and technology changed during the nineteenth century most impressive is his catalog of the feedback mechanisms that developed. In industry after industry organized scientific investigation became important. Firms began to look to science for assistance in production, and to that end supported laboratories and scientists charged with answering questions of importance for their industrial products.[9] Firms and agencies also began using the focus provided by technology to pose questions that led to the growth of propositional knowledge or science. Mokyr cites as the classic examples the 'emergence of thermodynamics as an endogenous response to theoretical problems posed by the operation of the steam engine and the work on electricity stimulated by the problems of long-distance telegraphy' (Mokyr, 2002, p. 96).

Another example is provided by the role that problems in the canning of food had on the development of bacteriology. In all of these cases new technologies led to new science and the feedback led to improved technology.

An additional feedback mechanism was generated by the development of equipment and instruments made possible by technological change. As Mokyr notes, at an earlier time, improvements in lens grinding led to the telescope and other instruments of science. Although the widespread use of glass may have come about as a by-product of the demand for wine, the use of glass and the development of precision grinding had profound impacts upon scientists' ability to evaluate ideas. New techniques of manipulating matter led to possibilities for further exploration of matter and that, in turn, often led to new techniques. Again, what changed in the course of the nineteenth century was the move away from science pursued as a hobby by leisured gentlemen or pursued by government agents as a sideline, to an organized and supported activity that made use of specialized equipment.

Finally, Mokyr suggests that a third feedback mechanism came through a change in 'rhetoric'.

> . . . techniques are not 'true' or 'false.' Either they work or they do not, and thus they confirm or refute the propositional knowledge that serves as their epistemic base. . . . Laboratory technology transforms conjecture and hypothesis into an accepted fact, ready to go into textbooks and to be utilized by engineers, physicians, or farmers. (Mokyr, 2002, p. 100)

In short, a 'cascading interaction' between propositional knowledge, or science, and prescriptive knowledge, or technological knowledge, has created a standard for 'truth' that is itself part of the technological process.

Writing almost 100 years after Veblen, Mokyr's account supports Veblen's. Technology and science have fed upon each other to change not only the way we live but the way we think about living.

SCIENCE, PROGRESS AND PRAGMATISM REVISITED

In Veblen's treatment, modern science is simply a continuation of mankind's efforts to account for the patterns observed in nature manipulated both by purposeful action and by the actions of idle curiosity. Scientific explanation has no claim for absolute or timeless authority to truth, for in Veblen's work (both in his essays of 1906, 1908 and later) there can be no such truth claims. There can only be claims against whatever standards of final validity have been produced by the idle curiosity of the time. All human standards of finality are subject to change and there is no universal or immutable standard to which we may appeal.

At the conclusion of his essay on 'The place of science' Veblen speculated about what might happen as science assumed a more important role as the standard of finality.

> But while the scientist's spirit and his achievements stir an unqualified admiration in modern men, and while his discoveries carry conviction as nothing else does, it does not follow that the manner of man which this quest of knowledge produces or requires comes near answering to the current ideal of manhood, or that his conclusions are felt to be as good and beautiful as they are true. The ideal man, and the ideal of human life, even in the apprehension of those who most rejoice in the advances of science, is neither the finikin skeptic in the laboratory nor the animated slide-rule. The quest of science is relatively new. . . . The [human] race reached the human plane with little of this searching knowledge of facts; and throughout the greater part of its life-history on the human plane it has been accustomed to make its higher generalisations and to formulate its larger principles of life in other terms than those of passionless matter-of-fact. This manner of knowledge has occupied an increasing share of men's attention in the past, since it bears in a decisive way upon the minor affairs of workday life; but it has never until now been put in the first place, as the dominant note of human culture. The normal man, such as his inheritance has made him, has therefore good cause to be restive under its dominion. (Veblen, 1906 [1990], pp. 30–31)

This was written 100 years ago. In 2007, however, it does seem that Veblen may have been prescient in thinking that the 'normal man' might become restive as science became more important. Certainly science has in many ways been put in 'the first place, as the dominant note of human culture' and it is this dominance that has come increasingly under question and attack.

The trends in acceptance of science since Veblen wrote have been both intertwined and yet conflicting. On the one hand, the pragmatists of Veblen's era foresaw the possibility that humans would learn to live with 'passionless matter-of-fact' explanations of all aspects of life. The promise of social science in the first half of the twentieth century was based firmly on the proposition that enlightened mankind would come to see that human cultures are the creations of mankind and would modify those cultures in the interests of both individual and species longevity (Mayhew, 1981). New technologies would be used to usher in the good life.

This quasi-utopian vision of the brighter future that would emerge with the dominance of technology and its hand-maiden science was strongest among economists in the American institutionalist tradition such as Marc Tool (2000) and Thomas DeGregori (1985) who cast Veblen's doubts and uncertainty about the future aside in favor of a technocratic vision. Continued human progress was not only definable and achievable, but virtually inevitable.

However, even among economists who were not so persuaded by the promise of technocratic society, there was considerable optimism about a more 'rational future'. Joseph Schumpeter was one who thought that the convergence of science and technology was itself both a consequence and a cause of a spreading appreciation among humans of a supracultural rationality, where rationality is defined as deliberate choice among alternatives arrayed according to a common standard of measurement. This is the commercial rationality that Schumpeter identified as product of the development of money as a numeraire and of the related emergence of the creative destruction of capitalism (Schumpeter, 1950, ch. XI). This view of the 'scientific' promise of economics has run through much of the optimism about economic development over recent decades. Armed with appropriate cost/benefit models, people can make rational choices, obtain the appropriate technologies and move into a better place.

What has gone wrong with these intertwined visions for a better future? It is certainly not the case that science has lost its claim as the final test of validity. Indeed, the approach of science has pervaded our languages and cultures so thoroughly that even those in opposition to the truths that most scientists support seek to frame their own arguments in the language of science. As I write this essay, proponents of 'intelligent design' as an alternative to evolutionary biology argue that their own approach is more scientific. And the social science journals are filled with mathematical notations that serve to disguise logical deductions made in closed systems as scientific discovery and proof. The idea of science reigns, even to the extent that attacks upon scientific truth must themselves take apparent scientific form. And yet, more and more people have come to doubt that science deserves the wide arena that it has been given in Western societies through much of the twentieth century. Veblen saw that 'modern Christendom' enjoyed superiority only in 'a fairly narrow range of intellectual activity'. As the hegemony of science in Western society expanded it has become more difficult for Westerners to see the limits of that range. Among aid officials, economic and political advisors, military personnel, missionaries and other emissaries of the West, humility in offering the advantages of modern science and technology has too often been replaced by a certainty that Western superiority was general. This, in combination with the inequities of material well-being associated with differences in rates of technological change, has made it seem that the Western, 'Christian' nations are both hegemonic and exploitative. Many modern political movements and a substantial scholarly literature rest on this concern and conviction.

In addition, in the West itself, and in the most 'Christian' of communities, the boundaries of science have come into conflict with other forms of belief. And, even among the thoroughly secular, the failure of science to answer such larger questions as 'Why?' and 'For what Purpose?' have contributed to science now being in doubt. It may well be that there is for mankind a metaphysical imperative. That is, it may well be necessary to recognize that mankind needs to ask and answer questions that cannot be answered by science, necessary, that is, to recognize that both religious and metaphysical discourse satisfy a fundamental human need.

This is a very uncomfortable conclusion for those of us who most admire Veblen and the other pragmatists of his era for their recognition that there was no final resting point in human evolution and no final arbiter of truth. Part of the pragmatic approach was a rejection of the necessity of either religion or metaphysics as anything other than elegant and frequently beautiful ritual or clever mind games. This core proposition is currently at stake. However, for the present, the only hope that can be offered is that we are in a period of doubt and of social evolution from which pragmatic accommodations to the human need to answer metaphysical questions may yet emerge. Veblen offered no certain answers.

However, it is worth remembering that when Veblen wrote he was struggling, as are we at the beginning of the twenty-first century, to understand how much of patterned human behavior is a result of inherited and biological characteristics, and how much a consequence of inherited and evolving culture. Debate on this important point has revived with the emergence of sociobiology, but Veblen himself in his later writing gave greater and greater weight to cultural evolution, even though he often returned in sardonic style, to statements of doubt about 'the normal man, such as his inheritance has made him'. Good modern social science continues to emphasize cultural evolution as the primary explanation of pattern variation among human populations over space and recorded history, variation that is of course always constrained by biological parameters.

Is it reasonable to think, therefore, that the importance of religious and metaphysical thought that is so obvious in the world today is a cultural phenomenon rather than a biological imperative? It seems at least possible that the failures of the past half century to embed sufficiently the processes of science, technological change and the economic changes that have resulted into larger matrices of society may be driving the desire for a return to certainty, or at least to a sense of 'the meaning of it all'. It may not be the biology of the 'normal man' that is to blame. At the beginning of this chapter I asked how far a physician from the USA, practicing medicine in a highly patriarchal country, should go in insisting on care for women and children when such care may necessarily trespass upon concepts of appropriate modesty of women and of male rights over both women and children. What happens in a situation where the technological requirements of a complex construction job contravene local concepts of on-the-job authority and control? To what extent, and how, should religious authority be challenged by health care officials when religious prohibitions against, let us say inoculations, threaten the health of a large group? Do the representatives of nations donating food to displaced or otherwise threatened populations have the right or responsibility to override, perhaps by force, local authorities in food distribution? Each of these difficult questions represents an interface between science and technology and deep cultural traditions. The failure of Westerners to recognize the cultural baggage of 'Christendom' that we always carry with us has made our answers offensive even when given great weight by the science and technology that has come over the past century from the West. Perhaps, closer to home, it has been an arrogant failure to recognize that very few of us are or want to be 'finikin skeptics' or 'animated slide-rules' all of the time. Most readers of this volume will be well aware of the arrogance of too many economists in asserting both at home and abroad that their proposed reforms are based on scientific truth and not derived from one of those aspects of culture that lies beyond the narrow realm of Western superiority. What should or can be shielded from science and what opened to its dispassionate glare remains a question to which Veblen gave no definitive answer. Such pragmatic modesty is also a valuable lesson.

NOTES

1. Such claims are common in political rhetoric ('America is the greatest nation') and in commonly asserted conflations of political and economic institutions with scientific and technological superiority. They also appear in scholarly discourse as, for example, in David Landes' *The Wealth and Poverty of Nations* (1998).
2. Why 'Christendom?' Partly, I suspect, because the term gives the sentence an ironic twist but also because an integral part of Veblen's analyses throughout his work stressed the cultural commonality of people of several nations who shared the cultural traits of which he was writing. Christianity as a religion was not, in Veblen's view, either a source or a consequence of the evolutionary sequence that he lays out but served simply as a useful identifier. In this he differed from modern analysts such as Landes (1998), and in more extreme and egregious form, Stark (2005) who have sought explanations for Western technological superiority in Judeo-Christian religious traditions.
3. Veblen may confuse the issue for a twenty-first century reader by saying that it is not clear whether the 'impersonal, dispassionate insight into the material facts' is a 'matter of habit or of racial endowment' or of both. It is important to remember that when Veblen was writing this article he was still struggling to understand the extent to which human variation was biological, and to what extent a matter of culture or habit. As Maynard illustrates, through the first decade of the twentieth century, Veblen continued to think that such variation was, at least in part, biological (Maynard, 2000, pp. 20–21). This was a common perception at the time, when Lamarckian understandings of genetics were more widely accepted, and if Veblen can be read as emphasizing culture as the explanation, this is more tribute to his emphasis on variation than it is to his clarity as to the distinctive roles of culture and biology. This lack of clarity will be important to my concluding argument.

4. A recent book, Louis Menand's *The Metaphysical Club: A Story of Ideas in America* (2001) and a classic account, Darnell Rucker's, *The Chicago Pragmatists* (1969), are both good treatments of the revolution in thought and its context. Confusion about the relationship of Veblen to his fellow pragmatists sometimes arises because of a linguistic difficulty. It also results from the fact that Veblen was looking for a different set of answers than were most of his fellow pragmatists who were more concerned with psychological/philosophical issues and less with the economic processes that held Veblen's attention. Veblen took great pains to distinguish between 'pragmatic action', action with a purposeful end, and action that was idle, which is to say without specific purpose. Because he was searching for the cause of change in human society, and because he found the cause in a propensity to idle action, this distinction was much more important for him than it was for the other pragmatists. Somewhat confusingly, he wrote that 'Pragmatism creates nothing but maxims of expedient conduct. Science creates nothing but theories' (Veblen, 1906 [1990], p. 19).

> What distinguishes the present . . . is (1) that the primacy in the cultural scheme has passed from pragmatism to a disinterested inquiry whose motive is idle curiosity, and (2) that in the domain of the latter the making of myths and legends in terms of inputed personality, as well as the construction of dialectical systems in terms of differential reality, has yielded the first place to the making of theories in terms of matter-of-fact sequences. (Veblen, 1906 [1990], p. 19)

In support of these arguments he cites both William James and Lester Frank Ward, both pioneers of philosophical pragmatism.

What Veblen is saying is that philosophical pragmatism, a way of thinking to which he adhered, saw ideas as immanent from always changing action and experience rather than better or worse reflections of fixed realities. The physical world both created and was created by active human agents. But he was also saying that deliberate and purposeful action based upon a prior understanding of that world would always be at cross-purposes with the experimentation, the playful, the idly curious actions that produced change in the ability to manipulate the world. Quite confusingly he used the word 'pragmatism' to describe such deliberate and purposeful action. This is probably understandable given that he was writing during the time when the notion of philosophical pragmatism, pragmatism writ large, was becoming well established as a separate and named body of thought.

In any event, and whatever the linguistic confusions that may have resulted, Veblen was in agreement with the pragmatist revolution, a revolution that held that people learned by doing things and that knowledge of action and effect in nature was accumulated, not as an approach to enduring truth, but in contingent manner. The contingent path of accumulation depends in large measure on purposeful action.

5. Veblen continued to use the language of the unilinear evolutionists of the late nineteenth century who classified the stages of human history as consisting of savage and lower barbarians. Veblen's prose is less offensive to the modern ear and still true to Veblen's arguments if we substitute a phrase such as 'our ancestors' for 'savage and barbarian peoples'.

6. Veblen obviously shared with Karl Marx (and others) a materialist conception of human history even though the lines of causality run quite differently in their work and led to different conclusions about what the future might hold.

7. Mokyr notes that Nathan Rosenberg (1976, 1994) and Paul David (1975) are among the few economists currently writing who have taken much interest in the role of additions to useful knowledge in economic growth. It is interesting that, as Mokyr says, 'Even the "New Growth Theory", which explicitly tries to incorporate technology as one of the variables driven by human and physical capital, does not try to model the concept of useful knowledge and its change over time explicitly' (Mokyr, 2002, p. 4).

8. Mokyr's chapter in *The Lever of Riches* (1990) on 'Understanding Technological Progress', is an excellent essay on the subject, and provides a good list of sources on the topic and specifically on the relationship of science and technology.

9. Mokyr cites Robert Fox and Anna Guagnini (1999) in substantiation of this claim. Janet Knoedler (1991) has also documented the importance of backward-linked industrial

research in the manufacture and processing of steel in the US, and the importance of this for the transition from 'rule-of-thumb methods' to science in the late nineteenth and early twentieth centuries.

REFERENCES

David, Paul A. (1975), *Technical Choice, Innovation, and Economic Growth*, Cambridge: Cambridge University Press.

DeGregori, Thomas R. (1985), *A Theory of Technology: Continuity and Change in Human Development*, Ames, Iowa: Iowa State University Press.

Dorfman, Joseph (1934), *Thorstein Veblen and His America*, 7th edn (1972), Clifton, NJ: Augustus M. Kelley.

Fox, Robert and Anna Guagnini (1999), *Laboratories, Workshops, and Sites: Concepts and Practices of Research in Industrial Europe, 1800–1914*, Berkley: Office for History of Science and Technology, University of California.

Handler, Philip (1980), 'Public doubts about science', *Science*, **208** (4448), 2.

Knoedler, Janet Therese (1991), 'Backward linkages to industrial research in steel, 1870–1930', dissertation, University of Tennessee.

Landes, David (1998), *The Wealth and Poverty of Nations: Why Some Are So rich and Some So Poor*, New York: W.W. Norton & Co.

Mayhew, Anne (1981), 'Ayresian technology, technological reasoning, and doomsday', *Journal of Economic Issues*, **XV** (2), 512–20.

Maynard, Raymond Anthony (2000), 'Thorstein Veblen on culture, biology, and evolution', dissertation, University of Tennessee.

Menand, Louis (2001), *The Metaphysical Club: A Story of Ideas in America*, New York: Farrar, Straus and Giroux.

Mokyr, Joel (1990), *The Lever of Riches: Technological Creativity and Economic Progress*, New York: Oxford University Press.

Mokyr, Joel (2002), *The Gifts of Athena: Historical Origins of the Knowledge Economy*, Princeton and Oxford: Princeton University Press.

Rosenberg, Nathan (1994), *Exploring the Black Box*, New York: Cambridge University Press.

Rosenberg, Nathan (1976), *Perspectives on Technology*, Cambridge: Cambridge University Press.

Rucker, Darnell (1969), *The Chicago Pragmatists*, Minneapolis: University of Minnesota Press.

Schumpeter, Joseph A. (1950), *Capitalism, Socialism, and Democracy*, New York: Harper and Row.

Stark, Rodney (2005), *The Victory of Reason: How Christianity led to Freedom, Capitalism, and Western Success*, New York: Random House.

Tool, Marc (2000), *The Discretionary Economy: A Normative Theory of Political Economy*, New Brunswick, NJ: Transactions Publishers.

Veblen, Thorstein B. (1906), 'The place of science in modern civilisation', *The American Journal of Sociology*, **XI** (March), reprinted in 1990, *The Place of Science in Modern Civilization*, New Brunswick and London: Transaction Publishers.

Veblen, Thorstein B. (1908), 'The evolution of the scientific point of view', reprinted 1990, *The Place of Science in Modern Civilization*, New Brunswick and London: Transaction Publishers.

2. Thorstein Veblen on the origins and meaning of private property

Robert E. Prasch

The great create an atmosphere which reacts badly upon the small. This atmosphere is easily and quickly felt. Walk among the magnificent residences, the splendid equipages, the gilded shops, restaurants, resorts of all kinds. Scent the flowers, the silks, the wines; drink of the laughter springing from the soul of a luxurious content, of the glances which gleam like light from defiant spears; feel the quality of smiles which cut like glistening swords and of strides born of place and power, and you shall know of what is the atmosphere of the high and mighty. Little need to argue that of such is not the kingdom of greatness, but so long as the world is attracted by this and the human heart views this as the one desirable value which it must attain, as long, to that heart, will this remain the realm of greatness. So long, also, will the atmosphere of this realm work its desperate results in the soul of man. It is like a chemical reagent. One day of it, like one drop of the other, will so affect and discolor the views, the aims, the desires of the mind that it will thereafter remain forever dyed. A day of it to the untried mind is like opium to the untried body. A craving is set up which, if gratified, shall eternally result in dreams and death. (Theodore Dreiser, *Sister Carrie*, 1900 [1981], p. 305)

Thorstein Veblen understood, in a manner that all-too-few modern economists do, that substantial disparities of wealth require validation. Done properly, such a validation enhances the self-esteem of the 'haves' while fostering a sense of acceptance among the 'have-nots'. Living as we are through a second Gilded Age, we should not be surprised to find that the juridical and economic theories that Veblen and others once so soundly refuted are being revived. With the revival of these once-discarded ideologies comes an equally pressing need to recover our understanding of their flaws. It is hoped that this chapter, in addition to the others in this volume, will contribute to the latter process.

Veblen's most well-known book was, and remains, *The Theory of the Leisure Class* (1899, hereafter the TLC). Unfortunately its rhetorical style, which was at least partially responsible for its success, also induced many readers to interpret it as a satire, thereby diminishing its force as a work of social analysis and commentary. Although the TLC is indeed an amusing book, it was and still is an error to undervalue its insights. Among the most crucial are important reflections on, and revisions of, conventional economic theories concerning such matters as the origin of property rights, our fundamental motivations as human beings, and the purpose and role of consumption in society.

Reviewing Veblen's early work on the origin of private property, human motivation and the theory of consumption serves an additional, pedagogical, purpose. As Douglas Dowd has observed, 'Although it provides the best introduction to Veblen's thought, it [the TLC] is more than an introduction. In it almost all his major ideas, and hints of most of the ideas he developed in later writings can be found' (Dowd, 1964, p. 6). One of these major ideas is that, as a consequence of our fundamental human motivations, our consumption patterns are both deliberate and structured. A critical contribution to this structure is our response to the consumption patterns of those around us. This insight has been largely ignored by economists, who generally begin their studies by supposing that society is made up of a set of discrete individuals seeking to satisfy their individually and autonomously determined pleasures at the least cost. Missed by this analysis is the fact that people are motivated, to a substantial degree, by their need for self-respect. Moreover, this need for self-respect is most readily fulfilled through the recognition and esteem of the larger community (Dowd, 1964, pp. 7, 13; TLC, p. 30; for more contemporary treatments along similar lines, see Sennett, 2003; Bourdieu, 1984).

While our sense of self-respect was once grounded in what Veblen termed our 'Instinct of Workmanship', he argues that the institutions and norms through which this instinct must be pursued have evolved in the context of a modern and increasingly urban society (Veblen, 1914). Of most importance, in an urban society people often desire the approval and esteem of others who only passingly know them and this fact induces a fundamental change in their search for self-respect. Specifically, the search for the respect and esteem of the community must increasingly be pursued through the adoption of readily understood 'signs' of merit. This insight led Veblen to posit that, under modern conditions, our creative impulses increasingly find their outlet in consumption: specifically consumption geared to display. Since the point of this consumption is to set us apart from the larger mass of people, it takes both invidious and conspicuous forms. This explains, at least partially, how modern social structures have induced a set of behaviors contrary to more conventional understandings of the human motivation to consume, including the economists' theories of utility, and even some of the more sophisticated theories of needs (Veblen, 1909).

Prominent among contemporary behaviors is a strongly-held desire, even a need, to engage in the observable use or display of expensive items: what

Veblen termed *conspicuous consumption.* Such consumption is largely but, in deference to the remnants of older traditions such as the proverbial work ethic, not entirely unproductive.[1] Its primary function is to establish the social status of an individual and his or her family though a public display of purchasing power. This practice creates and supports *invidious distinctions*; that is to say, it promotes and instantiates social rankings and other varieties of social stratification. From his analysis, Veblen believes that the most reliable way for one to distinguish oneself socially is to imitate society's elites. In a society built upon the unequal ownership of private property the standard and pattern of consumption to be embraced and emulated is that of the wealthy. Being wealthy, moreover, this elite is characterized by Veblen as the *Leisure Class,* a group whose assured access to wealth frees it from the many undignified and menial, but necessary and productive, tasks associated with earning a living through useful labor (TLC, chs. 2–4; 1899, 1898a).

THE ORIGINS OF PRIVATE PROPERTY

Joseph Dorfman has argued, correctly, that the TLC should be read as an extended response to the famous Social Darwinist, and noted apologist for modern social arrangements, Herbert Spencer. According to Dorfman, Veblen retained Spencer's idea that the norms and institutions of our society were a consequence of a long and continuing evolutionary process while simultaneously discarding Spencer's contradictory belief that, even as society went through these evolutionary processes the social institutions of private property and contract would remained essentially fixed (Dorfman, 1932).[2]

To Veblen, a social science influenced by Darwin's theory of evolution would be self-contradictory to the extent that it adhered to a 'Natural Law' understanding of private property. Beginning with his earliest writings Veblen set out to challenge the idea that private property was a 'natural' category, one that transcended historical or evolutionary processes (Veblen, 1899, 1898a, 1898b, 1898c). As he expressed it, 'The conjectural history of the origin of property, so far as it has been written by the economists, has been constructed out of conjecture proceeding on the preconceptions of Natural Rights and the coercive Order of Nature' (Veblen 1898a, p. 352). The problem was the following:

> This natural-rights theory of property makes the creative effort of an isolated, self-sufficing individual the basis of the ownership vested in him. In so doing it overlooks the fact that there is no isolated, self-sufficing individual. All production

is, in fact, a production in and by the help of the community, and all wealth is such only in society. (Veblen, 1898a, p. 353)

By contrast Veblen believed that property, in its conventional understanding as a right of exclusive disposal, was a consequence of a specific historical development. Moreover, like Henry Sumner Maine, he believed that our understanding of this institution could be enriched if its origins were considered in a scholarly manner (Maine, 1861 [1963]). The implication is that with a different sequence of circumstances or events, property law could have taken a completely different form.

By contrast with the 'conjectural' theory of private property that permeated nineteenth-century liberal thought, Veblen observed that the employment or use of convenient or useful devices, that is to say tools, occurred in all early societies. Moreover, the development and use of these tools occurred independently of today's notions of ownership:

> In all communities the members, both male and female, habitually appropriate to their individual use a variety of useful things; but these useful things are not thought of as owned by the person who appropriates and consumes them. The habitual appropriation and consumption of certain slight personal effects goes on without raising the question of ownership; that is to say, the question of a conventional, equitable claim to extraneous things. (TLC, p. 23)

Drawing upon his extensive knowledge of anthropology, Veblen inferred that humanity initially devised a 'division of labor' between women and men. This was a division explicitly based on relative status. It was not grounded, as some neoclassical economists would later conjecture, on a physiologically based comparative advantage. Predatory and honorific activities, including hunting and the performance of leading roles in religious ceremonies, became the tasks of men. Women were assigned the more mundane, repetitive and time-intensive tasks of food preparation and attending to the sundry chores associated with the maintenance of the family group or tribe.

The division of labor between the sexes initially took place before people were in the habit of recording their histories. Through tests of courage and strength, including battles between and amongst themselves, men assumed power over the goods, domesticated animals and women of rival family groups or tribes. In addition to enhanced status, victorious men derived sexual, material and other advantages from 'owning' the women they obtained through conflict. With so many advantages, it was not long before men came to extend this same 'ownership idea' to the women of their own family group or tribe. Over time, 'women as trophies' evolved into the broader notion that men owned women in general. 'From the ownership of women the concept of ownership extends itself to include the products of their industry, and so there arises the ownership of things as well as of persons' (TLC, p. 24; also Veblen, 1898a). To Veblen, then, the idea of private property was grounded in the search for status rather than in a quest for a more efficient means to enhance individual or social output.

CONTRASTS WITH THE RECEIVED THEORY OF THE ORIGIN OF PRIVATE PROPERTY

In his *Theory of Business Enterprise*, Veblen observed that 'The modern theories of property run back to Locke, or to some source which for the present purpose is equivalent to Locke; who, on this as on other institutional questions, has been proved by the test of time to be a competent spokesman for modern culture on these questions' (Veblen, 1904 [1978], p. 71). Veblen was at pains to undermine this important intellectual tradition, one that gained great currency when it was restated and thereby reaffirmed by the highly regarded legal theorist William Blackstone in his *Commentaries on the Laws of England* (Blackstone, 1765–69, bk. 2, ch. 1). Contrary to this tradition Veblen argued that the historical record affirmed that property rights were grounded neither in useful labor nor in occupancy nor any other tangible or intangible action that could provide a coherent foundation for a claim of a 'natural' right. Moreover, neither was our right to property founded upon a mythical or primordial 'Social Contract.' Presenting an alternative theory that bears an echo of Pierre Proudhon, Veblen argues that 'Property set out with being booty held as trophies of the successful raid' (TLC, p. 27). To Veblen, the historical foundation of the theory of property was appropriation by force, with a dual origin in a culture of barbarism and the search for status:

> The original reason for the seizure and appropriation of women seems to have been their usefulness as trophies. The practice of seizing women from the enemy as trophies, gave rise to a form of ownership–marriage, resulting in a household with a male head. This was followed by an extension of slavery to other captives and inferiors, besides women, and by an extension of ownership–marriage to other women than those seized from the enemy. (TLC, p. 23)

To Veblen private property evolved out of what today's conservatives term 'traditional marriage'. Both were a consequence of a human need to achieve and display social status. The advantage of women captives and property, suggests Veblen, was that each presented their owners with 'a durable result of their exploits' (TLC, p. 24).[3] It follows that the widely accepted claim of nineteenth-century liberal thought, from Henry Sumner Maine (1822–88) to Herbert Spencer (1820–1903) and William Graham Sumner (1840–1910), that society had undergone a tremendous evolution when it changed from a regime of status to one of contract, was greatly qualified, if not overturned. Veblen reconceived private property as being grounded in an older order of status seeking and consumption. What had changed, in Veblen's view, was the method by which we displayed our relative status under modern, what he called 'quasi-peaceable', conditions.

Veblen's reconceptualization of the emergence of private property is best understood in contrast to John Locke's *Second Treatise of Government* (1690). According to Locke, 'reason and revelation' mandated that each person's first responsibility was to maintain his own life, as this was God's greatest gift. This first duty implied that men had both the need to acquire and the right to possess those things that were necessary to accomplish this end. To obtain these several objects, he must 'mix his labor' with the produce of the earth. It was this effort, that of applying one's labor to the objects of nature, that was the foundation of each individual's right to ownership (Locke, 1690, ch. 5).[4]

Veblen upended this narrative. He argued that, in a society based on status, the process of attending to the maintenance of life and the mundane needs that sustained the community – the essence of productive labor – was not seen to be honorific. It followed that productive labor was beneath the status of the more esteemed members of the society. Lower-status persons, such as women and male captives, rather than higher-status males, must be the ones to perform the 'mixing of labor' referred to by Locke. Men, as a consequence of their superior status, were entitled to appropriate and consume a disproportionate share of what women and male captives produced. Property rights, then, were a consequence of one's status rather than one's labor. The ultimate foundation of this status was a person's power. It conveyed a right over women, slaves, children and any of the objects, services or psychic benefits they could each and severally provide. Property rights, in Veblen's alternative view, are a consequence of power and derive whatever transcendent meaning they have from the actual or potential exercise of that power.

To reiterate, the foundation of property rights was neither labor nor the accommodation of one's needs in a world of scarcity nor the sundry pleasures or conveniences collectively termed 'utility'. Rather it was a consequence of power and status. Beyond our basic needs, and an innate propensity to workmanship, the motivation to accumulate property developed out of people's need for status, which means the respect of one's community. Our need to establish and display our relative status is the ultimate foundation of our desire to deploy our wealth to establish 'invidious distinctions' between ourselves, our neighbors, and our rivals.[5]

Consistent with the structure of his argument, Veblen believed that the idea of a leisure class is closely tied to the idea of property. Indeed, as a matter of logic and necessity, the former depends upon the existence of the latter. Without some prior and recognized claim over property, people of all classes would have to perform productive work to meet their own immediate needs, or the needs of someone else with whom they can then barter. A world in which everyone engages in such productive activities is categorically inconsistent with the idea of a leisure class (TLC, p. 22).

For economists, it should be evident that Veblen's perspective was in opposition to the emerging neoclassical view that scarcity was the ultimate foundation of property rights (TLC, pp. 24–6). Indeed, this perspective was articulated by, among others, the most philosophically sophisticated of the founders of the neoclassical school of economics, Carl Menger.

> Thus human economy and property have a joint economic origin since both have, as the ultimate reason for their existence, the fact that goods exist whose available quantities are smaller than the requirements of men. Property, therefore, like human economy, is not an arbitrary invention but rather the only practically possible solution of the problem that is, in the nature of things, imposed upon us by the disparity between requirements for, and available quantities of, all economic goods. (Menger, 1871 [1994], p. 97)

Menger's perspective is not that of a discarded or eclipsed theory. It has been carried over into modern economic thought through a widely-celebrated article by Armen Alchian and Harold Demsetz. Drawing inspiration from a largely conjectural recounting of the early history of the North American fur trade, Alchian and Demsetz reassert Menger's argument that a coherent regime of property rights will emerge spontaneously from an underlying condition of scarcity (Alchian and Demsetz, 1973).

PRIVATE PROPERTY AND THE ECONOMIC STRUGGLE

To Veblen the available evidence failed to affirm that our modern notions of private property emerged out of the struggle for existence in a subsistence economy (TLC, p. 24). This, one of his more important conclusions, has been affirmed by several prominent anthropologists and anthropologically informed economists (c.f. Neale, 1984, 1987; Polanyi, 1944, 1968; Sahlins, 1972). None of this is to deny that for the poor, especially in a modern society where virtually all necessities are privately owned, needs will remain an important stimulus to effort. As Veblen argued, 'It is of course not to be overlooked that in a community where nearly all goods are private property the necessity of earning a livelihood is a powerful and ever-present incentive for the poorer members of the community' (TLC, p. 26). Additionally, it is well-known that the cost of meeting one's subsistence is generally higher in more developed societies. This is particularly evident when subsistence is understood in its most accurate sense as a minimal set of physical and social capabilities (Sen, 1999, ch. 4; Prasch, 2003). This latter tendency is marvelously captured by Joel Mokyr's quip that 'invention is the mother of necessity' (Mokyr, 1990, p. 151).

Property then is not about subsistence. For this reason it would be incorrect to infer that property is concerned with allowing us to consume what we must to attend to the needs and comforts of life (TLC, p. 25). With Veblen's understanding of the relationship between property and consumption in mind, it should not be too surprising to learn that several modern researchers have found no clear relationship between levels of consumption and people's 'utility' or happiness (Bowles, 1998; Lane, 2000; George, 2001; for a brief survey of current developments and their implications, see Brekke and Howarth, 2000). Happiness will, ideally, be a derivative benefit if the primary point of possession is to achieve and maintain status:

> The motive that lies at the root of ownership is emulation; ... The possession of wealth confers honour; it is an invidious distinction. Nothing equally cogent can be said for the consumption of goods, nor for any other conceivable incentive to acquisition, and especially not for any incentive to the accumulation of wealth. (TLC, pp. 25–6).

In our own era, the above conclusion is supported by the behavior of the most wealthy among us. Some of them, such as the Hilton sisters, appear to sincerely and enthusiastically relish the leisure and goods that they are able to access with their tremendous wealth. Others, such as Caroline Kennedy or Melinda Gates, seek satisfaction in careers as civil libertarians, philanthropists or in other relatively impecunious pursuits. Nevertheless, and this is a striking anomaly for the received, that is to say neoclassical, theories of motivation, many of our most extravagantly wealthy contemporaries work long and hard in the pursuit of ever-greater accumulations of wealth. This can be ascribed, not to any conceivable unmet need on the part of the wealthy, their children or their children's children, but to positional considerations:

> The possession of wealth, which was at the outset valued simply as an evidence of efficiency, becomes in popular apprehension, itself a meritorious act. Wealth is now itself intrinsically honourable and confers honour on its possessor. (TLC, p. 29)

When what Veblen terms 'invidious distinctions' are driving the search for ever-greater wealth, each level of accumulated wealth will, in time, come to be perceived as unsatisfactory (TLC, p. 31). For the reasons given above, the otherwise seemingly 'irrational' behavior of the wealthy is transformed into an observation that supports Veblen's theory: as social status is relative, and not absolute, no specific level of wealth can, on its own, provide a sense of satiation (TLC, p. 32).

If this perverse set of motivations exclusively afflicted the wealthy and the very wealthy, the problem could be contained or ignored. Sadly, this does not appear to be the case. The search for status induces even non-wealthy people to mimic the behavior and consumption patterns of the wealthy. 'To a great extent this emulation shapes the methods and selects the objects of expenditure for personal comfort and decent livelihood' (TLC, p. 32). The expenditure patterns and whims of the wealthy become normalized as more and more classes emulate their consumption standards. It is for this reason that 'For the great body of people in any modern community' there is 'a desire to live up to the conventional standard of decency in the amount and grade of goods consumed' (TLC, p. 102).

Inspired by the wealthy, a conventional standard of living is established in each and every era, society and even subculture within any given society. Simultaneously, a conventional mode of living and consuming that pays homage to the highest standards comes to be perceived by many of the non-wealthy to be desirable. As has been explained, observing these standards is often the basis for social recognition and even self-respect. But these standards can also assume an objective dimension in the sense that ascribing to them is essential if an individual or family is to command the degree of social regard or status that is necessary to function in their community (Perrot, 1981). An example would be the ostentatiously 'conservative' demeanor, social and political opinions, and clothing that were long a necessity for anyone wishing to pursue a career as a banker. In this manner conventional modes of consumption can transcend their mundane origins in expedience or fashion. At the extreme, these standards or conventions may come to be enforced through moral or legal sanction: 'certain convention-ally accepted ways and means come to be set up as definitive principles of what is right and good; while the ulterior purpose of it all is only called to mind occasionally, if at all, as an afterthought, by an effort of reflection' (Veblen, 1914, p. 8).

Elites, of course, must still confront their age-old problem of marking their status by distinguishing themselves from the mass. In the modern world of mass production, where the prices of passably good imitations of status goods are generally declining, the most effective manner of distinction is periodically to change the acceptable standards of deportment and consumption. As a consequence, the conventional standard of living, even within a given era, is necessarily subject to change. At times it is even subject to improvement. These dynamics lend a degree of specificity to the idea of a 'socially-determined subsistence' once articulated by classical economists such as Adam Smith, John Stuart Mill and Karl Marx. While each of these economists indicated that the level of subsistence was socially mediated and somewhat flexible, it was left to Veblen to provide a theory as to how the conventional standard of living could evolve in tandem with the development of wealth. In this manner Veblen's evolutionary interpretation of the changing standard of living was an important contribution to our understanding of consumption and its role and function in society.

THE EVOLUTION OF PROPERTY

In addition to its role as a measure and arbiter of relative standing within a society, property also serves to provide a visible and credible distinction between individuals and the larger society (TLC, p. 27; Bourdieu, 1984). A fundamental role of wealth, and a prominent reason to strive for it, is its deployment as a sign of merit or social distinction. The use of consumption as a sign of distinction becomes, according to Veblen, ever more important with the rise of industrial activity. The reason is that it is easier to recognize and evaluate the possession of property than 'heroic or signal achievement' (TLC, p. 29). Veblen acknowledges that property once served as a sign of some previous activity or service of use to the community, but that today the signal increasingly substitutes for such a contribution.

In our era, the form by which society once marked substantive merit or accomplishment has itself become the substance of such merit or accomplishment. An excellent example of this modified use of property is evident in our celebrity culture, where we admire the possession of great wealth for its own sake. Veblen observes that this tendency has become so pronounced that even criminals are admired provided they have accumulated (embezzled, or stolen) a great deal of wealth in the course of their crimes, and have the decency to display or otherwise deploy this wealth in a manner conforming to the canons of good taste (Michael Millikin, Ken Lay and Bernie Evers come immediately to mind in this context, but examples abound). 'The thief or swindler who has gained great wealth by his delinquency has a better chance than the small thief of escaping the rigorous penalty of the law; and some good repute accrues to him from his increased wealth and from his spending the irregularly acquired possessions in a seemly manner' (TLC, p. 117).

As a consequence of these trends those who fall behind in the race to acquire ever more wealth risk losing the esteem of the larger community. Since the conventional basis for evaluating the social status of so many people is shifting so regularly, it is not too surprising that a person's or family's status comes to be grounded, not in an antiquated 'producerist' sense of accomplishment, but rather in their ability to consume, or rather to consume conspicuously, at a level and in a manner consistent with their actual or imagined reference group. In our era status, and as a consequence self-esteem, can be substantially diminished in the event that one lacks access to the purchasing power that enables one to achieve a reputable display (TLC, pp. 30–31; see also Sennett, 2003).[6]

PROPERTY AND FREEDOM

It may be obvious, but in light of today's obfuscatory political discourse it is necessary to state, that property, specifically the ownership of property, is the essential basis of freedom in a property-based market society. *Formally*, since the Civil Rights Act was upheld by the United States Supreme Court in December of 1964, every American now enjoys an equal right to stay at every hotel and dine in every restaurant (*Heart of Atlanta Motel* v. *United States* 379, U.S. 241 (1964); *Katzenbach* v. *McClung* 379 U.S. 294 (1964)). Yet and this should be obvious though it is routinely overlooked, what makes these rights *substantive* is access to means of payment. This, for many people, is what is missing. In a property-based market society, one must have means of payment, that is to say actual or expected income, if one is to enjoy the goods and services that are available in such a society.

To anyone without means of payment, that is to say the poor, property rights are a regime of effective, if decentralized, constraints and prohibitions (Hale, 1943; Prasch, 2006). By contrast, to the wealthy a world of private property is one where they are indeed 'free to choose'. It is a smorgasbord of endless and delectable choices. These choices go well beyond selecting from among luxurious and tasteful goods and services. In the event of great inequality, these choices also include the purchase of other people's labor, dignity, sexuality, body parts, children and even their very persons. These 'free choices' also generally extend to disproportionate political influence, lenient treatment in the judicial system and exemption from the obligations of citizenship including jury duty and military service. To the wealthy, a society grounded exclusively in property rights really is indeed a realm of freedom – even license. As an additional benefit, the wealthy can also generally count on the fawning praise and admiration of the multitude. As Veblen pointed out so long ago, for many people this last benefit is a crucial pre-condition of their sense of self-worth and thereby self-respect. That wealthy persons would spend some of their substantial riches and influence to bring about a property-based market system, or to ensure the continuity and extension of such a political–economic regime in the event that it was already in place, can not be considered one of the unresolved mysteries of social science.

NOTES

1. This might be best illustrated through an example. The 'pick-up' truck was designed to be a multi-purpose light vehicle for work on a farm or construction site. Its powerful engine, its carrying capacity, its durability, etc., were all features that compensated for its lack of passenger comfort. Yet we are all familiar with the trucks owned by 'suburban cowboys' with their highly-polished and stylized bodies, chrome extras and hubcaps, elaborate music systems, etc. As suggested in the text these latter vehicles pay homage to the pick-up truck that remains a crucial tool in certain workplaces. But this nod to productive or industrial use is as far as it goes. The expensive and delicate modifications of such trucks make it plainly evident to one and all that the owner has both 'money to burn' and no occasion to use this truck in a workplace setting. It is in this sense that the suburban cowboy's truck simultaneously fulfills the role of conspicuous consumption while invoking, in a stylized way, an older set of values and traditions.

2. In the course of his writings Veblen also criticized the static preconceptions of other prominent traditions within economic thought, including the Classical, Neoclassical and Marxist schools (Veblen, 1906, 1907, 1909).

3. Veblen's notion that the institution of property emerged from the pursuit of status shares some similarities with that presented by Jean-Jacques Rousseau. However, these thinkers have different understandings of the origin of marriage as an institution. For Rousseau, rivalry between property-owning men was grounded upon a sex instinct, one that mandated that men impress potential mates with their prowess as demonstrated by the extent of their ownership. What Rousseau failed to explain was why men in the 'state of nature' would work so hard to accumulate the property necessary to attract women, when enslaving them would be so much easier (Rousseau, 1755).

4. The contrast with John Locke is much more than an instructive example in light of the importance of what Richard Hofstadter termed 'The Agrarian Myth' in American political and social consciousness (Hofstadter, 1955, ch. 2). As Hofstadter notes, Veblen directly challenged this myth in his discussion of the 'independent farmer' and 'the country town' in the course of his last book, *Absentee Ownership* (Veblen, 1923 [1997], pp. 129–65).

5. For a recent effort to establish this result empirically, see Johansson-Stenman and Martinsson (2006). Of course, as is well-known, Veblen himself illustrated these tendencies through the example of changing fashions in women's dress (TLC, ch. 7; 1894). See an excellent book by Philippe Perrot for a recent history that affirms Veblen's insights in the case of nineteenth-century France. It shows the importance of the convention of women bearing the burden, through their dress, of demonstrating the family's wealth and thereby upholding the family's status (Perrot, 1981).

6. Many of the best novelists of Veblen's time also wrote on these themes, as is evident in the quotation that began this chapter. In these novels a major character must acquire great wealth to sustain their repute in the community and thereby their sense of self-worth. Failure was socially and personally devastating. Dramatic and memorable examples of such characters include Lily Bart in Edith Wharton's *The House of Mirth* (1905), Curtis Jadwin in Frank Norris' *The Pit* (1903) and Hurstwood in Theodore Dreiser's *Sister Carrie* (1900).

REFERENCES

Alchian, Armen and Harold Demsetz (1973), 'The property rights paradigm', *Journal of Economic History*, **33** (March), 16–27.

Blackstone, William (1765–69 [1979]), *Commentaries on the Laws of England*, Chicago, IL: University of Chicago Press.

Bourdieu, Pierre (1984), *Distinction: A Social Critique of the Judgement of Taste*, Cambridge, MA: Harvard University Press.

Bowles, Samuel (1998), 'Endogenous preferences; the cultural consequences of markets and other economic institutions', *Journal of Economic Literature*, **36**(1) (March), 75–111.

Brekke, Kjell Arne and Richard B. Howarth (2000), 'The social contingency of wants', *Land Economics*, **76**(4) (November), 493–503.

Dorfman, Joseph (1932), 'The "satire" of Thorstein Veblen's theory of the leisure class', *Political Science Quarterly*, **47**(3) (September), 363–409.

Dowd, Douglas (1964), *Thorstein Veblen*, New York: Washington Square Press.

Dreiser, Theodore (1900 [1981]), *Sister Carrie*, New York: VikingPenguin.

George, David (2001), *Preference Pollution: How Markets Create the Desires We Dislike*, Ann Arbor, MI: University of Michigan Press.

Hale, Robert L. (1943), 'Bargaining, duress, and economic liberty', *Columbia Law Review*, **43**(5) (July), 603–28.

Hofstadter, Richard (1955), *The Age of Reform: From Bryan to F.D.R.*, New York: Vintage.

Johansson-Stenman, Olaf and Peter Martinsson (2006). 'Honestly, why are you driving a BMW?', *Journal of Economics, Behavior and Organization*, **60**, 129–46.

Lane, Robert E. (2000), *The Loss of Happiness in Market Democracies*, New Haven, CT: Yale University Press.

Locke, John (1690 [1952]), *The Second Treatise of Government*, New York: Macmillan.

Maine, Henry Sumner (1861 [1963]), *Ancient Law: Its Connection with the Early History of Society, and Its Relation to Modern Ideas*, Boston, MA: Beacon Press.

Menger, Carl (1871 [1994]), *Principles of Economics*, trans. James Dingwall and Bert F. Hoselitz, Grove City, PA: Libertarian Press.

Mokyr, Joel (1990). *The Lever of Riches: Technological Creativity and Economic Progress*, New York: Oxford University Press.

Neale, Walter C. (1984), 'The evolution of colonial institutions: an argument illustrated from the economic history of British Central Africa', *Journal of Economic Issues*, **18**(4) (December): 1177–87.

Neale, Walter C. (1987). 'Institutions', *Journal of Economic Issues*, **21**(3) (September), 1177–1206.

Norris, Frank (1903), *The Pit: A Story of Chicago*, New York: Grosset & Dunlap.

Perrot, Philippe (1981), *Fashioning the Bourgeoisie: A History of Clothing in the Nineteenth Century*, trans. Richard Bienvenu (1994), Princeton, NJ: Princeton University Press.

Polyani, Karl (1944 [1962]), *The Great Transformation: The Political and Economic Origins of our Time*, Boston, MA: Beacon.

Polyani, Karl (1968), *Primitive, Archaic and Modern Economies: Essays of Karl Polanyi*, ed. George Dalton, Garden City, NY: Doubleday & Co.

Prasch, Robert E. (2003), 'Technical change, competition and the poor', *Journal of Economic Issues*, **37**(2) (June), 479–85.

Prasch, Robert E. (2006). '"Free Entry and Exit" from the market: simplifying or substantive assumption?', *Journal of Economic Issues*, **40**(2) (June).

Rousseau, Jean-Jacques ([1755] 1964), *Discourse on the Origin and Foundations of Inequality Among Men* in *The First and Second Discourses*, trans. Roger D. and Judith R. Masters, New York: St. Martin's Press.

Sahlins, Marshall (1972), *Stone Age Economics*, Chicago, IL: Aldine-Atherton.

Sen, Amartya (1999), *Development as Freedom*, New York: Alfred A. Knopf.

Sennett, Richard (2003), *Respect in a World of Inequality*, New York: Norton.

Veblen, Thorstein (1894), 'The economic theory of woman's dress', reprinted in Leon Ardzrooni (ed.) (1934), *Essays in Our Changing Order*, New York: Viking.

Veblen, Thorstein (1898a), 'The beginnings of ownership', *American Journal of Sociology*, **4**(3) (November), 352–65.

Veblen, Thorstein (1898b), 'The instinct of workmanship and the irksomeness of labor', *American Journal of Sociology*, **4**(2) (September), 187–201.

Veblen, Thorstein (1898c), 'Why is economics not an evolutionary science?', *Quarterly Journal of Economics* (July), 373–97.

Veblen, Thorstein (1899 [1934]), *The Theory of the Leisure Class: An Economic Study of Institutions*, New York: Modern Library.

Veblen, Thorstein (1899), 'The barbarian status of women', *American Journal of Sociology*, **4**(4) (December), 503–14.

Veblen, Thorstein (1904 [1978]), *The Theory of Business Enterprise*, New Brunswick, NJ: Transaction Publishers.

Veblen, Thorstein (1906), 'The socialist economics of Karl Marx and his followers I', *Quarterly Journal of Economics*, **20**(4) (August), 575–95.

Veblen, Thorstein (1907), 'The socialist economics of Karl Marx and his followers II', *Quarterly Journal of Economics*, **21**(2) (February), 5, 299–322.

Veblen, Thorstein (1909), 'The limitations of marginal utility', *Journal of Political Economy*, **17**(9) (November), 620–36.

Veblen, Thorstein (1914), *The Instinct of Workmanship and the State of the Industrial Arts*, New York: Macmillan.

Veblen, Thorstein (1923 [1997]), *Absentee Ownership: Business Enterprise in Recent Times: The Case of America*, New Brunswick, NJ: Transaction Publishers.

Wharton, Edith (1905), *The House of Mirth*, New York: C. Scribner's Sons.

3. Capital and the modern corporation

Eric R. Hake

Thorstein Veblen's theory of the corporation, as laid out in *The Theory of Business Enterprise* and extended in *Absentee Ownership*, presents a critical and still timely insight into the nature of the modern industrial economy. His theory was developed during the dramatic industrial changes of the late nineteenth century as the United States shifted from farm to factory, and from rural and regional economies to national and international business. These changes did much to establish a course of institutional and economic evolution for the twentieth century. The rise of consolidated economic power, organized in the corporate form, was balanced in the early twentieth century by the growth of unions and an expanded federal government. But after a half-century of criticism directed at these institutions, American society is now seeing the demise of union influence and a shrinking of government responsibilities. While key differences remain between the beginning and the end of the twentieth century, in political rhetoric and economic practice there is resurgent support for an earlier, starker vision of unregulated capitalism. This trend requires that we reinvestigate that earlier period to understand more fully the motive force of the unregulated corporation.

No story this important could have been covered by only one author. Thorstein Veblen is only one of many who have attempted to understand the general outlines of the modern era. But Veblen's work can and should be singled out for two important reasons: the unified nature of his historically grounded theory and his willingness to discuss the potential flaws and limitations of the emerging industrial order. These features of his work are complementary. Veblen built an economic theory on the solid foundation of practical business relations – he did not begin with unrealistic assumptions or a narrow field of vision. He sought to understand the practical construction of economic activity in the modern era and discuss its potential limitations. His willingness to seek out the implications of convenient solutions kept him from writing a convenient theory or history, one that would avoid certain subjects or perpetuate the privilege of special interests. In pursuing this course, Veblen produced a wholly modern and unique theory of production, consumption and distribution that incorporates a fundamental attention to the potential flaws and limitations of this new industrial society.

The comprehensive sweep of his analysis created a modern theory of the firm, a reformulation which is at odds with the classical and marginalist conceptions of perfect competition. His analysis of the firm included the role of financial innovation, the inherently sociological qualities of capital and the impact of the then emerging corporate form on the reorganization and consolidation of ownership. To these ends he developed, in conjunction with his theory of the firm, theories of finance and of industrial organization. Lastly, he set this apparatus in motion, explaining the fluctuations of economic activity that would be produced by this new set of arrangements. In this manner he added a theory of the business cycle to his analysis. For many critics of traditional economic theorizing, Veblen presented a new way of developing economic models. Deductive logic and a belief in a natural order of society were cast off in favor of an inductive, historically grounded analysis of the economy as it existed. Rather than rely upon economists' definitions for key concepts, Veblen turned to the commentary of business people, grounding his economic theory in the day-to-day practices of business. In this way, he sought to explain the actual working of the economy, rather than to set forth a stylized and abstract theory based on principles foreign to business practice.

Secondly, Veblen also examined the potentially hazardous features of this new landscape. His signature literary style, a categorical explication of the logical failings of conventional wisdom peppered with biting sarcasm, suggests he relished the task. Unfortunately for economic science, his attempts to explain what he perceived as clear and consistent features of economic and social life were poorly received by a large majority of economists. It is an apparent sociological fact that no community takes pleasure in a comprehensive analysis of its guiding myths and most deeply held cultural beliefs. Veblen can be seen in the most sympathetic light, not as an intellectual combatant protecting an ideological position or defending a particular class of interests, but as someone committed to the scientific study of the economy.

For Veblen and his followers, the surest route to developing an economic science would be to build theories based on the practical operation of the economy and its actors. The employment of simplifying assumptions, while always necessary, must also be carefully evaluated, to ensure that assumed relationships are not simply ideological bias masquerading as unassailable bedrock. To be sure, a first step in the direction of unified economic theory would be a recognition of the multifaceted nature of human existence and an integration of the insights developed in other social sciences. Veblen clearly began his analysis of the modern economy by admitting the role and importance of several basic truths, such as the influence of culture, the social nature of human existence, path-dependent development, hysteresis and the role of power in economic relationships. To this end he constructed his theory of business and capitalism upon a close inspection and knowledge of practical business activities and practices.

To better understand Thorstein Veblen's theory of business enterprise, it might be best to start by deliberating upon his proposition that firms, in addition to making money by producing goods, can also earn income by reducing or limiting production. This simple proposition, when carried to its logical conclusion, alters our understanding of the nature and purpose of the firm's capital assets. In the presence of this option, the ability of the firm to issue securities for sale, borrow money and finance its business activities is increased. This ability in turn changes the method of capitalizing the firm and allows for a redistribution of income towards creditors. Once this new class of financial assets is legitimately added to the balance sheet, it changes our understanding of the amount of income that can be received by financial agents, managers or owners. When coupled with the mechanism of the stock exchange, this class of asset furnishes us with an additional insight into the dynamics of that market and its implications for understanding the business cycle, adding an important sociological dimension to the volatility of the firm's access to credit.

CAPITAL AND THE MODERN CORPORATION

The single most important organizational development in business during the modern era is the corporation and, within that institution, its most unique and valuable asset is capital. In the modern industrial society, the answers to the fundamental economic questions of what will be produced, how will it be produced and who receives the income derived from this production can all be found within the corporation.[1]

According to Thorstein Veblen, the most consequential development of the late nineteenth-century economy was the growth of absentee ownership (Veblen, 1923 [1964], p. 3; Veblen, 1904 [1988], p. 133). The appearance of the large-scale industrial corporation had allowed the owners of business and the recipients of industrial profits to become increasingly removed from the day-to-day operations of the firm. The mechanism that allowed this removal from routine operations to occur was the ability of the corporation to create and transfer ownership shares: dividing up the rights to profit into many individual shares that could be sold by the corporation. To explore the significance that Veblen attributed to the corporation and its mechanisms, however, it is necessary to understand his theory regarding the requirements of industrial advance and the motive force of profit.

THE MACHINE PROCESS AND COMMERCIAL LOGIC

Thorstein Veblen is widely credited as the founder of the only uniquely American school of economic thought. One of this school's principles is to attempt to integrate our understanding of culture – human social constructs – with an analysis of material economic conditions. This effort infused a common theme into Veblen's writings, that of the conflict between the social and physical features of human existence. Throughout much of Veblen's analysis, he employed the notion of a dichotomy or dualism; this dichotomy involved the material and physical realities of the world on the one hand and the cultural constructs devised by human society on the other. With this division, sometimes neatly and sometimes less neatly constructed, Veblen introduced the idea that there is a fundamental tension within much of human activity. This tension is also responsible for a fundamental limitation of more efficient and practical organization of human affairs.[2]

As stated, Veblen's application of culture as a category distinct from physical reality produced a revolutionary framework for studying the economy. In business activity, Veblen described the distinction between physical and social reality as the industrial/pecuniary dichotomy. This division was evident in the first sentence of the *Theory of Business Enterprise:* 'The material framework of modern civilization is the *industrial system* and the directing force which animates this framework is *business enterprise*' (1904b [1988], p. 1). Accordingly, the *industrial system* is governed by the physical laws that determine the mechanisms and physical constraints on the potential production and distribution of goods. The *pecuniary system* that organizes social action, on the other hand, is the result of our social constructions: the conception and legal articulation of private property, commercial law and financial contract. In Veblen's reconstitution of economic theory, the industrial system is embedded within the cultural rules of society.

Veblen stated that the modern industrial economy has its foundation in the machine process. Those industries most advanced have been those most amenable to the application of scientific measurement and causal analysis. But the machine process is more comprehensive than the aggregate of mechanical equipment. The machine process transforms and shapes both the raw materials and the practice of modern business. It is the aggregation of scientific knowledge and its application. This sets the modern stage of society on a uniquely different and more dynamic path than those preceding stages. The machine process can be found:

Wherever manual dexterity, the rule of thumb, and the fortuitous conjunctures of the seasons have been supplanted by a reasoned procedure on the basis of a systematic knowledge of the forces employed, there the mechanical industry is to be found, even in the absence of intricate mechanical contrivances. It is a question of the character of the process rather than a question of the complexity of the contrivances employed. (Veblen, 1904 [1988], p. 6)

The cultural force which animates this machine process is that of the business enterprise under the guiding concerns of profit. The goal of profit, a pecuniary motive, harnesses productive endeavors, coordinating ownership, trade and the allocation of property among individuals. As an example of this industrial/pecuniary dichotomy, consider bauxite. Bauxite has always contained aluminum ore, and the chemical reactions necessary to create aluminum are much older than the subject of chemistry. But the relationships and methods used to turn bauxite into aluminum, if there is to be any hope of some scale or regularity to the process, require a legal system of contracting, finance and the spur of the profit motive. Each of the latter is a social construction.

Accepting Veblen's application of the concept of culture, we can recognize that the relationship between industry and business may not be as consistently harmonious as is so frequently assumed. If a business wishes to profit by producing additional goods or by improving the methods for manufacture, there exists a happy confluence of industrial and business goals. But, if an opportunity exists to create profit by cutting output, interfering with supplies of raw materials, by withholding productive capacity, or by manipulating financial contracts and obligations to the detriment of trade, a wise businessperson would, it may be surmised, be equally inclined to seize the opportunity. In the latter case, it is plausible to believe that the forces of competition would ensure that such methods would be adopted. The firm that chose not to adopt such methods would simply lose competitive strength relative to its more aggressive rivals. Consequently, it is possible that the affairs of business will not always encourage the expansion of industry. Under the correct conditions, they will even thwart it (Veblen, 1901 [1990], pp. 288, 292).

Positing a theoretical explanation of industrial sabotage drew little support from professional economists or the business community. As a consequence of their predispositions and training, most economists ignore, or view as an aberration, the conflict between industry and business. In the conventional introductory analysis of marginal costs of production and revenue, there is little possibility of profit from the deliberate withdrawal of efficiency. The realization that firms operate within a monetary framework, and for that reason are interested in nominal money values in real time, is also obscured from view by the conventional representations of the marginal analysis of production costs. It becomes difficult to imagine the business goal of accumulating nominal profits could be achieved through the alteration and rescheduling of the financial contracts or assets of the firm, or the employment of new financial instruments – all of which are possible without recourse to changes in the output of the firm (Veblen, 1909 [1990], p. 249).

The Veblenian legacy has been diminished by more than just willful ignorance. While the dichotomy can be usefully applied, it should be recognized that the two forces are not polar opposites. Indeed, by assuming that they are mutually exclusive goals, this dichotomy can be easily criticized and dismissed (Uselding, 1980, p. 445; John, 1997, p. 165). Rather, as Veblen noted, if technological advance represents the surest way to pecuniary gain, the two goals are complementary. If the mere fact of industrial progress in the twentieth century provides sufficient proof to the faithful of the harmonious confluence of business and industrial pursuits, it seems the existence of two distinct words (profit and production) might be used by critics as sufficient evidence of their asymmetry.

AN EVOLUTIONARY THEORY

Another element of Veblen's core theoretical structure was the idea of constant social evolution. As technologies evolve and our cultural constructs slowly adapt or change, society is gradually being altered. As is generally known and understood, incremental change ultimately results in qualitative change. To describe this evolution, Veblen articulated a series of stages. This heuristic device of stages allowed Veblen to develop a taxonomy of material and social behaviors, and to explain their connection, alteration or the gradual lingering influence that extended beyond their originating stage.

In the larger sweep of human history, the contemporary stage of civilization was preceded by various stages of Savagery and Barbarism. Although these stages are in the past, some anachronistic habits remain embedded within modern practice. As explained by Veblen, examples of such phenomena would include most transparently 'The Barbarian status of woman'. Other examples are illustrated in his article, 'An early experiment in trusts' (Veblen, 1899, 1904a [1990]). But Veblen also maintains that, in the modern stage of civilization, societies and business practices have continued to evolve. Following the language of the German writers, Veblen characterized the economy of the early-modern period, the late eighteenth and early nineteenth centuries, as that of the 'money economy'. In the last decades of the nineteenth century, Veblen argued this system was giving way to the 'credit economy'.

What characterizes the early-modern scheme, the 'money economy', and sets it off in contrast with the natural economy (distribution in kind) that went before it in West-European culture, is the ubiquitous resort to the market as a vent for products and a source of supply of goods. The characteristic feature of this money economy is the goods market ... and to this early-modern system of industrial life the current doctrines of political economy are adapted, as indicated above. The credit economy – the scheme of economic life of the immediate past and the present – has made an advance over the money economy in the respect which chiefly distinguishes the latter. The goods market ... is still as powerful an economic factor as ever, but it is no longer the dominant factor in business and industrial traffic, as it once was. The capital market has taken the first place in this respect. The capital market is the modern economic feature which makes and identifies the higher 'credit economy' as such. In this credit economy resort is habitually had to the market as a vent for accumulated money values and a source of supply of capital. (Veblen, 1904 [1988], pp. 150–51)

This evolution of the credit economy altered the pre-existing forms of financial and legal arrangements. Veblen argued this alteration was necessary to culturally encapsulate the technological revolution in production, communication and transportation commonly referred to as the second industrial revolution. The significance of these business adaptations, however, was ignored or misunderstood by the majority of economists who continued to rely upon theoretical constructs formulated during the earlier, 'money economy', stage of development (Veblen, 1904 [1988], p. 133).

THE RISE OF THE NATIONAL MARKET

Introductions to the subject of industry and business typically assume that the purpose of the corporation and corporate finance is to provide the purchasing power necessary to invest in the machinery and technologies of mass production (McEachern, 2006, p. 294). For Thorstein Veblen, such an observation could not be more incorrect. Veblen argued that the rise of the modern industrial corporation represented a unique solution to the problems of excess capacity and increased competitive pressures that were ushered in by the creation of industrial society. Specifically, the corporation and its use of equity finance did not create mass production, it fixed it.

Unlike the conventional wisdom regarding the role of the corporation and corporate finance, Veblen's theory more closely fits the stylized facts. The Trust was the closest organizational precursor to the corporation, and its history was clearly an attempt to coordinate the productive capacity of disparate firms. With respect to the use of corporate finance, it is a well-documented fact that the vast majority of corporate stock issues have never been used to finance real investment (Eddy, 1937, p. 79; Myers, 2001,

p. 82). As a matter of timing, it is also unlikely that corporate finance could have created the investment necessary for modern industry. Simply put, modern industry began to appear before the full flowering of the modern corporate form. While the modern manufacturing techniques had generally been established in the primary industries by 1880, the modern legal form of the corporation was not fully established until the general revision of New Jersey's Corporate Statutes in 1896 (Chandler, 1977, *passim*; Seligman, 1976, p. 265). To illustrate the importance of these changes, a digression is warranted.

During the nineteenth century, the factory form of mass production that had developed in textiles, hog slaughter and armaments was expanded into a wider range of industries. By the 1880s, the fields of food processing, chemicals, petroleum, primary metals, machinery and transportation equipment had already seen significant investment in larger factories according to census analysis (O'Brien, 1988, p. 641). Having plowed their profits back into investments, regional firms had adopted the new technologies, increased factory size, and expanded the total productive capacity of the economy.

Coupled with these new factories and production technologies, expansion and integration of the railroad system and telegraph communications dramatically reduced the costs of transportation. Consequently, previously isolated regional firms were gradually subjected to national competition. The machine process crept forward with the expanding body of social knowledge, reorganizing and ordering all features of life that it came into contact with.

> [T]hroughout this period of industrial growth, changes in the processes of industry and in the localisation of the various industries had been going forward; due in great part to the growth and redistribution of the population and to continued extensions and enlargements of the transportation systems. New natural resources also continued to be drawn into the industrial system and to be engrossed by certain of the larger owners. All of which conspired to put these business concerns out of date and out of joint with the conditions of the market. Perhaps the gravest of the factors ... was the competitive character of their market ... because the productive capacity of the existing plants was already greater than the market would carry off at a profitable price. (Veblen, 1923 [1964], p. 335)

This process of industrial expansion, however, conflicted with traditional business arrangements. The business practices adopted during the stage of regionally segregated production were no longer profitable. The typical business response to this new competition and larger market was to expand production and reduce prices to sell more product. But this strategy was not profitable when total productive capacity exceeded total demand at the relevant reasonable price. Competition between firms became cut-throat in an attempt to secure market share and operate at full capacity (running full). Smaller firms were unable to compete against those firms which had adopted modern continuous production methods and larger firms engaged in destructive price competition. In several industries, prices fell below the cost of production. Bankruptcy, liquidation and financial crisis were the consequent dangers, as described by Veblen.

> These industrial business concerns, and their underlying companies and plants, had in their time been projected with a view to the traffic of a fairly open competitive market, and they had expanded by successive extensions and accretions, and so had grown to maturity under conditions which that traffic had created. With the progressive filling-out and closing-in of this market they found themselves, progressively, in the position of competitive producers for a closed market of variable volume ... And all the while their combined productive capacity rather exceeded the capacity of their market – at any such price as would afford them a 'reasonable profit' on their output. In this sense the market was closing in. It was becoming too narrow for a free run of output at the price-level at which these enterprises had been projected. The period of competitive business in the key industries was closing. So that the continued open competition among them became 'cut-throat competition'; such as to entail present and prospective decline of their earning capacity. (Veblen, 1923 [1964], p. 337)

Under the conditions of technological evolution, standard business practices and methods of organization were no longer profitable. Some solution was necessary. It is in this light we see the evolution of social practice (the new legal form and financial mechanisms of the corporation) reorganizing the ownership of industrial assets and profitably harnessing the new technologies.

> The conjuncture was essentially that of a sweeping transition and realignment, incident to the passing of the common run of the key industries from a footing of competitive business in an ample market to a footing of collusive traffic in a closed market too narrow for unguarded competitive production. (Veblen, 1923 [1964], p. 338)

THE CORPORATION AS LEGAL TRUST

By the 1890s, piecemeal consolidation of businesses in specific lines of industry had been attempted and found lacking. These quasi-legal consolidations included pools, associations, gentlemen's agreements and the Trust form of organization. The Trust form of organization, initially developed in refining industries such as petroleum, lead and sugar, issued trust certificates to the owners of competing firms, allowing the coordination of independent firms. The Sherman Anti-trust Act of 1890, while failing to stop the eventual consolidation of industry, did stop the use of trust certificates to coordinate the management of independent firms. Some other method of coordinating ownership was necessary.

While the possibility of creating a federal incorporation law was discussed during the Industrial Commission of 1900, legislation was never proposed. The states have retained their responsibility for controlling the creation (and receiving the charter fees) of corporations. This lack of uniformity allowed some states, such as New Jersey and Delaware, to experiment with new conditions and corporate privileges in response to business interests. Other states such as Ohio maintained more conservative laws governing incorporation. For New Jersey and others, the state revenue that could be generated from annual corporation charter fees certainly stimulated their willingness to reform the charter codes and grant specific privileges to the new corporations (Grandy, 1989, p. 678).

In the competition between states for corporate charters, New Jersey emerged as the clear winner. It incorporated more than half of all new corporate mergers in the decade that straddled 1900. After establishing the right to create a corporation through a standardized filing process in 1874, additional changes were made in 1888 and 1891. Ultimately, these revisions were included in the major and more substantial general revision of corporate law in 1896. Joel Seligman, one of the United States' leading scholars in securities law, has referred to New Jersey's 1896 revision as the basis for all modern corporate law (Seligman, 1976, p. 265).

With the active support of corporation lawyer James Brooks Dill, New Jersey Governor Leon Abbett and Secretary of State Henry Kelsey, New Jersey liberalized its General Incorporation Laws in 1888, establishing among other rights an absolutely lower and marginally declining tax rate on total capitalization (Grandy, 1989, p. 681). The next several years saw additional revisions that were accumulated in the General Revision Act of 1896. This act also included some new freedoms, and explicitly clarified some of the lingering confusions regarding tax rates, director liabilities and total capitalization. In 1893, the right of any New Jersery corporation to hold the shares of any other corporation was established. The right to pay for tangible and intangible assets, services and corporate stock with fully paid corporate stock was established in 1889 and extended in 1896 with the provision that the director's valuation of assets acquired would be accepted, except in the case of fraud. This last clause proved especially important in facilitating the acquisition of assets that had no replacement or production costs (Borgmeyer, 1900; US Industrial Commission, 1901, pp. 265–91; Stimson, 1892).

Unrelated to the corporate charter law, New Jersey's repeal of the state Antitrust law in 1892 also helped reduce fears of future litigation for merger activity. At the same time New Jersey was liberalizing these features of its business law, other states were busy prosecuting firms accused of stifling competition. Examples include New York's prosecution of the North River Sugar Refining Company in 1888 (later American Sugar Refining NJ); Ohio's 1891 prosecution of Standard Oil of Ohio, and the Distiller's and Cattlefeeder's Trust decision to avoid litigation by becoming incorporated in Illinois (Hake, 1994, p. 32). Prosecution by other states made New Jersey even more attractive to firms seeking the right to merge. Ultimately, by 1896, the New Jersey corporations had an unlimited lifespan, limited liability of shareholders and protection for directors in case of bankruptcy, the right to consolidate businesses within similar lines of industry and unlimited capitalization.

These key changes in New Jersey corporate law (and to a lesser extent Delaware, Pennsylvania and New York) provided a new mechanism to organize the ownership of manufacturing, a reorganization similar to that already experienced by the railroad industry. The opportunity provided by this revised corporate form and an emergent speculative demand for new security issues on the secondary market culminated in the American merger movement of 1895–1904. Following the Trust Movement of the 1880s and a small merger boom of 1889–93, the turn of the century merger period created more than 400 mergers from 3000 previously independent firms (Hake, 1994, p. 3; Lamoreaux, 1985; Nelson, 1959).

In the standard scenario, a corporate promoter would arrange for the creation of a new corporation and secure from existing company owners an option to acquire their property or outstanding stock with shares of stock in this new corporation. By granting the new corporation directors unlimited capitalization and the right to acquire any assets with new issues of stock at any price they deemed appropriate, the New Jersey Law provided a valuable tool for reorganizing the ownership of existing productive capacity. Indeed, the only limit on the ability of the new corporation to create and consolidate ownership was the willingness of speculators on the secondary market to acquire shares. In this way, the stock market became a system for the continual extension of credit to the firm. The two primary uses of these stock issues were the generation of working capital (underwritten for cash) and the reorganization of industrial ownership (sold or swapped for stock). The ability of the corporation to consolidate industry and receive this injection of liquidity is ultimately based on the expectations and mood of the speculative secondary market. In periods of speculative excitement, the ability to float new stock accelerates, thereby adding to firm liquidity or additional mergers and acquisitions.

In the standard merger scenario, a merger promoter would arrange the acquisition of several competing firms' assets or capital stock with newly issued shares of a corporation created specifically for the purpose of merging the former competitors into one company. For all interested parties, such as the banks and trust agencies underwriting the new company, the former business owners and the speculative promoters, payment would be made in the new shares of the company. Some interested parties would require some portion of their payment in cash. The merger promoter's ultimate decision regarding the capitalization of the new firm became a function of the total costs necessary to satisfy the various constituents. In this way, the value of the stock payment used to pay the financier and others for their services became a part of the new firm's capital stock. The shares of the new company could then be floated on the secondary exchange. The willingness of speculators on the secondary market to acquire these new shares was the ultimate determinant of whether the combinations could be formed: they were the granters of the credit necessary to consolidate ownership.

It should not be surprising, however, that in a period of such dramatic upheaval and reorganization a certain over-exuberance on the part of company financiers was apparent. In the decades following the end of the nineteenth century, more than half of the corporations created through mergers between 1895 and 1904 failed. Some industries were unable to coordinate production successfully and still others were experiencing continued technological innovation. In these cases, new developments, such as vertical and conglomerate mergers, appeared in later years. But, in the success stories of first mergers, and in the new mergers that were yet to appear, the corporate form was the mechanism of coordination.

Thus, the merger period of 1895–1904 represents a watershed in American industrial and financial development. The importance of this legal innovation as a solution to the problem of excess capacity and unprofitable organization is not determined by the number of original corporations that failed, but by the ubiquity of its use in modern industrial societies. During the late nineteenth century, the corporate form was adapted to manufacturing concerns and proved to be a suitable method for organizing industry on a coordinated national level. The size and number of security issues by manufacturing companies had been greatly expanded with a consequent expansion of the secondary market. Additionally, the types of securities issued and the methods of corporate finance had both been altered and found agreeable (Navin and Sears, 1955; Dewing, 1922). The modern industrial corporation had arrived.

THE ORIGIN AND EVOLUTION OF CAPITAL

In describing the role of the corporation and corporate finance in the modern era, Veblen argued that the productive assets of the corporation were evolving to include new forms of capital. The attempt to establish a definitive explanation of capital, however, was not unique to Veblen. Capital has long been a problematic concept, an asset that is difficult to define and measure but whose existence nevertheless establishes the right to income for the owner of business, altering the marginal shares of laborer and rentier. Consequently, the history of economics includes a history of capital controversies, one that quickly and inevitably enters the territory of competing ideologies.

The reason for this ideological undertone is transparent. Without capital, there would be no capitalism. Capital is that asset that accelerates the productivity of labor and leads to the creation of material wealth. The creation of capital is therefore crucial to economic development. But how is capital created? Through greater savings? By lowering interest rates? Through more competition between firms? The existence of capital is also a primary determinant of income distribution. The ownership of such powerful material would necessarily provide a handsome income, and the existence of capital and the right to profit could reduce (or increase) the income shares of those who provide labor or raw materials. Unfortunately, capital as an asset has proved hard to define, much less measure, and so the determination of the proper share of gross income that can be attributed to capital owners also remains vague. Like many divisive subjects, its status vacillates between heated debate and taboo (Tuttle, 1903; Weston, 1951; Cohen and Harcourt, 2003).

In Veblen's work, the changing and evolving nature of capital represented the key development of the modern corporation. These changes in the nature of capital affected the distribution of income, the organization of industry, and had implications for the business cycle. He included an in-depth discussion of capital in *The Theory of Business Enterprise* (Chapters 5 and 6) and *Absentee Ownership* (Chapter 12). His fullest treatment, however, appeared in the *Quarterly Journal of Economics*. In this journal, Veblen presented his most complete treatment of the theory of capital by dividing the subject in two. The resulting articles were published in August and November of 1908. 'Capital I' (1908b [1990]) was an explanation of the sociological origins of capital. 'Capital II' (1908c [1990]) explored the growing significance of capital as a pecuniary asset.

Capital I: The Productivity of Capital Goods

When most economists refer to capital, they generally conceive of it as a stock of physical productive assets, 'industrial equipment, raw materials, and means of subsistence' (Veblen, 1904b, [1988], p. 134).[3] To make these physical objects productive, however, there must be some knowledge of how to use the equipment, the ways and means of using the object. Without that knowledge, the physical object would have no use and therefore would not be considered a capital asset. This can be seen most easily with capital assets in various cultural contexts or under changing technological circumstances. In primitive cultures, a length of cord or digging stick will only have productive power if social knowledge of how to use these items exists. Likewise, capital goods received from other societies may often go unused or underutilized, unless they can be adapted for use in the existing social/ economic stage of existence. Its application, and potential productivity, is then not a function of the object itself, but the cultural circumstance and knowledge base of the community deploying it. In a similar manner, capital goods of antique vintage, adapted to an earlier industrial circumstance, may become irrelevant and unused. The existing social circumstance and state of industrial knowledge in this case determines whether the asset is a capital good or simply a discardable object (Veblen, 1908b [1990], p. 327). As Veblen described, the existence of a generalized body of knowledge, and the ability of a culture to generate that knowledge, are the source of the productive capabilities of the physical objects referred to as capital. Most importantly, the capital objects themselves may be of a transitory or easily duplicated nature, even though the knowledge base that informs their creation is not so transient. Capital is therefore a social phenomenon, and is a consequence of the social characteristics of human society to innovate, communicate and accumulate knowledge (Veblen, 1908b [1990], pp. 324–5).

   In most phases of human civilization, it can be generally argued that the common stock of knowledge regarding the ways and means of physical production is considerably greater than the ability of any one individual to create or use it. Despite this complexity, for most of human history, the physical equipment – what is usually referred to as capital – has been relatively insignificant. It is not until the later stages of civilization that the material artifacts necessary to exploit the existent social stock of knowledge become more specialized and exacting, to the point they can no longer be worked in common or easily constructed. At this latter point, property rights in capital equipment begin to take shape, and the restriction of access becomes possible. At this point, the ability for an individual or small group of individuals to extract income from the common stock of knowledge as it is embodied in or used in conjunction with specific material artifacts becomes the conventional and accepted practice (Veblen, 1908b [1990], p. 331).

To clarify the matter, Veblen extended his analysis to show the similarities between recent claims to property over modern capital and earlier claims that were established over other sources of wealth such as landed estates, labor (as in the example of slavery) and cattle. Except in the shape of the physical artifact, Veblen argues the claim, as a property right, to corner the usufruct of common knowledge of the producing community in the era of modern capital was no different from the income shares that were earlier claimed as a consequence of the ownership of estates composed of land, slaves or cattle. Those sources of income could be considered a return on the capital investments associated with earlier states of technological knowledge (Veblen, 1908b [1990], pp. 333–4).

The landlord's, slave-owner's or capital owner's preferential position to claim a portion of the net product consists of their legal right to 'decide whether, how far, and on what terms men shall put this technological scheme into effect in those features' which involve the use of their physical equipment (Veblen, 1908b [1990], p. 338). Under those circumstances where the state of technology is such that virtually everyone has the capacity to acquire and deploy the community's accumulated stock of immaterial equipment, the satisfaction of social goals may be efficiently met by the classical system of natural liberty and free competition. But, as technology advances, the minimum efficient unit of industrial equipment necessarily extends beyond the capacity of the individual to construct or acquire it. In these latter circumstances, equality before the law as conceived in the eighteenth-century vision of *laissez faire* was no longer sufficient to produce equal opportunity (Veblen, 1908b [1990], p. 340).

To this point, Veblen's explanation of the role of capital has focused specifically on a given stock of capital: an explanation of the sociological basis of capital's productivity has been extended to show the impact of technology on the relative share of income going to the owner of capital equipment. Veblen argued that a given stock of capital equipment was profitable, and capable of producing some material return, because of its location within a specific community's knowledge and capacities. As technology advanced, the ability of business interests to assume a larger portion of the net product, to corner the productive capacity of knowledge was made more explicit by the increased scale of capital equipment.

But, for Veblen, the unique feature of the modern age was not the origin of capital's productivity, but rather the ability of business to finance the acquisition and accumulation of capital. To understand the importance he attributed to financial capital, Veblen wrote his second essay, 'On the nature of capital: II. Investment, intangible assets, and the pecuniary magnate'.

Capital II: Investment, Intangible Assets and the Pecuniary Magnate

> The pivotal factor in the business enterprise of this new era is the larger use of credit which has come into action during the last few decades; larger in absolute scale and volume as well as the ratio which it bears to those underlying tangible assets on which it is conceived to rest. (Veblen, 1923 [1964], p. 326)

In his first essay on capital, Veblen dealt with the subject along much the same lines as the Smithian tradition: capital was depicted as a physical object, a 'productive good' in his terminology. While Veblen argued that the profitability of those capital goods depended upon the degree to which the social store of knowledge had been successfully cornered by private business, the type of capital, as useful devices or machines, was at least familiar to the general line of discussion. In his second essay, however, Veblen turned his attention to the role of liquid or pecuniary capital. It was this component of capital, liquid capital as a financial asset rather than merely a piece of equipment, that he considered the most striking feature of the modern era. While this class of 'intangible' assets had already seen some earlier articulation, the new circumstances of business, the creation of the industrial corporation and corporate finance, adapted these earlier theoretical constructions and greatly expanded their relative significance.

For Veblen, the idea that capital was limited solely to physical productive assets was a theoretical construction more suited to the time of Adam Smith, when the conditions of the money economy prevailed. According to the testimony included in the Industrial Commission Reports of 1900 the businessman's notion of capital had been dramatically changed by the circumstances of continuous production. In modern times, as the wider use of credit, corporate finance and the mechanism of the corporation had come to dominate business relationships, the businessman's notion of capital had evolved. To remain relevant to the advancing methods of business, Veblen argued that the economist's theory of capital also needed to evolve (Veblen, 1904 [1988], p. 134).

> A modern science has to do with the facts as they come to hand, not with putative phenomena warily led out from a primordial metaphysical postulate, such as the 'hedonic principle'. To meet the needs of science, therefore, such modern concepts as 'capital' and 'income' must be defined by observation rather than by ratiocination ... As it plays its part in these affairs of business, the concept of capital is, substantially, a habit of thought of the men engaged in business, more or less closely defined in practice by the consensus of usage in the business community. A serviceable definition of it, therefore, for the use of modern science, can be got only by observation of the current habits of thought of business men. This painfully longwinded declaration of what may appear to be a patent truism so soon as it is put in words may seem a gratuitous insistence on a stale

commonplace. But it is an even more painfully tedious fact that the current polemics about 'the capital concept' goes on year after year without recognition of this patent truism. (Veblen, 1908a [1964], p. 150)

Adopting the language of business, Veblen stated that capital could be either *tangible* or *intangible*. Tangible assets were capital goods, physical equipment that could yield an income when applied to the act of production. Intangible assets also yielded an income, but their immaterial nature encompassed a wide range of market conditions, business arrangements and the outcome of influence and force. Crucial to the circumstances of modern industry, larger and larger portions of the assets claimed by the corporation were falling under the heading of intangible assets (Veblen, 1908c [1990], p. 353).

These intangible assets greatly increased the firm's access to credit by increasing the total quantity of capital owned by the firm. Unlike tangible assets, this class of assets did not have technological serviceability. But, like tangible assets, they had the ability to yield an income. Claiming these intangibles as a valuable source of wealth in the corporation meant an increase in the total value of assets recorded on the balance sheet of the corporation. In the practice of corporate finance, these assets could then be capitalized and securitized – turned into shares of ownership to be sold for cash, services or the outstanding stock of competing firms.

In addition to physical productive equipment, what kinds of assets provide their owner with a right to income? Veblen began by discussing those intangible assets most closely situated to actual tangible assets. It is reasonable, then, in this first case, to think of legal rights to produce particular types of goods, or legal protections for a particular method of manufacture (Veblen, 1908c [1990], p. 362). Starting with those intangible assets in closest proximity to the tangible act of production, it is apparent that patents, trademarks and brand names provide their owner with some enhanced right to income. It is reasonable to assume a firm with a patented production process, or a specific brand name, can be assured of a higher return on investment, when compared to a competitor producing a similar unpatented, unbranded, good. The value of that patent, trademark or branded name could then be calculated as some percentage return on investment above the normal rate of return. The legal costs of developing and protecting this technique could then be considered an undertaking with a projected rate of return. This vision of intangible assets fits closely with those notions then coming into vogue among businesses. An intangible asset, then, provides some percentage return on tangible capital stock above what could be expected under normal business conditions.

Goodwill, an accounting and business term that has a long history of confounding accounting conventions, can be seen as one step removed from the physical nature of the patented production process. As a term and capitalizable asset that predated the late nineteenth century, a working definition of goodwill had previously been adopted, at least for general purposes of discussion. Under these terms, goodwill was seen as a return associated with stable business relations, 'a kindly sentiment of trust and esteem on the part of a customer...' (Veblen, 1908c [1990], p. 363). If a customer had been well served by a particular vendor in past contracts, then that customer would be more willing to establish a stable business relationship, returning to the producer as a repeat customer. The intangibility of this asset can be easily seen. While it had been suggested that goodwill resides in the favorable quality of the goods for sale, or in the positive mood of the shopkeeper, its existence is most clearly traced back to the habits and routines of customers. For a variety of reasons, a customer could choose to continue to do business, or could search for an alternative supplier, the relatively low price, high quality or the pleasant demeanor of the owner notwithstanding. The only substantive evidence of this phenomenon, however, is a slightly higher and more durable level of business income.

As each example of intangibility moves by degrees from the realm of tangible productive effort, it is useful to remember that *any asset that yields an income can be considered an item of wealth to be capitalized by the firm*. It is at this most abstract statement of the degree of intangibility that Veblen's industrial/pecuniary dichotomy becomes most apparent. Because activities in restraint of trade can generate profits (or stave off losses), it is possible to consider such an activity to be the basis of a new intangible asset. Some method of justifying, explaining and making concrete the higher rate of profit is necessary.

Within the ethereal realm of loosely defined business relations and the relevant degree of industrial competition, there are business arrangements, such as the exercise of market power, that allow for increased profits. In the most extreme case, the position of monopoly can be seen as providing a uniquely large and stable profit margin. The creation of intangible assets, then, represents the capitalization of this market power, helping to solidify the position of powerful business interests. Despite its earlier pleasant image, from the Veblenian perspective, it is apparent that goodwill is more easily understood as capitalized restraint of trade. Indeed, goodwill and the more general class of intangible assets are convenient legal fictions created by the desire to capitalize the privilege of market power. Profits generated by the production of goods are created by tangible assets. Profits generated in other ways, such as the restraint of trade, are created by intangible assets.

> On this showing it would appear that the substantial difference between tangible and intangible assets lies in the different character of the immaterial facts which

are turned to pecuniary account in the one case and in the other. The former, in effect, capitalise such a fraction of the technological proficiency of the community as the ownership of the capital goods involved enables the owner to engross. The latter capitalise such habits of life, of a non-technological character – settled by usage, convention, arrogation, legislative action, or what not – as will effect a differential advantage to the concern to which the assets in question appertain. (Veblen, 1908c [1990], p. 365)

While this distinction between tangible and intangible assets is useful, and becomes more clearly significant in its application to corporate finance and the behavior of the business cycle, Veblen did not think the distinction between the two was necessarily hard and fast. Indeed, intangible assets could be used to acquire tangible assets, and vice versa. The printing of advertisements involves manufacture, but it is undertaken for the purpose of generating intangible assets. Conversely, an intangible asset may be seen as enhancing the value of goods being sold. In still another transmutation, the added increment of income from a monopoly position may be used to acquire new productive equipment (Veblen, 1908c [1990], p. 367).

For those accustomed to thinking of capital as capital equipment, the conversion of tangibility into intangibility, and back, would be difficult to understand. For Veblen, it was relatively simple. Recognizing that assets are always calculated as a pecuniary business item, the value of the asset is a matter of capitalization. The determination of the capital asset as tangible or intangible is then merely a question of imputing value to a particular article or class of articles (Veblen, 1908c [1990], p. 367). Initially, that imputing of value was done through recorded production costs. As assets became more intangible, value could be determined by the decision of the director's valuation, or the price at which the investing public was willing to buy shares of capital.

Having solidified the distinctions between tangible and intangible assets, Veblen developed an additional layer of intangibility, an extended class of assets which provide income to the 'pecuniary magnate'. This capital financier benefited from judicious manipulations of the market for vendible capital. This higher stage of finance was important to Veblen's discussion of the modern system, business enterprise on the higher plane, that provided a more reliable source of income and profit than even the engrossing of productive efficiency undertaken by the lesser capitalist–employer still emerging in the late nineteenth century (Veblen, 1908c [1990], pp. 373–86). But this discussion is best continued after exploring the relationship between intangible assets, merger finance and the stock market.

Following Veblen, the concept of an intangible asset was based on practice that pre-dated the modern industrial firm. Goodwill as a concept had its origins in the friendly relations between the shopkeeper and customer of Adam Smith's time (Dicksee and Tillyard, 1906; Hughes, 1982). The development of financial arrangements utilizing the class of intangible asset and further extensions of credit through the primary, secondary and tertiary collateralization of assets had also seen more recent development in the railroad finance and reorganizations of the third quarter of the nineteenth century (Veblen, 1904b [1988], pp. 119, 140). What was different in the development of the modern industrial enterprise of the late nineteenth century, however, was the scale and speed with which the expansion of credit had occurred. The quantity of intangible assets assumed to exist in relation to the physical equipment of the firm was unprecedented, and so too was the speed with which the firms were constructed and capitalized.

> But as the possibilities of this expedient have grown familiar to the business community, the time consumed in perfecting the structure of debentures in each case has been reduced; until it is now not unusual to perfect the whole organization, with its load of debentures, at the inception of a corporate enterprise. In such a case, when a corporation starts with a fully organized capital and debt, the owners of the concern are also its creditors; they are, at the start, the holders of both common and preferred stock, and probably also of the bonds of the company – so adding another increment of confusion to the relation between modern capital and credit, as seen from the old-fashioned position as to what capitalization and its basis should be. (Veblen, 1904b [1988], p. 119)

The concept of capital was not the only common business term altered by the increased use of intangible assets. The basis for the capitalization of the firm underwent substantial transformation. As new assets were added to the balance sheet, old rules for calculating the value of capital stock that could be created were violated and discarded. According to the old rules of corporate finance, the ability to issue capital stock was limited to the book value of tangible assets included on the balance sheet. Shares were issued with a par (face) value, so that the total value of stock issued would equal the value of productive firm assets.

With the increased use of intangible assets, this rule was no longer applicable. Intangible asset value was difficult to determine. Within the practice of business and accounting, it now became necessary to determine a more encompassing method for calculating the value of a firm's capital stock. Once this was accomplished, Veblen claimed, the addition of intangible assets helped turn debits into credits and loans into assets. The traditional language of business was to a certain extent subverted by the new circumstances.

> The line between credit and capital, or between debt and property, in the values handled throughout these strategic operations of coalition, remains somewhat uncertain. Indeed, the old-fashioned concepts of 'debt' and 'property', or

'liabilities' and 'assets', are not fairly applicable to the facts of the case – except of course, in the way of a technical legal distinction. (Veblen, 1904b [1988], pp. 125–6).

Business competition helped to accelerate this blurring of credit and capital. Because the goal of increasing profit can be met by either increasing the total volume of business or increasing the rate of capital turnover, credit extensions become an important business strategy. The competition between firms promotes the full exploitation of these credit extensions. In this way, indebtedness comes to serve much the same purpose as the improvement of the processes of industry (Veblen, 1904b [1988], p. 95). Once the new methods of financing activity became generally accepted, firms that chose not to take fullest advantage of the improved access to financial resources for increased capitalization would find themselves unable to compete with those firms that had been more aggressive in applying these new methods.

Through a process of trial and error, it became apparent that some new method of capitalizing the firm was appearing in the new combinations and larger corporations of the late nineteenth century. Realizing that the value of the assets, whether tangible or intangible, existed in their ability to generate income, some promoters and financiers began to argue that the firm should be able to capitalize these assets according to the earnings of the corporation. The practice was already underway in the railroads and in Great Britain, and according to testimony before the US Industrial Commission, it was in practice in the US, at least de facto if not de jure (Hake, 1998, p. 149). This new method of valuing a firm frequently contrasted the older method of valuing the firm as a 'going-concern' with the (appreciably smaller) value of its physical assets. As noted by John R. Dos Passos, a Chicago lawyer and corporate promoter:

Capitalization is of two kinds; there is a capitalization based upon the actual value of the property and a capitalization upon earning power, these are the two methods. You will find two classes of people in this country – one in favor of the former method and one in favor of the latter. (U.S. Industrial Commission, 1901, p. 1149)

For Veblen, capitalization based on earning capacity meant a greatly expanded access to credit. A firm could have very limited tangible equipment but, if they were profitable, they could issue a greater magnitude of stock.

Under the exigencies of the quest of profits, as conditioned by the larger industry and the more sweeping business organization of the last few decades, the question of capital in business has increasingly become a question of capitalization on the basis of earning-capacity, rather than a question of the magnitude of the industrial plant or the cost of production of the appliances of industry. (Veblen, 1904b [1988], p. 89)

And, further, Veblen argued:

> Capital in the enlightened modern business usage means 'capitalized presumptive earning capacity', and in this capitalization is comprised the usufruct of whatever credit extension the given business concern's industrial equipment and good-will will support. (Veblen [1904] 1988, p. 127)

In this way, with the rise of the modern industrial corporation a cumulative change in finance and accounting was possible. The spasm of horizontal merger activity from 1895 to 1904 provides ample indication of the manufacturer's willingness to embrace the financial methods first articulated in the railroad reorganizations. These changes in capitalization technique and increased access to credit have as their genesis the acceptance of market power or preferential advantage as a legitimate component of business capital.

And what mischief such a simple addition could make. As an example, suppose a firm decides to pay for the services of a lawyer or financier with some newly-issued company stock. The lawyer is then able to sell those securities on the secondary market as compensation. But the value of those shares, issued for perhaps a transitory and momentary obligation, remain as evidence of capital on the balance sheet of the firm.[4] What might have previously been considered a liability of the corporation becomes viewed as an asset and is reflected in greater market capitalization.

> Answering to the essentially timeless character of the gains accruing to the financial agent, the earnings of the promoter engaged in transactions of this class are also not of the nature of profits per cent per time unit, but rather a bonus which commonly falls immediately into the shape of a share in the capitalization of the newly organized concern. ... It is worth noting that the cost of reorganization, including the bonus of the promoter and the financial agent is, in the common run of cases, added to the capitalization; that is to say, as near as this class of transactions may be spoken of in terms borrowed from the old-fashioned business terminology, what answers to the 'interest' due the creditor on the credit extension involved is incorporated in the 'capital' of the debtor, without circumlocution or faltering. (Veblen, 1904b [1988], pp. 124–5)

Alternatively, suppose a firm has the option to acquire the assets of a competitor and on doing so, destroys them. By reducing potential future competition, the earning capacity of the firm's existing assets can increase, and so too could the price of its existing stock and its ability to issue new capital stock.

As a final case, assume a combination has the ability to acquire several competing firms, each of which has its own share of intangible assets. In acquisition, the new corporation could include the value of all previously outstanding goodwill. To that value it could add an additional increment of goodwill to the balance sheet, to support the capital stock that must be distributed to the lawyers and underwriters as payment for services rendered (Veblen, 1904b [1988], p. 126). This practice, of successive layers of goodwill accruing to the corporation, makes theoretical sense only when goodwill is seen as a legal fiction to allow the capitalization of additional expected earning capacity. It does not make sense according to the earlier conception of goodwill, as positive business relations.

As if by magic, the expected increase in future earning capacity associated with the restraint of trade made possible by the new business arrangement can be used to finance the creation of the new corporation (Veblen, 1904b [1988], pp. 121–2). How much capital stock can the firm create in this way? As much as the market will bear. The mood of speculative investors becomes a primary determinant of the ability to reorganize the ownership of productive assets through merger.

VALUATION OF ASSETS

Following Veblen's analysis, the concept of intangibility alters the definition of capital, increases access to credit and changes the distribution of income associated with the corporation. The issue and sale of stock based on intangible assets provide a new mechanism to reorganize the ownership and industrial organization of productive assets. This new source of income also changes the corporation's basis for capitalization, shifting from a simple capitalization of physical productive equipment to a capitalization based on the expected earning capacity of the corporation. What has only been mentioned tangentially to this point is the method used to determine the value of that capital stock.

Through this review of the articulation and application of the concept of intangibility, the issue of valuation has remained in the background. It should come as no surprise that Veblen argued the method of valuing capital stock was also evolving. Initially, the imputation of the value of capital was done through the recorded costs of acquiring physical assets. This method seemed best fitted to a circumstance where the value of capital stock was based on productive capacity, and the time horizon of production was finite. But, as the process of continuous production emerges, and the value of capital stock is assumed to include the degree of competition and relative position of a firm in relation to its markets for inputs and outputs and the overall market power of the industry in which it operates, this method proves to be less reliable.

Of course this change occurred by degrees. As corporate laws changed to allow the use of stock to acquire stock in other companies or to acquire services, the value of capital stock took on a more indefinite nature. Increased managerial discretion during the turn of the century mergers provided a greater degree of latitude in the valuation of capital. The penultimate change, however, came with the growth of the secondary stock market and the constantly shifting value of industrial securities. Ultimately, the final decision of valuation becomes the secondary market in securities, the willingness of speculators to trade in the stock of the corporation. Lacking a substantive market price for physical assets, the value of the firm is determined by the opinions of the general business community.

> In effect, the adjustment of capitalization to earning-capacity is taken care of by the market quotations of stock and other securities: and no other method of adjustment is of any avail, because capitalization is a question of value, and market quotations are the last resort in questions of value. The value of any stock listed on the exchange, or otherwise subject to purchase and sale, fluctuates from time to time; which comes to the same thing as saying that the effectual capitalization of the concern, represented by the securities quoted, fluctuates from time to time. It fluctuates more or less, sometimes very slowly, but always at least so much as to compensate the long-period fluctuations of discount rates in the money market; which means that the purchase price of a given fractional interest in the corporation as a going concern fluctuates so as to equate it with the capitalized value of its putative earning-capacity, computed at current rates of discount and allowing for risk. (Veblen, 1904b [1988], fn. p. 118)

Once the capitalization of stock becomes a function of expected earning capacity, the uncertainty of the future necessarily becomes a part of that calculation. Consequently, the potential for the shifting opinions of that portion of the public that buys or sells stock is included in the value of capital. The potential for instability in the financial position of the firm, as well as managerial or speculative subterfuge, is therefore increased. On the one hand, the access to a valuable stream of credit – the capitalization of the expected earnings of the corporation – becomes dependent upon this sub-set of popular opinion. On the other hand, if it is possible to convince the stock-buying public that a firm has a likelihood of future profits, the firm's access to credit increases. Potentially, this increased credit could be used to create the conditions of increased profitability, or the momentary increase in fortunes could be used to divert income through the fortuitous sale of large stock positions.

This extension of instability into the basic elements of the balance sheet has important implications for the behavior of the business cycle. During periods of business optimism, the investing public will provide a ready demand for industrial securities. The effective capitalization of currently existing shares will also be increased. This will increase the liquidity of the firm, recapitalizing the firm and providing an increased ability to float new securities. In this respect, it is worth noting that the majority of cash raised by the initial sale of stock is used for purposes of adding to working capital, a phenomenon evident in the combination plans of the late nineteenth century and in modern practice (Fazzari and Petersen, 1993, p. 328; Hake, 1994, pp. 61, 76). These additions to working capital provide the firm with the ability to smooth earnings over time, increase the rate at which profits can be plowed back into investment and manage the debt obligations of the firm.

While this feature of the intangibility of assets is beneficial to the management of the firm's financial positions, periods of optimism can also increase the fragility of the economic system. As stock prices increase, the equity footing of the firm becomes thinner and the effective market capitalization of the firm expands relative to the value of underlying tangible assets.

> The run of business exigencies on which an era of prosperity goes forward may be sketched in its general features somewhat as follows: Increased demand and enhanced prices ... increase the prospective earnings of the several concerns engaged. The prospective earnings may eventually be realized in full measure, or they may turn out to have been putative earnings only; that is largely a question of how far in the future the liquidation lies. The business effect of increased prospective earnings, however, is much the same whether the event proves the expectation of increased earnings to have been well grounded or not. The expectation in either case leads the business men to bid high for equipment and supplies. Thereby the effective (market) capitalization is increased to answer to the increased prospective earnings. This recapitalization of industrial property, on the basis of heightened expectation, increases the value of this property as collateral. The inflated property becomes, in effect, collateral even without a formal extension of credit in the way of loans ... during the free swing of that buoyant enterprise that characterizes an era of prosperity contracts are entered into with a somewhat easy scrutiny of the property values available to secure a contract. So that as regards this point not only is the capitalization of the industrial property inflated on the basis of expectation, but in the making of contracts the margin of security is less closely looked after than it is in the making of loans on collateral. (Veblen, 1904b [1988], pp. 197–8)

An additional feature of the buoyant stock market is its effect on mergers and acquisitions. Because corporate stock represents shares of ownership in the enterprise, the secondary market becomes a market that facilitates the reorganization of industrial assets. A period of positive public sentiment increases the effective capitalization of the firm and the ability of the firm to issue stock. This increases the firm's ability to buy, sell or swap stock to reorganize the ownership of existing industrial assets through mergers, acquisitions or spin-offs. A prominent example that occurred during the recent technology bubble was AOL's purchase of the publishing giant Time-Warner. Under these conditions of strong public sentiment regarding the potential future earning capacity of the firm, the market stands ready to absorb the large issues of securities necessary to effect these alterations of industrial ownership.

Over an extended period of optimism, the thinner equity footing of capital ultimately increases the fragility of the balance sheet. If investor confidence in the future value of the firm is shaken, it is possible to experience a sudden and discontinuous decline in the sentiment of the stock-owning public and thereby the effective capitalization of the firm. This, in turn, reduces the firm's access to working capital, thereby increasing the volatility of the earnings stream, and potentially leading to a collapse of the liability structures that were predicated on the value of the firm's assets. The potential volatility of asset valuation can, of course, be magnified across the business landscape, contributing to the fluctuations of the business cycle.

> Of the three phases of business activity, depression, exaltation, and crisis, the last named has claimed the larger and livelier attention from students, as it is also the more picturesque phenomenon. An industrial crisis is a period of liquidation, cancelment of credits, high discount rates, falling prices and 'forced sales', and shrinkage of values. It has as a sequel, both severe and lasting, a shrinkage of capitalization through the field affected by it. (Veblen, 1904b [1988], pp. 190–91)

From the perspective of Veblen, capitalism in the modern age finds itself in a peculiar position. Capital, the unique property claim that determines so much of the distribution of income and the ownership of profit, is more expansive yet stands on much softer ground than in the era of the money economy. The value of capital is no longer the book value of physically productive assets. Capital has become a function of the general stock-buying public's opinion regarding the ability of the firm to achieve and exercise market power. The corporate form provides the constituent framework for the organization of industry, the distribution of incomes and the extension of credit. Under such conditions, the ability to organize and reorganize the productive capacity of the economy provides an alternative to financial crisis and liquidation. The role of speculation is increased as the pursuit of income through the manipulation of expectations and the trading of vendible capital comes to provide greater potential returns than simple production for sale. The potential for catastrophic adjustment, a sudden precipitous decline of the value of a firm's capital assets and its access to credit, could be considered a summary effect of this new system.

FINANCIAL INNOVATION AND THE GROWTH OF THE SECONDARY STOCK MARKET

While Thorstein Veblen later came to be criticized for a lack of empirical testing, it is apparent that his theory comes directly from the practical affairs of business and a close observation of those developments. In this sense, his is an organic conception of the modern industrial economy. Much of the substance of his argument regarding corporate finance comes, almost directly, from the comments provided by business leaders that can be found in the US Industrial Commission Reports. If his theoretical description of the modern industrial economy is to be dismissed, such a dismissal should include an explanation as to why his ostensible errors were shared by so many prominent business leaders of the early twentieth century. In developing an explanation of the role of the modern corporation, and its use in reorganizing the manufacturing capacity of the United States in the late nineteenth century, it would seem reasonable to take as a basis for argument the commentary of business leaders such as Charles Flint, John Dos Passos, James B. Dill, John W. Gates, Francis L. Stetson, Henry H. Rogers and Henry O. Havemeyer – the men who were responsible for the creation of U.S. Steel, Standard Oil, American Steel and Wire, and the American Sugar Refining company, to name just a few. Their discussions of the workings of corporate finance are a commentary that few economists have tried to integrate into a theoretical framework.

Veblen's theory, as outlined above, is best understood as the potential tendency of the new circumstances of business. It is as reasonable to suppose that in some lines of industry the new forms of merged corporations and modern financial structures are less likely to be adopted because of the unique circumstances of some trades (Veblen, 1908b [1990], p. 347). Similarly, even those industries more fully reorganized through the corporate form still retained some portion of tangible assets and productive equipment, and so the ability of capital to be entirely converted into intangibility represents some unachievable theoretical upper bound.

Despite this caveat, Veblen's theory of the corporation closely overlays many developments observed over the late nineteenth century. The scale and scope of the increased use of intangible assets explored by Veblen can be seen in both the financial innovation of the corporation and the consequent growth of the secondary market for these instruments. Manufacturing firms adopted many financial innovations from railroad reorganizations. These financial innovations also allowed the creation of combination or reorganization plans utilizing multiple stock issues that were formalized through legal agreements prior to the formation of the new corporation.

Prior to 1889, the few industrial firms that had stock on the New York Stock Exchange listed common stock, bonds or trust certificates. By 1904, the standard plans for combination involved a stock swap or stock acquisition of constituent firm assets. The capitalization of the new firms utilized common stock, preferred stock, bonds, debentures and collateral trust bonds. General conventions were adopted for the valuation of the various classes of securities issued by the corporation. Common stock was frequently valued according to intangible assets or some multiple of earnings and offered as a bonus on preferred stock. Preferred stock was frequently valued according to the physical assets of the firm. According to the industrialists involved in the combination movement, these new financial instruments, and the ability to capitalize the firm in excess of tangible assets, were crucial to the process of reorganization. To entice constituent owners and the general public to accept new company shares, some opportunity for both guaranteed return (preference shares) and speculative gains (common stock) was necessary. While bonds could have been issued to meet some of the combination's financial obligations, there was no market for bonds unsecured by collateral. The common stock and preference shares provided the opportunity for speculative returns, and the market was eager to accept that risk (US Industrial Commission, 1901, pp. 1149–50).

As the quantity and variety of newly issued securities multiplied, the secondary market for industrial securities grew rapidly (Navin and Sears, 1955, p. 129). This expansion is consonant with Veblen's description of the increased reliance upon the extension of credit. Prior to the first small wave of merger activity from 1889 to 1893 there were 28 firms listed on the miscellaneous and industrial securities index of the New York Stock Exchange, 21 of which were associated with the railroads as land, water power, tunnel and bridge companies. By the end of the great merger wave, in December 1904, there were 183 companies listed on the exchange, of which 133 were mergers. During the same period of time, the number of firms offering more than one type of corporate stock, such as common and preferred shares, increased from three to 113 (Hake, 1998, pp. 155–6). It is evident that the rise of the corporation through merger was crucially important to the growth of the industrial securities exchange, the types of securities being issued and the marketing practices employed in their sale.

Veblen's observation that the stock market represented the ultimate and final arbiter of the effective capitalization of the firm was substantially grounded on the commentary of the businessmen before the Industrial Commission. William H. Moore, one of the more prolific promoters involved in organizing National Steel, Diamond Match and the National Biscuit Company, among others, argued that firms were not over- or under-valued as a result of the trading prices of stock – instead, the trading price represented their true valuation (US Industrial Commission, 1901, p. 962). Henry O. Havemeyer, president of the American Sugar Company, made the simple point that a more profitable firm, irregardless of its tangible assets, should be worth more money (US Industrial Report, 1900, p. 111). With reference to the testimony of financiers, lawyers and promoters involved in sugar, steel, tobacco and silver combinations, Veblen summarizes:

> Earning capacity is practically accepted as the effective basis of capitalization for corporate business concerns, particularly for those whose securities are quoted on the market. It is in the stock market that this effective capitalization takes place. But the law does not recognize such a basis of capitalization; nor are business men generally ready to adopt it in set form, although they constantly have recourse to it, in effect, in operations of investment and credit extension. (Veblen, 1904b [1988], pp. 138–9)

Veblen provides a unique vantage point on the American economy by directing the attention of economists towards the actual financial practices of business. While economic histories of the United States have integrated the rise of the modern industrial enterprise and explored the technological changes that precipitated the merger movement, they have yet to develop an explanation of *how* these mergers were carried out, or discuss the significance of those methods (Lamoreaux, 1985; Chandler, 1977). This apparent oversight might be explained, in part, by a reluctance to evaluate the rise of the corporation as a legal entity, driven forward by the force of motivated, politically connected and, at times, anti-social interests. Focusing on the technological revolutions harnessed by the benefits of corporate coordination, perhaps, provides a more palatable history.

THE CREDIT ECONOMY IN THE TWENTY-FIRST CENTURY

> The rapidity of Enron's decline is an effective illustration of the vulnerability of a firm whose market value largely rests on capitalized reputation. The physical assets of such a firm comprise a small proportion of its asset base. Trust and reputation can vanish overnight. A factory cannot. ... The difficulty of valuing firms that deal primarily with concepts and the growing size and importance of these firms may make our economy more susceptible to this type of contagion. (Alan Greenspan, 2002)

Much has changed since the appearance of the modern industrial corporation one hundred years ago. Changes in technology, the complexity of financial instruments and in the regulatory framework have each affected the organization of industry. Despite this, the basic mechanism described in Veblen's theory of capital and its articulation through corporate finance and the business cycle remains applicable to modern economic developments. There are several practical research applications for Veblen's analysis including economic history, economic theory and the recent developments of the late twentieth century.

Considering Veblen's importance to the history of economics and his application of his own theory to economic history, it is disappointing that his theory of the credit economy has not been adopted by mainstream economists. Certain features outlined by Veblen have been generally accepted, such as the technological advances of modern manufacturing and the excessive competition that appeared in the 1880s. But his notion that corporation finance provided a valuable organizational mechanism which was especially useful in the era of modern production has not seen general adoption. In terms of his dichotomy, the technological aspects have been recognized, but the notion of the corporation as a pecuniary/ legal solution that evolved in response to these technological innovations has not. In part, this lack of recognition has become entrenched in the study of the corporation because of the overwhelming influence, in business and economic history, of Alfred Chandler's unique vision: a tradition of writing and theorizing that recognizes, but minimizes, the significance of the evolution in the financial practices associated with the rise of the corporation. In the aftermath of the proliferation, application and broad adoption of Chandler's vision, some general criticisms have begun to appear, and perhaps as a consequence some renewed attention to the relevance of Veblen's analysis will be possible (John, 1997, p. 199).

The limited pursuit of the interrelated issues of financial innovation and evolution has led to a division between what are today the accepted theories in accounting and business history. In particular, the capital theory developed by Veblen has clear connections to the entity concept of accounting theory developed most fully by Andrew Paton (Hake, 2001, p. 426). Additionally, while accounting historians have more fully explored the significance of Paton's theory and the evolution of accounting conventions, business and economic historians have not integrated these same insights into their theory of the rise of the corporation (Previts and Merino, 1998, p. 223; Johnson, 1975, p. 448).

With respect to theory, Veblen's analysis of business enterprise incorporated several concepts that have been the subject of sustained disagreement and debate within the economics and accounting professions. Disagreement concerning the nature, relevance and recording of capital, goodwill and the intangibility of assets accelerated even as Veblen wrote, and these debates have continued throughout the twentieth century (Tuttle, 1903; Kendrick, 1961; Hughes, 1982). Several episodes of this ongoing debate, such as the Cambridge capital controversies, have been particularly dramatic although they have failed to leave behind a coherent and mutually agreed upon foundation for continued analysis (Cohen and Harcourt, 2003, p. 207). Throughout these discussions, the occasional vitriol of the debate has even raised the question as to whether these discussions established scientific law (Nelson, 1949) or mythical legitimation of the economic order (Montagna 1986). Perhaps seeking to evade such outcomes, more recent theoretical discussions have avoided Veblen's observations regarding the nature of capital as a socially determined flow of credit. Instead, the majority of economists continue, almost instinctually, to rely upon a concept of capital as tangible productive capital, despite the now-evident theoretical and practical flaws of that position. Perhaps, as Avi Cohen and Geoffrey Harcourt maintain, the debate will re-emerge (Cohen and Harcourt, 2003).

While it appears unlikely that Veblen's writings will alter today's standard construction of capital theory, his analysis is relevant to John Maynard Keynes' observations on speculation and Hyman Minsky's important work on financial fragility. The potential connections between these theories have been most fully developed by J. Patrick Raines and Charles G. Leathers (1992, 1996, 2000) and Robert Dimand (2004). This perspective is particularly relevant and applicable to the dynamics of financial innovation and capital market expansion that have occurred over the final decades of the twentieth century. As Veblen noted one hundred years ago, financial innovation and the expansion of effective capitalization can be credited for simultaneously increasing the flexibility of individual firms, the fragility of the aggregate economy and the redistribution of income.

Developments over the past 25 years have led to a renewed relevance of Veblen's analysis of capital and corporate finance (Ranson, 1983, 1987). The pro-business political environment that produced a dramatic phase of deregulation, merger and accelerating stock markets (1982–2000) has provided fertile new ground for some of the dynamics described above. Some examples of this applicability include the expansion of intangible assets and increase in effective capitalizations that spurred a dramatic increase in merger activity in industries as varied as meatpacking and electricity distribution companies (Hake and King, 2002; Hake, 2005). Craig Medlen (2003) has developed this relationship between effective capitalization and merger activity into a more general formulation of Veblen's theory, one which he argues predicts better than other more popular constructions of merger activity such as Tobin's Q.

Veblen's analysis of the role of intangible assets is also relevant to the rapid growth (and collapse) of commercial Internet companies and the many allegations of securities fraud that began to appear in 2000. In the dot-com bubble of the late 1990s, the balance sheets of many companies included fabricated definitions of intangible assets, such as eyeballs, degree of mindshare, and stickiness, that justified the large stock market issues and capitalizations that dwarfed the value of their profitable 'old-line' competitors. This attempt to increase balance sheet assets so as to maintain some vague relationship with the expanding effective capitalization of companies is an example of the stock market dynamic described by Veblen. With the bursting of expectations in mid-2000, the dramatic collapse of dot-com effective capitalization and the subsequent expunging of goodwill accounts have been well documented in the business press (Hake, 2004).

With respect to the allegation of securities fraud and the manipulation of stock prices for the profit of corporate managers and financiers, the current episode has produced a wide-ranging literature (Bebchuk, Fried and Walker, 2001), some of which recognizes Veblen's contribution (Cornehls, 2004; Ganley, 2004). Veblen noted that the increased use of intangible assets associated with the corporation provided greater latitude for the manipulation of public opinion regarding the expected earning capacities of firms. Through sagacious withholding and planting of information and rumor, Veblen argued corporate managers and other financial interests could find easy profits with the strategic sale of stock. The Veblenian perspective realizes that the growing sophistication of financial instruments, deregulation and the use of managerial incentives such as stock options increase opportunities for fraud. This route to profit is a feature of the system and not simply an unintended aberration. Regulation of some form is necessary to curtail it (Trebing, 2004, p. 4).

While the analysis of corporate fraud is perhaps the most widely recognized aspect of Veblen's theory of the business enterprise, it represents only the first, elemental, step in the development of his larger analysis: of greatest importance is his more general proposition that the judicious expansion of productive capacity and efficiency along technical lines is not the only route to profit. Business logic, then and today, requires that firms actively seek out all sources of income, including the conscientious withdrawal of efficiency that is sometimes known as deceit and industrial sabotage. From this initial assumption Veblen builds his own, highly original, analysis of capital assets, industrial organization, capital markets and the dynamics of business cycles.

CONCLUSION

As illustrated in the course of this chapter, Veblen hoped to produce a functioning theory of the emerging industrial economy through his inductive and evolutionary approach to economics. Working directly from the business press and the commentary of lawyers, financiers and industrialists as compiled in the United States Industrial Commission Report, Veblen argued that the economy was undergoing a profound shift as it entered the modern era. This new footing of business could be contrasted with the previously existing 'money' economy whose most important sources of growth were the expansion of manufacturing activities. Under this older dispensation, a formal theory of capital, assets, debts and profit had been established by the classical economists. This theory conveniently dovetailed with the then-prevalent practices of business and accounting. It explained in a ready and coherent fashion the affairs of business under the approximate conditions of free competition and limited industrial capacity relative to the general run of the market.

With the rise of the industrial corporation, however, Veblen argued that a new phase of economic development had been established. Adopting and codifying the industrial and financial practices that had appeared piecemeal with the rise of the railroads in the third quarter of the nineteenth century, a new system for organizing production was developed. These new financial and manufacturing practices were necessary as the scale of industry expanded and the total level of production began to expand beyond the immediate demands of the market. The corporation appeared as a mechanism capable of coordinating large-scale production and distribution. This mechanism included, when needed, the limitation of output and the establishment of a more complete system of price (and demand) management. Under the new conditions of business, the terminology and concepts that were applicable to the earlier stages of business were no longer germane.

The introduction of intangible assets into the balance sheet, and the capitalization of the corporation, subverted the old definitions of assets and credits, muddying the clear distinctions that were previously assumed. Continuous production processes, when coupled with an infinitely lived business enterprise, required a redefinition of the concept of profit. The stock market, usually seen as a market of ownership shares, became the ultimate arbiter of the effective capitalization of the firm, and the market for the extension of credit necessary for working capital. The growing intangibility of the corporation's assets increased access to credit and its ability to reorganize the ownership of existing industrial assets. While increasing the flexibility in ownership that serves as an alternative to financial panic and liquidation, the large increase in intangibility also served to increase the potential for volatility and even dramatic declines in firm valuations. As has been shown, a crisis of speculative confidence could translate directly into a curtailment of credit and thereby induce a precipitous decline in the value of the corporation's assets. Within this new framework, opportunity for profit-seeking behavior was certainly expanded. The manipulation of financial values as a source of profit, either through the manipulation of the internal records of the firm or through the sagacious timing of stock sale, became an important line of business.

Veblen specifically called upon the economists of his time to recognize the distinction between the modern industrial economy and the circumstances of purely competitive markets, formulate a new theoretical construction and begin exploring the operation of the new system. In large measure, this revolution in economic thought has not occurred. The Keynesian revolution, and the counter-revolution that followed it, have clearly introduced new concepts and the theories of economics and finance have each continued to evolve. But the more thorough-going critique proposed by Veblen, a rebuilding of the theory of the firm on the corporate model and its integration with a theory of industrial organization and business cycle dynamics, has not been accepted. Within the past decade, there has been much discussion suggesting a growth of methodological diversity within the economics discipline. Perhaps this diversification, if fully carried out, will ultimately allow for a reassessment and reintegration of Veblen's early and still applicable insights.

NOTES

1. Through the system of corporate finance, the corporation is able to acquire, create and consolidate the ownership of productive assets. Ownership of corporate stock also determines the allocation of income and capital gains generated by the corporation. It is remarkable, then, that within the economics profession the analysis of the corporation and its operations has not been codified into the general theory of the discipline. Advanced courses in macroeconomics or microeconomics, to say nothing of principles courses, contain only footnotes on the corporate form. There is no theory of the firm that addresses the unique qualities of the modern corporation. The study of industrial organization is also limited by the presumed homogeneity of business forms: purely competitive and monopolistic industry are apparently populated by firms that differ only in their size relative to their markets for inputs or outputs. There is no theory of money supply and demand based on the corporation, and scant discussion of the actual operation of capital markets. The universe of economic agents is limited to the trinity of households, government and firms. If you wish to understand the operation of the corporation, its emergence and its influence, you must decamp to a business school, study law or finance, or take an increasingly rare business history class.
2. It is worth noting how this awareness of culture placed him at odds with the community of economists. This gulf was to last throughout much of the twentieth century. Only over the past 20 years have more economists begun to seriously consider a discussion of culture relevant to the study of the economy, and this reconciliation is constructed in a most particular and circumscribed way (Greif, 1997, p. 401; Greif, 1998, p. 80). Clearly, Veblen's insights have not penetrated to the level of standard practice, and it appears to be unlikely to threaten conventional lines of inquiry and analysis for several more decades. However limited in practical application, it does appear a renewed experimentation in methodological practice suggests that at least some of this these developments are gaining a broader foothold (Hands, 2001).
3. Current training in graduate microeconomics takes this limited definition of capital as its starting point and narrows it even further. Hal Varian's textbook begins analysis of

capital with the discussion of the capital asset pricing model (CAPM) developed in the 1970s, which is referred to as the 'grandfather of them all' (Varian, 1992, p. 371). The new standard textbook in graduate microeconomics makes two explicit references to the treatment of production and capital. To begin, 'the firm is viewed merely as a "black box", able to transform inputs into outputs' (Mas-Colell, Whinston and Green, 1995, p. 127). In the treatment of asset markets, the authors do recognize both real assets and financial assets, but the model continues by assuming only real assets: those items that produce physical goods such as a durable piece of machinery or a futures contract for the delivery of copper. To save notation, these real assets are then assumed to only produce outputs in amounts of a single identical type of physical good (Mas-Colell, Whinston and Green, 1995, p. 699).

4. While the inflation of capital assets through the inclusion of various debts (such as lawyer's fees or promoter's profit) was more transparent in Veblen's time because of the use of par-stock, a modern consequence of this phenomenon can be seen in the discussion of expensing stock options. If stock issues associated with options were rationally discounted by the investing public, their price would be quite low. They add relatively little to the value of the firm or its capital.

REFERENCES

Bebchuk, L., J.M. Fried and D.I. Walker (2001), 'Executive compensation in America: optimal contracting or extraction of rents', Ropes and Gray Berkeley Olin Program in Law and Economics, Working Paper Series no. 50.

Borgmeyer, Charles L. (1900), *The American Corporation Legal Manual*, Plainfield, NJ: The Corporation Legal Manual Co.

Chandler, Alfred D. (1977), *The Visible Hand, The Managerial Revolution in American Business*, Cambridge, MA: Harvard University Press.

Cohen, A. J. and G.C. Harcourt (2003), 'Retrospectives: whatever happened to the Cambridge capital theory controversies?', *Journal of Economic Perspectives*, **17**(1), 199–214.

Cornehls, J.V. (2004), 'Veblen's theory of finance capitalism and contemporary corporate America', *Journal of Economic Issues*, **38**(1), 29–58.

Dewing, Arthur Stone (1922), *Corporation Finance*, New York: Ronald Press.

Dicksee, Lawrence Robert and Frank Tillyard (1906), *Goodwill and Its Treatment in Accounts*, reprinted 3rd edn (1976), New York: Arno Press.

Dimand, R.W. (2004), 'Echoes of Veblen's theory of business enterprise in the later development of macroeconomics: Fisher's debt–deflation theory of great depressions and the financial instability theories of Minsky and Tobin', *International Review of Sociology*, **14**(3), 461–70.

Eddy, G. (1937), 'Security issues and real investment in 1929', *Review of Economic Statistics*, **19**(2), 79–91.

Fazzari, S.M. and B.C. Petersen (1993), 'Working capital and fixed investment: new evidence on financing constraints', *Rand Journal of Economics*, **24**(3), 328–42.

Ganley, W.T. (2004), 'The theory of business enterprise and Veblen's neglected theory of corporation finance', *Journal of Economic Issues*, **38**(2), 397–403.

Grandy, C. (1989), 'New Jersey corporate chartermongering, 1875–1929', *Journal of Economic History*, **49**(3), 677–92.

Greenspan, A. (2002), 'Federal reserve board's semiannual monetary policy report to the Congress', Committee on Financial Services, U.S. House of Representatives;

retrieved 10 July 2006 (http://www.federalreserve.gov/boarddocs/hh/2002/february/testimony.htm).

Greif, A. (1997), 'Cliometrics after 40 years', *American Economic Review*, **87**(2), 400–404.

Greif, A. (1998), 'Historical and comparative institutional analysis', *American Economic Review*, **88**(2), 80–84.

Hake, E. (1994), 'The role of financial and legal innovation in the rise of the modern credit economy: evidence from the American merger movement, 1870–1904', dissertation, University of Tennessee, Knoxville.

Hake, E. (1998), 'Financial innovation as facilitator of merger activity', *Journal of Economic Issues*, **32**(1), 145–70.

Hake, E. (2001), 'The stock watering debate: more light, less heat', *Journal of Economic Issues*, **35**(2), 423–30.

Hake, E. (2004), 'The appearance of impairment: Veblen and goodwill-financed mergers', *Journal of Economic Issues*, **38**(2), 389–95.

Hake, E. (2005), 'Financial illusion: accounting for profits in an Enron world', *Journal of Economic Issues*, **39**(3), 595–611.

Hake, E. and M.B. King (2002), 'The Veblenian credit economy and the corporatization of American meatpacking', *Journal of Economic Issues*, **36**(2), 495–506.

Hands, D. Wade (2001), *Reflection without Rules: Economic Methodology and Contemporary Science Theory*, Cambridge, UK and New York: Cambridge University Press.

Hughes, Hugh P. (1982), 'Goodwill in accounting: a history of the issues and problems', CBA Business Publishing Division, Georgia State University, Atlanta, research monograph 80.

John, R.R. (1997), 'Elaborations, revisions, dissents: Alfred D. Chandler, Jr.'s The Visible Hand after twenty years', *Business History Review*, **71**(2), 151–200.

Johnson, H.T. (1975), 'The role of accounting history in the study of modern business enterprise', *Accounting Review*, **50**(3), 444–50.

Kendrick, J.W., (1961), 'Some theoretical aspects of capital measurement', *American Economic Review*, **51**(2), 102.

Lamoreaux, Naomi R. (1985), *The Great Merger Movement in American Business, 1895–1904*, Cambridge, UK and New York: Cambridge University Press.

Mas-Colell, Andreu, Michael D. Whinston and Jerry R. Green (1995), *Microeconomic Theory*, Oxford, UK and New York: Oxford University Press.

McEachern, William A. (2006), *Economics: A Contemporary Introduction*, 7th edn, Mason, OH: South-Western College Publishers.

Medlen, C. (2003), 'Veblen's Q – Tobin's Q', *Journal of Economic Issues*, **37**(4), 967–86.

Montagna, P. (1986), 'Accounting rationality and financial legitimation', *Theory and Society*, **15**(1/2), 103–38.

Myers, S.C. (2001), 'Capital structure', *Journal of Economic Perspectives*, **15**(2), 81–102.

Navin, T.R. and M.V. Sears (1955), 'The rise of a market for industrial securities, 1887–1902', *Business History Review*, **29**(2), 105–38.

Nelson, E.G. (1949), 'Science and accounting', *The Accounting Review*, **24**(4), 354–9.

Nelson, Ralph (1959), *Merger Movements in American Industry 1895–1956*, Princeton, NJ: Princeton University Press.

O'Brien, A.P. (1988), 'Factory size, economies of scale, and the great merger wave of 1898–1902', *Journal of Economic History*, **48**(3), 639–49.

Previts, Gary John and Barbara Dubis Merino (1998), *A History of Accountancy in the United States: The Cultural Significance of Accounting*, Columbus, OH: Ohio State University Press.

Raines, J.P. and C.G. Leathers (1992), 'Financial innovations and Veblen's theory of financial markets', *Journal of Economic Issues*, **26**(2), 433–41.

Raines, J.P. and C.G. Leathers (1996), 'Veblenian stock markets and the efficient markets hypothesis', *Journal of Post Keynesian Economics*, **19**(1) 137–51.

Raines, J. Patrick and Charles G. Leathers (2000), *Economists and the Stock Market: Speculative Theories of Stock Market Fluctuations*, Cheltenham, UK and Northampton, MA, USA: Edward Elgar.

Ranson, B. (1983), 'The unrecognized revolution in the theory of capital formation', *Journal of Economic Issues*, **17**(4), 901–13.

Ranson, B. (1987), 'The institutionalist theory of capital formation', *Journal of Economic Issues*, **21**(3) 1265–79.

Seligman, J. (1976), 'A brief history of Delaware's general corporation law of 1899', *Delaware Journal of Corporate Law*, **1**, 249–87.

Stimson, Frederic Jesup (1892), *American Statute Law, An Analytical and Compared Digest of the Statutes of All the States and Territories Relating to General and Business and Private Corporations*, Boston: The Boston Book Company, reprinted in US Industrial Commission Report, 2, 265–91.

Trebing, H.M. (2004), 'Assessing deregulation: the clash between promise and reality', *Journal of Economic Issues*, **38**(1), 1–27.

Tuttle, C.A. (1903), 'The real capital concept', *Quarterly Journal of Economics*, **18**(1), 54–96.

US Industrial Commission (1900–1902), *Report of the Industrial Commission*, Washington, DC: Government Printing Office, vol 1–19.

US Industrial Commission (1901), *Report on Trusts and Industrial Combinations*, Washington, DC: Government Printing Office.

Uselding, P. (1980), 'Business history and the history of technology', *Business History Review*, **54**(4), 443–52.

Varian, Hal R. (1992), *Microeconomic Analysis*, 3rd edn, London and New York: W.W. Norton & Company.

Veblen, Thorstein (1899), 'The Barbarian status of women', *American Journal of Sociology*, **4**(4), 503–14.

Veblen, Thorstein (1901), 'Industrial and pecuniary employments', reprinted 1990 in *The Place of Science in Modern Civilization*, New Brunswick, US and London: Transaction Publishers, pp. 279–323.

Veblen, Thorstein (1904a), 'An early experiment in trusts', reprinted 1990 in *The Place of Science in Modern Civilization*, New Brunswick, US and London: Transaction Publishers, pp. 497–509.

Veblen, Thorstein (1904b), *The Theory of Business Enterprise*, reprinted 1988 New Brunswick, US and London: Transaction Press.

Veblen, Thorstein (1908a), 'Fisher's capital and income', reprinted in Leon Ardzrooni (ed.) (1964), *Essays in Our Changing Order*, New York: Augustus M. Kelley, pp. 148–74.

Veblen, Thorstein (1908b), 'On the nature of capital: I. The productivity of capital goods', reprinted 1990 in *The Place of Science in Modern Civilization*, New Brunswick, US and London: Transaction Publishers, pp. 324–51.

Veblen, Thorstein (1908c), 'On the nature of capital: II. Investment, intangible assets, and the pecuniary magnate', reprinted 1990 in *The Place of Science in Modern Civilization*, New Brunswick, US and London: Transaction Publishers, pp. 352–86.

Veblen, Thorstein (1909), 'The limitations of marginal utility', reprinted 1990 in *The Place of Science in Modern Civilization*, New Brunswick, US and London: Transaction Publishers. pp. 231–51.

Veblen, Thorstein (1923), *Absentee Ownership and Business Enterprise in Recent Times*, reprinted 1964, New York: A.M. Kelley.

Weston, J.F. (1951), 'Some perspectives on capital theory', *The American Economic Review*, **41**(2), 129–44.

4. Pecuniary institutions: their role and effects

Glen Atkinson

Mainstream economic theory has tended to limit economic inquiry to the behavior of rational individuals. In order to model this behavior, these individuals are neither empowered nor constrained by economic institutions. They cannot act; they merely choose from alternatives presented to them by the market. This might have been a fairly useful framework for understanding an economy dominated by self-sufficient tillers of the soil. The irony is that those folks did not participate in a market system. Even Ronald Coase (1937), the founder of New Institutional Economics (NIE), had to ask how an organized business firm could exist and be consistent with an economic system founded on radical individualism. Coase accepted the existence of the firm but had it act as if it were an individual minimizing transactions costs to maximize profits. Thus an institution, the business firm, was introduced with no real effect on rational economic behavior. This solution resonated with mainstream economists because it could be modeled.

Original Institutional Economists (OIE) had taken an entirely different tack in incorporating institutions into economic theory. According to the OIE pioneers such as John R. Commons and Thorstein Veblen, human individuals have great mental power and they act with purpose. However, these individuals are shaped from birth by social institutions such as the family and the community. Their actions are influenced by the values and traditions of these institutions as well as by rational calculations. Though their actions are shaped by customs and habits, they use their intellect as well to act to change their circumstances. Compared to the individual depicted in mainstream economics, this is a very complex organism, and its behavior is difficult to capture in a model, especially models that neglect history, culture and the evolving institutional structure. Rather than considering the firm as a fictional, rational individual, OIE scholars understand the firm to be a going concern that organizes the talents and roles of interdependent individuals to promote cooperation. The going concern will evolve owing to forces from the external environment as well as the changing personalities within the firm.

Among the most significant contributions OIE scholars made to economics was the recognition and study of the effects of pecuniary institutions on the stability of production and the distribution of income received from that production. The OIE scholars observed that, as economies evolved from self-sufficiency to handicraft production to machine-based industrial production, the role and effects of pecuniary institutions also evolved. They had a unique understanding of the co-evolution of finance and production that, if properly understood, will provide insight into economic problems of advanced countries in the twenty-first century. Reviving those insights is the purpose of this chapter.

The discussion begins with an explanation as to how the growth of pecuniary institutions began in the handicraft stage of production. This discussion is based mainly on the work of John R. Commons, who investigated the consequences of the widening of the market in the United States that led to a continental market. This evolution from local to national markets set the conditions for the factory system. The development of the factory system was only possible with the concurrent development of pecuniary institutions to finance the required fixed and working capital. The twin development of factories and modern finance created not only an industrial society but a pecuniary culture as well that shaped our habitual assumptions. The second step in the discussion will be to explain the continuation of the co-evolution of production and finance in the machine age. This section depends heavily on the work of Thorstein Veblen, particularly *The Theory of Business Enterprise* (1904 [1932]). The third section explains how Wesley C. Mitchell used Veblen's theory of business enterprise to investigate and develop his theory of the modern business cycle. The fourth section will concentrate on problems of economic instability and the maldistribution of wealth and income over the last thirty-five years. The final section is a brief summary.

It is argued in this chapter that the investigations and theoretical framework developed by Commons, Veblen and Mitchell provide superior insights into today's economic successes and maladies. The modern economy evolved along the path described by the earlier OIE scholars. In order to understand the maladjustments in today's economy, we need to understand the path that led us here. The key to following the path is to understand that for the OIE scholars the basic role of pecuniary institutions is to create and allocate property rights in intangible assets. The continuum in this path from self-sufficient production to the modern economy is the increasing role of intangible property relative to bricks and mortar. The importance of intangible assets defines the modern business cycle (irrational exuberance) and plays a major role in the widening of the gap between the rich and the poor in some developed countries.

The purpose of this chapter is not intended to be simply an exercise in the history of economic thought. Instead, if we understand the origins and blazing of the path that led to the domination of the habitual assumptions of finance over those of production, we can gain an understanding of the fragility of the economy that accompanies the impressive economic prosperity. Though we are shaped by our history, there is no predetermined path stretching before us. However, we do need to understand the path we have traveled to this point and challenge our habitual assumptions to avoid becoming locked in an undesirable groove.

This generation of institutional economists has the tools to lead a public discussion on how we might maintain our prosperity while reducing the threat of financial fragility that can lead to economic distress.

THE ORIGINS OF MODERN PECUNIARY INSTITUTIONS

The origins of pecuniary institutions that are of concern in this chapter are those that led fairly directly to the development of the industrial economy. For example, the commercial expansion ignited by early European imperialism and colonization had to be financed. One could make a good argument that those adventures planted the seeds that led to subsequent industrialization. However, the early phase of this colonial expansion of the market was mainly limited to commerce and the development of financial institutions to facilitate trade in the wider markets that were developing (Atkinson, 2004; Commons, et al., 1918). Unfortunately, the path of economic history and development has poor identifying boundaries. One has to slice into this ongoing process and my point of departure is to begin with the American experience that was documented by Commons, Veblen and Mitchell.

Commons developed his theory of institutional economics from his investigations into the interaction of law and economics and specific labor disputes. One of the most important contributions to his theoretical construct was his investigation of the evolution of the shoemaking industry in America from 1648 to 1895. He began by investigating court documents in Philadelphia in 1789 concerning an action brought by master shoemakers against journeymen accusing the latter of forming a combination and engaging in a conspiracy to raise their wages (Commons, 1923, p. 226). The evidence in this case led Commons to conclude that the interstate commerce clause of the United States Constitution provided the legal impetus for an ever-widening market. Among other consequences of this development were the separation of functions of the master craftsman from the merchant and the rise of the logic of finance in the production process (Atkinson, 2004).

Settled shoemakers in American cities were faced with what they considered to be unfair competition from itinerant shoemakers who boarded with the customer's family to make shoes. The settled shoemakers, who produced with the assistance of journeymen associates, felt that production arrangements of itinerants were leading to lower quality standards of production. These craftsmen operated from shops rather than working in homes and negotiated price *and* quality of the merchandise with the customer at the time the order for a pair of shoes was placed. This was not speculative production for future consumption but bespoke work instead. Bespoke work means that the sale is consummated before the work begins. There is virtually no risk and no need for financing a stock of inventory. Also the shoes were made with hand tools owned by the journeymen, which meant that there was no need to finance fixed capital.

In order to stifle the competition from itinerant producers the settled shoemakers sought and won legal authority to form a guild. This first guild was established in Boston in 1648 with the purpose of stymieing a 'race to the bottom' in terms of quality of merchandise. Guilds were then established in other cities on the eastern seaboard. All of these guilds served local, citywide markets because there were no continental markets during the colonial period.

Things began to change with improvements in transportation and the adoption of the US Constitution. The interstate commerce clause of the Constitution prohibited legal barriers to commerce between the states and better transportation facilities allowed this commerce to take place. This enlarged sphere of commerce placed the new nation on the path to eventual industrialization.

How did this industrialization come about? First, some master guild craftsmen became a bit more ambitious and required their journeymen to produce shoes to stock an inventory for off-the-shelf sales. This created a labor conflict that was resolved in the 1789 trial of the Boot and Shoemakers of Philadelphia. The journeymen objected to the speed-up of work required of them to stock the shops and were found guilty by the court of a conspiracy to raise wages. This action allowed the masters to press for more speed-up of work to produce a stock of shoes to haul to the wider region. Thus production was transformed from bespoke, to shop work, to speculative output. This move to production for a wider market led to a separation of the production function from the merchant function.

Here occurs the separation of the merchant-function from the employer-function. The bargaining specialist, the merchant–capitalist, need no longer be one who has knowledge of the technical process of the trade. These [technical functions] he turns over to a subordinate or to a master workman, who now merely becomes the labor contractor; while for himself the merchant capitalist retains those functions calling for his special skill in sizing up the market, driving a bargain, and commanding credit. (Commons et al., 1918, p. 101)

Speculative production required a large inventory of merchandise, and a lag between the cost of production and realized income. Soon the financial load for this stock of inventory exceeded the ability of the master to raise the funds. The master craftsman had become an employer, but an employer with no real capital and no relationship with the consumers, since these were the days before brand names. Thus he had no means to finance the lag between production and receipt of income.

The wholesale merchant, who took the stock of goods to the retail merchants in the region, found a way to fulfill the financing function.

The earliest loans on evidences of intangible capital were made by merchants. A merchant would agree with a manufacturer, who had contracts or notes, to honour orders that he issued to his workmen in lieu of cash wages. He would then redeem the orders in merchandise. Such accounts would run until the manufacturer's customers made their remittances. ... It will readily be seen that business was considerably hampered under a credit system that did not recognize intangible evidences of property. The small producer especially suffered under these conditions. (Commons, et al. 1918, p. 89)

This new financial process was an early step in the creation of intangible property and a transformation of pecuniary institutions. Production could not occur if purchasing power could not be created on the anticipation of sales. Orders for future, prospective sales were turned into money to finance current production. This was a major extension of the path transferring authority from productive enterprises to pecuniary institutions. The term 'what the market will bear' was coming to signify not only what the consumer was willing and able to pay but also the terms and conditions of the loans to finance production. Financial markets had to be satisfied before consumer markets could be created.

Eventually banks began to buy these notes and provide financial backing based solely on intangible property (Atkinson, 2004; Commons et al., 1918). This was the beginning step toward what Commons would later call Banker Capitalism. First, the producer was separated from the merchant capitalist. Then the merchant and financial functions were separated and performed by two different individuals. The economy was on the road to financial capitalism. The evolving economic system was becoming much more productive, the separation in time between production and purchase of the commodity by the consumer was creating the conditions that cause modern business cycles.

Remarkably this was before factory production and widespread use of the machine process. The situation that has been discussed so far is limited to production with hand tools. The financial burden was created by the need for working capital to stock inventory. These events did lay the groundwork and create the conditions that led to factory production (Atkinson, 2004, p. 47). The relationship of the evolving pecuniary institutions and the machine process is the topic of the next section.

PECUNIARY INSTITUTIONS AND THE MACHINE PROCESS

The logic of factory production emerged in the final days of hand-tool production. As the pace of work needed to be speeded up to feed the wider national markets, scientific management was introduced to rationalize the flow of work. When machinery was introduced to produce larger volumes of commodities, the interstices had to be minimized to maximize the flow of production. Imagine the flow of a log as it is transported through a sawmill and transformed into finished lumber. The machines have to be located in the appropriate sequence and workers situated so they can keep the machines humming. A broken conveyer chain will stop the whole flow and a slow worker will reduce the output of all the other workers. If the supply of logs is inadequate or low-quality, output is stopped or slowed.

Now follow the lumber to the construction site. The construction process is more akin to the layout of the hand-tool era. Different skills are needed to lay the foundation, raise the walls, put on the roof or install the plumbing. The components do not flow as in a factory but the workers and materials must be in the right place at the right time. The building construction will be slowed if the skilled workers or materials for the next step are not ready.

If the demand for new buildings slows, the effects will feed back on the sawmill and timber industries. If the lumber industry cannot keep pace with the demand for construction, it will slow construction and increase the cost. In sum, production done with machines takes on the logic of machines. Cause and effect are obvious and careful sequencing is essential. Standardization of machines, factory layout and even consumer products fit this scheme of production. This was the secret of Ford's Model T and it remains the secret of McDonald's hamburgers.

It was Veblen's contention that the logic of this type of production was at odds with the pecuniary logic of business executives (Veblen, 1904 [1932]).

'The adjustments of industry take place through the mediation of pecuniary transactions, and these transactions take place at the hands of the business men and are carried on by them for business ends, not for industrial ends in the narrower meaning of the phrase' (Veblen, 1904 [1932], p. 19).

For the purpose of this chapter, Veblen made two very important points. First, he was interested in the purpose and effects of the combination and merger movement of the last quarter of the nineteenth century (Veblen, 1904 [1932], pp. 61–4). What was the economic purpose of merging many small firms into one large enterprise? The mergers were not driven by the requirements of the machine process but by pecuniary logic (Hake, 2004). In other words, the combined operation was no more industrially efficient than the separate units were. However, they were more profitable for the owners. To fully understand this point, we need to go to the second point, which is the importance of intangible property in the modern business enterprise.

Commons documented the shift in legal rulings of the U.S. Supreme Court that recognized the exchange value of property in addition to its use value. The cases began with the Slaughter House cases in 1872 and the issue was finally resolved in the Minnesota Rate Case of 1890 (Commons, 1924 [1968], pp. 11–18). The issue in dispute in these cases was whether the government was taking property if it regulated prices without taking or otherwise interfering with the use of the owners' tangible property. Under the legal doctrine of exchange value, property can be taken if a regulation affects the market value even though the property remains intact with the owner. For example, a regulation that limits the fares a railroad can charge can reduce the market value of the firm. The Court finally and clearly concluded in the Minnesota case that the Constitution protected exchange value as well as physical property. This decision reflected common business practices as they were emerging.

Without mentioning these cases, Veblen was arguing that this concept of ownership was at odds with industrial efficiency in the machine age. Remember that producers in the hand-tool era were pursuing a livelihood rather than the accumulation of financial assets. Veblen observed the increasing separation of management and ownership in the large firms that were being created through mergers. He wanted to understand the objectives and strategies of this new class of business executives. The objective of owners and managers of factories was profit or accumulation of financial wealth. Their motive was pecuniary rather than pride of workmanship or industrial efficiency. They spent more time with financial agents than time on the factory floor.

It is an habitual assumption that these managers and owners were trying to maximize profits but that is too narrow a concept to capture their strategy. They did manage the affairs of the firm to be able to report healthy profits but the promise of profits may be more important in the financial world than actual, historical profits. Their main goal was capitalized value of the firm as reported in financial markets. As Veblen stated,

> ... under this system of corporation finance the affairs of the corporation are in good part managed for tactical ends which are of interest to the manager rather than to the corporation as a going concern. (Veblen, 1904 [1932], p. 80)

The traditional way of reporting the value of the firm was as its use value and that could be measured by the replacement cost minus depreciation of the capital equipment and structures. This measure had little meaning in the new regime of financial capitalism. Again, according to Veblen:

> The business interest of the managers demands, not serviceability of the output, nor even the vendibility of the output, but an advantageous discrepancy in the price of capital which they manage. (Veblen, 1904 [1932], p. 79)

The difference between the replacement cost of the physical capital and the value of the going concern in the financial markets is intangible property. Intangible value is based on what financial investors *expect* the value of the firm to be in the future. The investors' eyes are on the ability of the managers to make a deal that will boost stock prices rather than on the industrial efficiency of the firm. The requirements of the machine process and the pecuniary culture of the business enterprise are ill matched. According to Veblen,

> ... the fortunes of property owners are in large measure dependent on the discretion of others – the owners of intangible property; and the management of industrial equipment tends strongly to center in the hands of men who do not own the industrial equipment, and who have only a remote interest in the efficient working of this equipment. (Veblen, 1904 [1932], p. 86)

This behavior has three serious consequences that we continue to experience today. First, the pursuit of financial wealth determines how fully we use labor and machinery in the factories and mills. Because the value of intangible property is based on expectations and speculation, its value can swing widely based on mass optimism and pessimism. Financial wealth can be created without any addition to the stock of material capital and it can disappear without any destruction of industrial equipment. During depressions we witness idle workers along with idle machinery. In the examples given above, the production in the sawmill and construction site can shut down even though there are ample raw materials, machinery and labor. In the next section, we show how Wesley Mitchell used Veblen's theory of business enterprise to study and explain the modern business cycle. Second, the distribution of wealth and income is determined by an individual's ability to participate in financial markets rather than productive effort. Big wealth rests on a foundation of capitalized goodwill rather than production. It is impossible to explain the skewed distribution of wealth and income in the world or the nation based on talent, intelligence, ambition, effort or skill. Property institutions are required to permit such accumulations of wealth. Third, modern business enterprises finance public elections and high-level appointments to non-elected positions. Since governments determine what is property and enforce those rights, those who have access to and influence on those officials can have their intangible assets protected. 'But since the advent of constitutional government and parliamentary representation, business ends have taken the lead of dynastic ends in statecraft, very much in the same measure as the transition to constitutional methods has been effectually carried through. A constitutional government is a business government' (Veblen, 1904 [1932], p. 135). These three concerns will be discussed in the next two sections.

PECUNIARY INSTITUTIONS AND THE MODERN BUSINESS CYCLE

The widening of the market in the hand-tool era led to the acceptance of financing of intangible property. What were being financed were the wages of workers and inventories. The only collateral was the orders for merchandise, and the promise to pay could not be fulfilled if the product was not sold. The production for the wider market created the need for faster production and the hand tools were replaced over time by machinery located in factories. With this development more inventories *and* the machinery to create the additional output had to be financed. As Veblen noted, the market value of the physical equipment was much less than the total value of the firm including intangible value. Eric Hake provides a recent view of this situation (Hake, 2004).

Wesley C. Mitchell, as a founding member of the National Bureau of Economic Research, set his goal to provide measurements to explain the fragility of the economy caused by these pecuniary institutions. Mitchell observed that we have an embarrassment of riches in theories of the business cycle (Mitchell, 1927 [1949], pp. 47–8). He noted that business is affected by physical, psychological, political, economic or social factors that can be local, national or global in scope. Mitchell, 1927 [1949], p. 3) noted that orthodox economists, beginning with Adam Smith, had paid scant attention to the problem of business cycles. Skeptics of the classical tradition in economics who were aware of the harm caused by the oscillations in business activity were curious about their causes. Many of the economists who were aware that the market economy was not a smoothly adjusting mechanism as depicted in orthodox economics developed theories of the nature and causes of the fluctuations in business activity. Unfortunately they did not support their theories with systematic statistics. Instead, they offered selective facts that supported their position.

Mitchell wanted to change this approach by developing a consistent and comprehensive set of income and product accounts that would be able to support or reject the theories. However, he had to have a theory in mind to be able to collect and classify the data. For Mitchell, data collection was not a random activity. After reviewing and categorizing dozens of theories, he settled on the theory of business enterprise where profit and financial accumulation were the main goals (Mitchell, 1927 [1949], pp. 42–4, 62). As the economy was transformed from subsistence, to hand-tool production for the market, to an industrial system based on the machine process, finance became more and more important. Curiously, as machines became more widespread for production, finance became more critical in sustaining the smooth flow of production and income. Intangible property became the dominant influence on the market operations.

This is not the place to give a full review and discussion of Mitchell's accounting system. Rather the intent of this section is to demonstrate that Mitchell's statistical framework was designed to reveal pecuniary institutions as the source of business instability.

> Efficiency in producing goods is important to an individual chiefly because of its bearing on his ability to make money; money making is important to a nation chiefly because of its bearing on efficiency in production. Natural resources, mechanical equipment, workmanlike skill, and scientific technique are factors of fundamental importance under any form of organization. But where business economy prevails natural resources are not developed, mechanical equipment is not utilized, workmanlike skill is not exercised, scientific discoveries are not applied, unless conditions are such as to promise a money profit to those who direct production. (Mitchell, 1927 [1949], pp. 65–6)

This statement captures the dichotomy between the machine process and business enterprise as expressed by Veblen. It is also consistent with the concept of the transaction developed by Commons where property rights had to be established before production and exchange could take place (Commons, 1934 [1961], p. 58). Ownership determines who directs production.

So how can these insights be used to develop a theory of business cycles? The business enterprise must finance production for income to be received in the future. In the machine age, this requires massive quantities of working and fixed capital that must be financed. Of course, if there is a steady flow of income business operations will be smooth. However, resource shortages, tight credit and especially a fall in investor or consumer confidence will disrupt these operations and these disruptions can spread widely throughout the economy. Since production and profits depend on the expectation of future sales and this production is financed on credit, a wave of pessimism can sweep through the financial markets. This tendency is exacerbated in an economy where the large part of the firms' value is goodwill or intangible property.

The task that Mitchell set for himself was to develop a set of statistics and to analyze the relationships between these series of statistics to see if the profit or money economy was the foundation upon which a theory of the modern business cycle could rest. As a consequence, much of his work was directed to the development of statistical instruments to measure money flows.

Veblen explained that the habits of thought of those who worked in the machine process were at odds with the habits of thought of the pecuniary culture. The people working in the machine production environment thought in terms of linear, machine-like cause and effect (Veblen, 1904 [1932], pp. 9–15, 144–76). Those who worked in pecuniary pursuits thought in terms of power relationships and symbols of that power such as property rights and money. The pecuniary agents controlled the machine process without adequate knowledge of it. Furthermore, the pecuniary interests were supported by natural law philosophy, which meant that pecuniary operations did not have to be examined or justified; they were considered part of nature's plan. In short, pecuniary institutions were ceremonial. While no clear alternative was proposed, Veblen seemed to support the abolishment of parliamentary governments and the constitutional systems that supported them because they served business ends rather than the means to support the livelihood of the common man (Veblen, 1904 [1932], pp. 133–7). At the very least, he advocated a radical reconstruction of government and legal institutions to be better aligned with the industrial facts of the early twentieth century.

Commons also objected to justification of any institutional structure or system by appealing to natural law. However, the evidence suggests that he recognized the functional aspects of pecuniary institutions. Rather than abolition, he would reform them by public collective action. Commons offered the profound insight that the control of industrial processes by pecuniary institutions and logic had caused a reversal of the flow of cause and effect. The linear cause–effect relations still applied to the machine process. Commons made the following brilliant and crucial observation about the way pecuniary institutions and the rise of a pecuniary culture affected the sequence of cause and effect.

> Production and consumption cannot be carried out without first obtaining legal control. Possibly this changes the idea of causation. It places causation definitely in the future instead of in the past, where it was placed by the labor theories of Locke and the classical and communist economists; or instead of in the present sensations of pain and pleasure of production or consumption of the hedonic economists since the time of Bentham. It becomes a *volitional* theory of future consequences of present negotiations and transfers of legal control, determining whether production shall go on or slow down or stop, or determining the extent to which future consumption will be expanded or contracted or pauperized. (Commons, 1934 [1961], p. 7)

Randall Wray has made this same observation more recently.

> With the evolution of capitalism and the development of large-scale production, monetary relations gained prominence. The capitalist required credit (money functioning as a unit of account) to obtain labour and raw materials in order to produce goods to be sold in markets. The primary purpose of money in a capitalist system is to transfer purchasing power across time from the future to the present. (Wray, 1994, p. 93)

Thus cause and effect are different in the machine process and the pecuniary culture but this does not mean we opt for linear cause–effect systems. Instead, collective action is required to ensure that pecuniary control of the machine process is reasonable. 'If there is an object, so constructed that it ties the future to the present independent of individual wills in each bargaining transaction, then that comes within the proper meaning of objectivity. A thing does not need to be physical in order to be "objective". It needs only to be independent of any individual will. With this understanding, then it is collective action which is the object, and which can be made a subject-matter of political economy' (Commons, 1934 [1961], p. 521).

It is clear that Commons did not consider the pecuniary structure to be a part of the natural order governed by natural law. His theory starts with volition but that volition must be governed by public policy in order to keep the machines running. Who is included and who is excluded in the policy deliberations is crucial.

Likewise, Mitchell considered the uncertainty caused by the monetary economy to be the culprit causing economic instability. Mitchell's approach was to use quantitative measurement to confirm this theory and, some time in the future, to develop policy prescriptions to dampen the cycles.

THE FINANCIALIZATION OF THE ECONOMY

According to Yuval Yonay, OIE and neoclassical economists had equal influence and prestige between World War I and World War II (Yonay,

1998, p. 53). However, the influence of OIE scholars on professional and popular thought began to wane following World War II. Though the measurements of Mitchell and his student Simon Kuznets were used in post-WWII macroeconomics, they were encapsulated within the neoclassical synthesis of Keynesian economics. Neoclassical Keynesianism favored linear, mechanistic models and ignored the role of pecuniary institutions and uncertainty that was stressed by OIE scholars and Keynes himself. The debate in the mainstream was limited to whether fiscal or monetary policy was most effective in stabilizing the economy. In some sense this was progress because the debate had shifted from whether economic stabilization was necessary to the question of the most effective tools for stabilization. However, it was accepted by mainstream economists that all of this could be measured with probability distributions rather than an admission of fundamental uncertainty. In an article published in 1937, Keynes made it clear that his theories of saving and investment were not based on probability (1937, p. 218). Post Keynesians, such as Paul Davidson, have been especially forceful in distinguishing probabilistic risk from uncertainty. Davidson makes a link with OIE by stating that 'Government needs to set the "rules of the game" in such a way as to eliminate the anti-social results of the decision making under uncertainty, although it need not get involved in the nitty-gritty decisions regarding the allocations of real resources, like planning at the factory level' (Davidson, 1991, p. 142; Keynes, 1937).

A brief sketch of this recent history will remind us of the transformation that occurred in a few decades following World War I. The Great Depression was effectively ended by war production. Immediately following war hostilities, pent-up consumer demand boosted the economy as production was shifted from military to civilian goods and services. Returning veterans entered the manufacturing sector of the economy that was highly unionized because of New Deal legislation. Employment was reasonably steady and wages for semi-skilled workers were good. The economy was also bolstered by subsidies to veterans for housing and higher education as well as tax-financed construction of such infrastructure as the interstate highway system.

Kevin Phillips called this period the Great Compression (Phillips, 2002, pp. 76, 137). He cited data from the Economic Policy Institute to show that, between 1947 and 1979, income for families in the lowest quintile increased by 120 per cent compared to the highest quintile that increased by 94 per cent. The increases of the middle quintiles fell in between these two. This was sharply reversed in the 1977–94 period when the lowest quintile experienced a *decline* while the top 1 per cent realized a gain of 72 per cent in after-tax income. Only the top two quintiles saw a positive change in income during this period, and the fourth quintile enjoyed only a 4 per cent increase (Phillips, 2002, p. 137). Phillips labeled this latter period 'the Great Inversion'.

What accounts for this dramatic reversal? Phillips blames government policy and the financialization of the economy, and these tendencies were reinforcing. According to Phillips, 'Not even a full book – perhaps not even a full shelf of them – could begin to do justice to the role of the federal income-type taxation in shaping, favoring, and from time to time to even helping to realign wealth in the United States' (Phillips, 2002, p. 223).

The Economic Recovery Tax Act of 1981 accelerated depreciation rates in order to reduce the tax liability of corporations. One provision of that Act, called 'safe harbor leasing', allowed companies that had more depreciation allowances and investment credits than taxable income to sell them to profitable companies that needed tax deductions. General Electric was able to wipe out its tax liability for 1981 plus receiving $110 million in refunds for previous years. 'The sum of corporate-claimed depreciation for 1982–1987 totaled $1.65 trillion' (Phillips, 2002, p. 221). The firms with extra depreciation allowances tended to be the old industrial firms with low profits and lots of physical capital. The firms of the new economy that relied on intellectual capital rather than buildings and machinery, and consequently had insufficient depreciation allowances to cover their taxable income, tended to be the buyers in this market.

The 1981 Act led to a near disappearance of corporate tax revenues and a public outcry for another tax reform. The answer was the Tax Reform Act of 1986. This Act decreased depreciation allowances and closed other tax loopholes. Famously, it taxed income from capital gains at the same rates as ordinary income for the first and only time in the history of our income tax. The removal or reduction of loopholes expanded the tax base, allowing for a reduction in rates. However, 'Behind this façade of eliminating "tax preferences" for the rich and powerful' the Act had some 650 special provisions usually called 'transition rules' or 'technical corrections' invariably disguised, albeit thinly, in dense language' (Phillips, 2002, p. 221).

During this period when corporate and individual tax rates were coming down, especially for the rich, Social Security and Medicare taxes were increasing. In 1983, Alan Greenspan, later Chairman of the Federal Reserve Board, led this movement to shift more of the burden to working families. 'In 1985, for example, a two-earner family making $25,000 a year paid more in FICA taxes than in income taxes; by 1995, expanding FICA earnings coverage and higher rates made them the greater burden for two-thirds of U.S. families' (Phillips, 2002, p. 221).

The effects of the 1981 and 1986 income tax reforms were not only to shift the burden from the wealthy to the less well-off, but to favor financial assets over tangible capital. Phillips called this strategy 'financial mercantilism', where the United States 'had quietly embraced a "financial strategy" in lieu of an "industrial strategy"' (Phillips, 2002, p. 228).

This shift from factory production to finance led to the loss of jobs and diminishing quality of jobs for the working class. The effects of this shift were exacerbated by the rising burden of FICA taxes and the loss of employment-related benefits for workers. The widening of the gap between the rich and not-rich was also propelled by the larger proportion of non-employment income received in the booming financial markets because it takes money to participate in financial markets. Few noticed that finance, insurance and real estate (FIRE) moved ahead of manufacturing in its contribution to GDP during the 1990s (Phillips, 2002, p. 144). It should come as no surprise that the FIRE sector led all other sectors in campaign contributions in the 2000 campaign cycle (Phillips, 2002, p. 322).

James Crotty has recently commented on the effects that the financialization of the economy has had on non-financial corporations (NFCs) (Crotty, 2005, pp. 77–110). Prior to Phillips' Great Inversion, managers of industrial firms could rely on patient capital and plan their investment strategies for the long haul. Before the rise of institutional investors almost all corporate stock was owned by households. Throughout the 1950s, households owned 90 per cent of the corporate stock, usually for long periods of time. By 2000, the share owned by households stood at 42 per cent, compared to 46 per cent owned by institutions (Crotty, 2005, pp. 87, 91). This decline in access to patient capital led to '... a shift in beliefs and behavior of financial agents, from an implicit acceptance of the Chandlerian view of the large NFC as an integrated, coherent combination of relatively illiquid assets assembled to pursue long-term growth and innovation, to a "financial" conception in which the NFC is seen as a "portfolio" of liquid sub-units that home office management must continually restructure to maximize the stock price at every point in time' (Crotty, 2005, p. 88). In other words, the industrial firm has become primarily a pecuniary institution.

These 'portfolio firms' were forced to adopt a new type of manager and management. The conglomerate merger movement of the late 1960s and early 1970s led to a '... change in the perception of the proper role of top management, from one in which managers were expected to be expert in key aspects of the main business of the firm to an evolving view of top executives as generalists who could manage any kind of enterprise, even if they knew little about the details of its business' (Crotty, 2005, p. 89). The era of conglomeration was supplanted by the strategy of hostile takeovers of the 1980s. These takeovers were primarily financed by debt and forced 'the financial or portfolio view of the firm on NFC management. Financial market pressures could now force divestment of subunits that failed to meet investor expectations for just a year or two' (Crotty, 2005, p. 90). William

Lazonick and Mary O'Sullivan have concluded that 'The experience of the United States suggests that the pursuit of shareholder value may be an appropriate strategy for running down a company – and an economy. The pursuit of some other kind of value is needed to build up a company and an economy' (Lazonick and O'Sullivan, 2000, p. 33).

Thus the planning horizon has been shortened to the demands of financial markets rather than the requirements of product development and industrial strategies of firms. The pecuniary culture appears to have gained commanding control over industry as Veblen suggested several decades ago.

SUMMARY AND IMPLICATIONS

John R. Commons identified the creation of the gap between production and finance in his study of shoemakers during the handicraft stage of production. In his study that began as an investigation of deteriorating working conditions, he found that production for wider markets led to a need to finance inventories. The financier was soon able to influence the trade-off between the price and quality of commodities in order to satisfy the requirements of financial markets. The emphasis on low prices and low quality of commodities sparked a move to a new path of industrial development. Working conditions declined as work had to be speeded up to meet these demands. The factory system emerged out of the need to speed up and this led to the need to finance factory machinery (Atkinson, 2004, p. 47). This is where Thorstein Veblen picked up the story to describe the widening dichotomy between the motives of industrialists and those of financiers. Wesley Mitchell took these observations of the shift from production for use to controlling production for accumulation of financial assets to develop his theory and measurement of modern business cycles.

The requirements of wider markets, which began as an accident, set us on a path-dependent process. We have moved from customized, hand production through a centralized factory system to a global network of production directed by supply-chain managers. These firms have become portfolio firms required to maximize stock prices and financial accumulation. This motive can be at odds with the motive to maximize production while improving the conditions for workers in their far-flung operations. However, we must admit that material conditions have improved for many people as we moved along this path. It is difficult to imagine the feast of goods and services we (some of us) now enjoy if we had stuck with handicraft production. That is not to ignore the pain and suffering of the millions of people left out of this bonanza for the few of us. Nor should we be satisfied that we have a glut of such frivolous commodities as high-tech television sets, cosmetic surgery or diet colas while many people do not have access to safe and effective schools or basic health care. We were shocked, or feigned shock, at the images of the living conditions we saw on our digital, high-definition television sets of many victims of the hurricane Katrina. However, we probably do not have to give up our luxurious gadgets in order to help the underprivileged out. Instead, we need to remove the chokehold that pecuniary institutions have on our productive institutions. We need to stop the siphoning of purchasing power from NFCs by pecuniary agents and redirect that purchasing power to producers. We need to downsize the FIRE sector.

Fortunately institutional economists know that this path that we are on is not inexorable. Policies can be developed to ensure that the sacrifices of workers are not greater than the gain in their material welfare. Policies can be developed to spread the benefits of production more widely. Finally, we should not continue to allow financial accumulation to determine the composition of the output of our productive institutions. Pecuniary institutions should be enabling, not determinative. As Commons so eloquently said, we need to understand the '*volitional* theory of present negotiations and transfers of legal control, determining whether production shall go on or slow down or stop, or determining the extent to which future consumption will be expanded or pauperized' (Commons, 1934 [1961], p. 7).

REFERENCES

Atkinson, Glen (2004), 'Labor and the menace of competition', in Dell P. Champlin and Janet T. Knoedler (eds), *The Institutionalist Tradition in Labor Economics*, Armonk, NY: M.E. Sharpe.

Coase, Ronald A. (1937), 'The nature of the firm', *Economica*, **4** (November), 386–405.

Commons, John R. (1923), 'American shoemakers, 1648–1895', in *Labor and Administration*, New York: Macmillan.

Commons, John R. (1924), *Legal Foundations of Capitalism*, reprinted 1968, Madison: University of Wisconsin Press.

Commons, John R. (1934), *Institutional Economics: Its Place in Political Economy*, reprinted 1961, Madison: University of Wisconsin Press.

Commons, John R., David J. Saposs, Helen L. Sumner, E.B. Mittleman, H.E. Hoagland, John B. Andrews and Selig Perlman (1918), *History of Labor in the United States*, vol. 1, New York: Macmillan.

Crotty, James (2005), 'The neoliberal paradox: the impact of destructive product market competition and "modern" financial markets on nonfinancial corporation performance in the neoliberal era', in Gerald Epstein (ed.), *Financialization and the World Economy*, Cheltenham, UK and Northampton, MA, USA: Edward Elgar.

Davidson, Paul (1991), 'Is probability relevant for uncertainty? A post Keynesian perspective', *The Journal of Economic Perspectives*, **1**(Winter), 129–43.

Hake, Eric R. (2004), 'The appearance of impairment: Veblen and goodwill-financed mergers', *Journal of Economic Issues*, **2**(June), 389–95.

Keynes, J.M. (1937), 'The general theory of employment', *The Quarterly Journal of Economics*, **2**(February), 209–23.

Lazonick, William and Mary O'Sullivan (2000), 'Maximizing shareholder value: a new ideology for corporate governance', *Economy and Society*, **1**(February), 13–35.

Mitchell, Wesley C. (1927), *Business Cycles: The Problem and Its Setting,* reprinted 1949, New York: The National Bureau of Economic Research.

Phillips, Kevin, (2002), *Wealth and Democracy*, New York: Broadway Books.

Veblen, Thorstein, (1904), *The Theory of Business Enterprise*, reprinted 1932, New York: New American Library, A Mentor Book.

Wray, Randall (1994), 'Monetary policy', in Geoffrey M. Hodgson, Warren J. Samuels and Marc R. Tool (eds), *The Elgar Companion to Institutional and Evolutionary Economics*, Aldershot, UK and Brookfield, USA: Edward Elgar.

Yonay, Yuval (1998), *The Struggle Over the Soul of Economics*, Princeton, NJ: Princeton University Press.

5. Veblen's missing theory of markets and exchange, or can you have an economic theory without a theory of market exchange?

William T. Waller

The analysis presented in this chapter is based on a series of observations about current economic theorizing. The first is that modern neoclassical economics is not about the economy, meaning its subject matter does not include the processes of production, consumption, savings, investment or government policy of any sort. Neoclassical economics is about how a highly stylized conception of human behavior manifests itself in market exchange processes. All human behavior in this framework of analysis is considered either by the impact it has on market exchange, how it is deficient because it is not a market exchange, or how it could 'really' be understood if it is considered as if it were a market exchange. Consequently, neoclassical economics is a theory about *market* exchange: it is not a general theory of exchange or market exchange as it actually occurs in the economy.

Considered in this way the purpose of markets in neoclassical economic theory takes on a slightly different cast. If neoclassical economics is a theory about the outcome of market exchange and not a theory of exchange, what purpose do markets serve in the overall neoclassical framework? For those who explore the history of economic thought the answer is obvious. The textbooks of a generation ago that introduced the foundation of neoclassical economics were titled *Price Theory*, but the previous generation's textbook caught the crux of the matter more succinctly in J.R. Hicks' classic *Value and Capital*. Neoclassical economic theory is about the way markets equate price and value. This is worth emphasizing: economic equilibrium is when price comes to be equivalent to the value of a commodity (in this case the subjective value of the marginal purchaser and seller) and that value is the social value of that commodity. The efficiency claims of neoclassical economics are based on this equivalence and not the particular social structure that generates it. For this reason neoclassical economics is uninterested for the most part in the process of how prices are actually set and prefer the tidier, less troublesome, route of assuming that competitive markets are the means by which prices in the real world are set rather than exploring the untidy processes of administered pricing that actually sets the vast majority of prices in most modern industrial economies. A similar observation is made by David Levine (Levine, 1975, p. 74).

The second observation is that all exchange is not market exchange. Neoclassical economic theory does not have a general theory of exchange, but instead treats all exchange as market exchanges, proto-market exchanges or failed market exchanges. The disciplines of anthropology and sociology have treated exchange as a more general category where market exchange is but one subset of the more general category that also includes gifts, ceremonial exchanges and barter, to name but a few. For the most part the practitioners of these disciplines have focused on the more general category and have not vigorously contested the neoclassical account of market exchange (Plattner, 1985, pp. viii–ix).

The third observation is less obvious. At an international conference on 'Thorstein Veblen as a Systematic Thinker', several years ago, Geoffrey Hodgson made some comments that caught me by surprise.[1] The aspect of his comments that caught my attention was that Thorstein Veblen did not have a theory of markets. I cannot accurately recall the rest of his comments since that particular comment immediately caused my mind to start thinking through the Veblen canon to assess this aspect of Hodgson's comments. Eventually, I found myself in agreement with Hodgson on this point. Markets as a social institution receive limited attention in Veblen's theorizing. Veblen is of course aware of them, he discusses particular markets, but he does not spend much intellectual effort in explicating an evolutionary theory of economic behavior concerning markets as structured human behavior.

At first, this observation struck me as another mystery in Veblen's work. Ignoring market mechanisms, which for many economists are, if not the central social institution, at the very least incredibly important in modern industrial economies and international trade, seemed puzzling.

My own scholarly work actually began with exploring social reciprocity (non-market exchanges) in market economies. I had found that non-market exchanges were a very large and significant element in market economies. This led me to consider that maybe this omission of market mechanisms was not a great mystery in Veblen's work but instead an effect of his realization that markets simply were not as significant as they appeared in the canonical neoclassical and classical texts. Certainly my own work and the broader discussion of exchange in the disciplines of anthropology and sociology seemed to suggest this might be the case.

As we re-examine the development of exchange theory it is also important to note that the purpose of addressing exchange is different for neoclassical economists, anthropologists and sociologists, and institutional economists. While I have noted that neoclassical economists are concerned with the equivalence of price and value, and that their stylized conception of market exchange is how they achieve this equivalence, other scholars, including Veblen and later institutionalists, have a different purpose in mind.

In this chapter I explore theories of exchange and the use to which they are put with particular emphasis on Veblen and institutional economics. But to do so requires taking a complex path. I will be looking simultaneously at exchange in general and market exchange as a specific type of exchange: I believe the ethnographic record supports such an approach as not being particularly controversial. I will begin by looking at the way these concepts are theorized in economics, beginning with classical economic thought and proceeding to neoclassical thought. Then I will look at how exchange has been theorized in the anthropological and sociological literature. I will follow with an exploration of the concepts of exchange in general and market exchange in particular in institutional economics. In these explorations the focus will be primarily (but not exclusively) on canonical texts. The reason for this is to demonstrate how the various theories and conceptualizations of exchange and market exchange enter into the overarching theoretical framework that motivates these different approaches. The goal of this exploration is twofold. First, I seek to explicate the role of exchange in these systems of thought. Second, I wish to offer an assessment of what we can say about exchange theory and market exchanges in institutional economics in particular.

ADAM SMITH AND THE CLASSICAL ECONOMISTS

It makes sense to start at the beginning and that takes us to Adam Smith.

> . . . [The division of labour] is the necessary, though very slow and gradual, consequence of a certain propensity of human nature which has in view no such extensive utility; the propensity to truck, barter and exchange one thing for another.
>
> Whether this propensity be one of those original principles in human nature, of which no further account can be given; or whether, as seems more probable, it be the necessary consequence of the faculties of reason and speech, it belongs not to our present subject to enquire. It is common to all men, and to be found

in no other race of animals, which seem to know neither this nor any other species of contracts.

... Nobody ever saw a dog make a fair and deliberate exchange of one bone for another with another dog.[2] (Adam Smith, *The Wealth of Nations*, Cannan Edition, p. 13)

[2.] It is by no means clear what object there could be in exchanging one bone for another. (Edwin Cannan, ed. *The Wealth of Nations* by Adam Smith, Cannan Edition, p. 13)

This often cited passage by Adam Smith and the editorial footnote by Edwin Cannan have been a source of humor for generations of economists since the publication of the Cannan Edition of Smith's classic text in 1904. It encapsulates much of the confusion regarding exchange within neoclassical economics.

In the first sentence Adam Smith argues that the division of labor is a result of a 'propensity of human nature'. This is consistent with Smith's underlying natural rights epistemology which assumes that there are structures in the universe which have a fixed and unchanging character that, under the correct institutional structure that he broadly defines as 'Natural Liberty', cause the various elements of reality to function and exist in harmony. When Smith's phrases are rather simply rearranged they illuminate another unchanging element of human nature: 'Similarly the propensity of human nature ...', '... to truck, barter and exchange one thing for another ...', '... has in view no such extensive utility ...', when compared to the division of labor. Here is a key element, often overlooked in Smith's theory. Exchange is natural behavior. It requires no extrinsic motivation whatsoever. Or alternatively, exchange is not motivated by self-interest. To understand exchange in Smith's work we have to look at his views on human nature expressed in *The Theory of Moral Sentiments* (Smith, 1759 [1982]).

Smith writes on the nature of moral faculties:

Upon whatever we suppose that our moral faculties are founded, whether upon certain modification of reason, upon an original instinct, called a moral sense, or upon some other principle of our nature, it cannot be doubted, that they were given to us for the direction of our conduct in this life. They carry along with them the most evident badges of this authority, which denote that they were set up within us to be the supreme arbiters of all our actions, to superintend all our senses, passions, and appetites, and to judge how far each of them was either to be indulged or restrained. (Smith, 1759 [1982], p. 165)

Note that we have primary 'senses, passions, and appetites' that our natural moral faculties are supposed to help us regulate. He makes this clear when he writes: 'Our moral faculties are by no means, as some have pretended, upon a level in this respect with other faculties and appetites of our nature, endowed with no more right to restrain these last, than these last are to restrain them (Smith, 1759 [1982], p. 165).

He then goes on to describe the character of these natural faculties of all kinds.

> Since these (natural faculties), therefore, were plainly intended to be the governing principles of human nature, the rules which they prescribe are to be regarded as commands and laws of the Deity, promulgated by those vicegerent which he has thus set up within us. All general rules are commonly denominated laws: thus the general rules which bodies observe in the communication of motion, are called the laws of motion. But those general rules which our moral faculties observe in approving or condemning whatever sentiment or action is subjected to their examination, may much more justly be denominated such. They have a much greater resemblance to what are properly called laws, those general rules which the sovereign lays down to direct the conduct of his subjects. (Smith, 1759 [1982], pp. 165–6)

Smith has differentiated two different types of propensities of human nature: 'Original principles in human nature, of which no further account can be given.' These seem to be of the character of biological appetites and instincts; that Smith describes as 'senses, passions, and appetites'. These motivate behavior that Smith refers to above as 'laws of motion'. These are contrasted with principles of human nature that he describes as 'the necessary consequence of the faculties of reason and speech'. Since it is moral reasoning that Smith is concerned about it is clear that these are the capacities and aspects of human nature that are to regulate the behavior motivated by the so-called laws of motion.

This discussion clarifies the humorous aspect of the Smith and Cannan quotes: If dogs had the propensity to truck, barter and exchange as an element of their canine nature it would motivate exchange of identical bones between dogs. But similarly this propensity should motivate exchange between humans of identical objects as well. Exchange is motivated by biology for its intrinsic character! As we will see, the notion that the motive for exchange is gain or benefit of any kind is a modification and addition to this element of human nature.

The question of whether any human action is motivated by the opportunity of material benefit for Smith can only be answered by looking at how he understands the relationship between self-interest and duty as moral principles. Smith clearly states that the selfish passions require regulation by moral principles because they occupy a middle place 'between the social and unsocial affections' (Smith, 1759 [1982], p. 172). In his discussion of utility (which includes the utility of goods and services) Smith argues that utility is a principle that influences conduct that is often the 'secret motive

of the most serious and important pursuits of both private and public life'
(ibid, p. 181, IV.1.7). However, it too, must be mitigated by other moral
principles. It is worthwhile to consider Smith's analysis of utility in detail.
He describes the appetite that motivates the behavior.

> The poor man's son, whom heaven in its anger has visited with ambition, when he
> begins to look around him, admires the condition of the rich. He finds the cottage
> of his father too small for his accommodation, and fancies, he should be lodged
> more at his ease in a palace. He is displeased with being obliged to walk a-foot,
> or to endure the fatigue of riding on horseback. He sees his superiors carried
> about in machines, and imagines that in one of these he could travel with less
> inconveniency. He feels himself naturally indolent, and willing to serve himself
> with his own hands as little as possible; and judges, that a numerous retinue of
> servants would save him from a great deal of trouble. He thinks if he had attained
> all these, he would sit still and contentedly, and be quiet, enjoying himself in the
> thought of the happiness and tranquility of his situation. He is enchanted with
> the distant idea of this felicity. It appears in his fancy like the life of some superior
> rank of beings, and, in order to arrive at it, he devotes himself forever to the
> pursuit of wealth and greatness. (Smith, 1759 [1982], p. 181, IV.1.8).

Then he describes the resulting behavior: 'To obtain the conveniences
which these afford, he submits in the first year, nay in the first month of
his application, to more fatigue of the body and more uneasiness of mind
than he could have suffered through the whole of his life from the want of
them' (Smith, 1759 [1982], p. 181, IV, 1.8).

Obviously, this is not an anticipation of the behavioral assumption of
modern neoclassical economics that humans try to maximize net returns.
Smith is clearly describing a faulty cost–benefit analysis.

Some might conclude that the 'poor man's son's' experience is the result
of information costs or some other contrivance of the so-called 'new institutionalism', but consider the rest of Smith's analysis:

> He studies to distinguish himself in some laborious profession. With the most
> unrelenting industry he labours night and day to acquire talents superior to all his
> competitors. He endeavours next to bring those talents into public view, and with
> equal assiduity solicits every opportunity of employment. For this purpose he
> makes his court to all mankind; he serves those whom he hates, and is obsequious
> to those whom he despised. Through the whole of his life he pursues the idea of
> a certain artificial and elegant repose which he may never arrive at, for which he
> sacrifices a real tranquility that is at all times in his power, and which, if in the
> extremity of old age he should at last attain to it, he will find to be in no respect
> preferable to that humble security and contentment which he had abandoned for
> it. It is then, in the last dregs of life, his body wasted with toil and diseases, his
> mind galled and ruffled by the memory of a thousand injuries and disappoint-
> ments which he imagines he has met with from the injustice of his enemies, or
> from the perfidy and ingratitude of his friends, that he begins at last to find that
> wealth and greatness are mere trinkets of frivolous utility, no more adapted for

procuring ease of body or tranquility of mind than the tweezer-cases of the lover of toys; and like them too, more troublesome to the person who carries them with him than all the advantages they can afford him are commodious. (Smith, 1759 [1982], p. 181, IV.1.8)

This individual systematically miscalculates what is in his own self-interest. And what purpose does this behavior really serve in Smith's view – not some unfolding, expression of unchanging human nature. The purpose of the acquisition of these objects and services is not the utility of their use or the life of ease they provide for the body and soul of the acquirer; but instead that 'they more effectively gratify the love of distinction so natural to man'. The purpose of the acquisition of goods and services is to achieve some invidious distinction from others who are observing the trinkets; the method of achieving this distinction is conspicuous consumption! But even this purpose is doomed to fail the test of self-gratification.

But in the languor of disease and the weariness of old age, the pleasures of the vain and empty distinctions of greatness disappear. To one, in this situation, they are no longer capable of recommending those toilsome pursuits in which they had formerly engaged him. In his heart he curses ambition, and vainly regrets the ease and the indolence of youth, pleasures which are fled for ever, and which he has foolishly sacrificed for what, when he has got it, can afford him no real satisfaction. In this miserable aspect does greatness appear to every man when reduced by spleen or disease to observe with attention his own situation and to consider what it is that is really want to his happiness. (Smith, 1759 [1982], p. 182)

When Smith considers this type of behavior in the real world where human beings have the capacity to consider the moral sense of sympathy, generosity, duty, justice, compassion and self-regard, he concludes that it is the *systematic misperception of self-regard* that drives economic behavior.

It is this deception which rouses and keeps in continual motion the industry of mankind. ... They [the rich] only consume little more than the poor, and in spite of their natural selfishness and rapacity, though they mean only their own convenience, though the sole end which they propose from the labours of all of the thousands they employ, be the gratification of their own vain and insatiable desires, they divide with the poor the produce of all of their improvement. They are led by an invisible hand to make nearly the same distribution of the necessaries of life, which would have been made, had the earth been divided into equal portions among all its inhabitants, and thus without intending it, without knowing it, advance the interest of society and the multiplication of the species. (Smith, 1759 [1982], pp. 184–5)

This analysis of Adam Smith's understanding of exchange has two purposes. First, is to note that exchange behavior is motivated by a natural propensity. Smith does not attach to exchange any generic end-in-view or purpose.

Put simply, exchange is natural and thus not necessarily connected to any particular set of institutions, including markets. Second, is to establish that Smith's notion of exchange should not be interpreted through the lens of later marginal utility theory explanations of exchange, as Cannan appears to be doing in his critical response to Smith reproduced above.

EXCHANGE: THE NEXT GENERATION

While classical economists after Smith considered a number of motivations for economic behavior, including utilitarian explanations, the dominance of Say's Law eliminated the need for any serious consideration of the motivation of exchange: the act of production created the demand that was to be satisfied. The need to reopen this question seems to have been motivated by Karl Marx. Marx's theories of exchange are interesting in their own right, but in the interest of brevity they are not discussed in this chapter.

The Marginalists

The Marginalists, employing the work of William Stanley Jevons in particular, substituted an explanation of exchange behavior as motivated by self-interest, and characterized as maximization or optimization of the abstract notion of utility by individual consumers for Smith's natural propensity. Marginal Utility was also both the measure of the commodity's value (to consumers) and a determinant of price in competitive markets.

There are two problems with this theoretical innovation: it does not work and no one believes it. The first claim, that marginal utility theory does not explain either market demand or consumer behavior or price, is certainly familiar to institutional economists. In his famous essay 'The limitations of marginal utility' (1909 [1990]), Veblen argues that, with regard to human behavior, the theory of marginal utility simply assumes all that it purports to explain scientifically. Veblen observes:

> The cultural elements so tacitly postulated as immutable conditions precedent of economic life are ownership and free contract, together with such other features of the scheme of natural rights as are implied in the exercise of these. These cultural products are, for the purpose of the theory, conceived to be given a priori in unmitigated force. They are part of the nature of things; so that there is no need of accounting for them or inquiring into them as to how they have come to be such as they are, or how and why they have changed or are changing, or what effect all this may have on the relations of men who live by or under this cultural situation. (Veblen, 1909 [1990], p. 236)

After historically particular institutions are assumed to be timeless universal constructs the marginalist theorists compound their initial errors by adding:

> ... as their common point of departure the traditional psychology of the early nineteenth-century hedonists, which is accepted as a matter of course or common notoriety and is held quite uncritically. The central and well-defined tenet so held is that of the hedonistic calculus. Under the guidance of this tenet and of the other psychological conceptions associated and consonant with it, human conduct is conceived of and interpreted as a rational response to the exigencies of the situation in which mankind is placed; as regards economic conduct it is such a rational and unprejudiced response to the stimulus of anticipated pleasure and pain. (Veblen, 1909 [1990], p. 234)

When these assumptions are combined they allow for the deduction of a theory of action that would be necessarily (logically) true in the event that the postulated assumptions were both correct and the conditions they represent immutable in time, space and cultural context. But Veblen notes the peculiarity of this approach for a modern science of economics.

> ... it is the peculiarity of the hedonistic economics that by force of its postulates its attention is confined to this teleological bearing of conduct alone. It deals with this conduct only in so far as it may be construed in rationalistic, teleological terms of calculation and choice. But it is at the same time no less true that human conduct, economic or otherwise, is subject to the sequence of cause and effect, by force of such elements as habituation and conventional requirements. But facts of this order, which are to modern science of graver interest than the teleological details of conduct, necessarily fall outside the attention of the hedonistic economist, because they cannot be construed in terms of sufficient reason, such as his postulated demand, or be fitted into a scheme of teleological doctrines. (Veblen, 1909 [1990], p. 239)

Veblen concludes that when the real activities of real people in modern industrial economies are forced into being interpreted exclusively in hedonistic terms the real behavior disappears from the theory entirely (Veblen, 1909 [1990], p. 250).

When considering Jevons's theory of marginal utility, Veblen is right on target. Jevons's innovation consists of combining the notion of the margin with the concept of utility. Interestingly, Jevons, an outspoken anti-Ricardian, seems to have taken his concept of the margin from Ricardo's theory of rent. His notion of utility is from Bentham. And the first use he put this conceptual combination to is a theory of exchange. The theory results in the familiar conclusion that, in a system where two utility maximizing individuals trade two commodities in competitive markets, the ratio of prices will be equal to the ratio of the two individuals' marginal utilities. Formally speaking, the only assumptions necessary to provide a consistent theory of exchange are the psychological a priori assumptions that individuals always maximize their total utility and an a priori assumption that markets are purely competitive.

Thus, as a theory of actual human exchange behavior, Jevons's theory depends on the correspondence of his a priori assumptions to reality. As Veblen correctly notes, these a priori assumptions are unsupportable. So as a theory of actual human exchange Jevons's theory is derived from two highly questionable, if not demonstrably false, a priori assumptions – and while this does not make its conclusions necessarily false, it is a very unsound basis for further theorizing. This might partially explain why Jevons's contemporaries were not quick to embrace the theory.

Greater acceptance of the theory of marginal utility came with its incorporation into Alfred Marshall's theory of supply and demand. Marshall incorporates the theory of marginal utility as an underpinning for his theory of demand. He adds this to his theory of supply that he based on marginal cost considerations deriving from production. Thus supply is still based in production as it was in classical economics, whereas demand is determined by consumption. Prices are determined by the interaction of the two forces, so the labor theory of value of classical economics can be dispensed with. There is a satisfying behavioral symmetry with the assumptions of utility maximization and profit maximization derived from Marshall's general argument that behavior is rationally determined by a comparison between benefits and costs.

Value is now a function primarily of consumption and therefore utility. But what of exchange? Jevons only needed two consumers with different positive marginal utilities and markets to motivate exchange. Supply and demand theory still requires a consumer with positive marginal utility and competitive markets, but it also requires a supply of goods. Since the supply function is based on cost of production, albeit marginal cost of production, there is no guarantee that supply will be forthcoming at a price any consumer is willing to pay. Put simply, Jevons's theory of market transactions is dependent upon the existence of the dual coincidence of wants; but Marshall's exchange theory depends on it as well because he has substituted the firm for the second consumer with a differing marginal utility.

The consequence of this substitution of the firm for the second consumer in Marshall's theory as a theory of exchange is that it requires additional assumptions to be a theory of exchange behavior. Marshall's framework either requires the assumption that the dual coincidence of wants exists, or that all human exchange behavior is dependent on the pre-existence of a widely accepted form of money. Of course if we assume that the dual coincidence of wants exists we do not need money as a means of exchange, but the absence of money creates problems for a whole other area of economic theorizing.

For the purpose of understanding theories of exchange, the significance of Marshall's innovation is that it adds more underlying, intriguingly problematic assumptions as necessary conditions to explain human exchange behavior. Consider that this is a self-inflicted problem. With Smith's attribution of a propensity to exchange to human nature, people will exchange regardless of either utility or the satisfaction of the dual coincidence of wants, or the pre-existence of competitive markets. At least as a theory of exchange it is difficult to see how marginalism is an improvement.

Many authors have speculated why marginalism and neoclassical economics were adopted. Mark Blaug in his classic *Economic Theory in Retrospect* (1978) evaluates four different theories. He describes the reasons for the 'marginalist revolution' as '(1) an autonomous intellectual development within the discipline of economics; (2) the product of philosophical currents; (3) the product of definite institutional changes in the economy; and (4) a counterblast to socialism, particularly to Marxism' (Blaug, 1978, p. 314).

Blaug rejects all of these as sufficient explanations for the adoption of marginalism; indeed, he rejects the notion of a revolution altogether in favor of a more prosaic and circumspect analysis of multicausal, incremental change. Guy Routh's analysis gives more credence to reason number four, marginalism as a reaction to Marxism, at least among Austrian economists (Routh, 1975, pp. 257–60). Wesley Clair Mitchell comes down on the side that Marshall's theory of price determination was more appealing and complete than the theories of his predecessors (including Jevons's).

> Amidst all the confusion and the lack of symmetry, Marshall said that the theorist should follow the scheme of demand and supply in all exchanges. He will recognize that the studies of cost of production explain the factors on which supply depends in the case of problems that cover a time long enough for new goods to be produced. And on the other side, he can use the utility analysis as an explanation of the factors on which demand depends. In this way, Marshall was able to find a place within one and the same body of theory for what Jevons had conceived to be, and what Austrians continued in good part to believe, two more or less antagonistic elements: the element of cost analysis and the element of utility analysis. In short, Jevons's contribution was absorbed into a fuller analysis by Marshall. (Mitchell, 1948, in Dorfman, 1967, p. 102)

Essentially, Marshall abandons exchange theory by simply assuming people are naturally motivated to engage in exchange in order to satisfy wants and avoid irksome activity. He focuses on price determination in markets. Marshall, according to Mitchell, employed a deductive methodology based on assumed premises and then deduced logical conclusions from them usually using demand and supply schedules. Nevertheless, Marshall saw himself as engaged in 'the study of man in the actual business of life' (Mitchell, 1948, in Dorfman, 1967, p. 218). Mitchell further notes that 'Hardly more than Mill does he attempt inductive verification of his assumptions, or of the conclusions deduced from them. But he believes that his assumptions are substantially valid representations of prevailing practices' (Mitchell, 1948, in Dorfman, 1967, p. 219). Apparently this advance in the theory of price seems to have been sufficient to deflect any further concerns in the mainstream of economics.

But these attempted modifications were insufficient. E.Z. Downey's classic article, 'The futility of marginal utility' (1910 [1987]), demonstrates this insufficiency by expanding upon Veblen's critique, noting that the neoclassical theory not only fails to explain the motivation for human exchange behavior, but additionally, fails as an explanation of either demand or price. Downey notes that the so-called explanation of market price in marginal utility theory is really just a restatement of the problem of explaining price in terms incomprehensible to the layman. Indeed, it is a tautology. He provides an example worthy of careful reexamination, a model of a decrease in hog prices in Chicago over ten days in 1914.

> The marginal-utility theory has it that the price, on any given day, is fixed at a point between the 'marginal price-offer' and the 'marginal refusal price' – by which terms is meant the money expression of the 'subjective value' of hogs to the 'marginal buyer' and 'marginal seller' respectively. It is clear, then, that the price of hogs fell because the 'marginal price-offer' and the marginal refusal price simultaneously declined. (Downey, 1910 [1987], p. 54)

But then he notes:

> But is this anything more than a puzzling restatement of the problem? It says only that the 'marginal buyer' was disposed to pay less, and the 'marginal seller' willing to take less, on October 14 than October 4. As to the reasons for this change of heart we are left completely in the dark. And we are just as little enlightened as to the forces which fix the price on any given day. The 'marginal price-offer' is simply the lowest offer any buyer can make without being outbid by other buyers. Likewise, the ' marginal refusal price' is simply the highest price any seller can ask without being undersold by other sellers. If there is a 'perfect market', so that all hogs of a given grade are sold for the same price – which, of course, never occurs – 'marginal price-offer' and 'marginal refusal price' will coincide, or nearly coincide, with each other and with market price. But the 'marginal' bid and offer are only in an infinitesimal degree the *cause* of the market adjustment; they count for no more in that adjustment than do any other bids or offers. The 'margin' of price-paying or price-refusing disposition is what it is only because of the action of all the buyers and sellers in the market. And the action of buyers and sellers is what it is only because of all the forces which bear upon hog supply, on the one hand, and upon the demand for hogs on the other. That is to say, the 'margin' is

the resultant of all those forces which fix market price. The 'margin' is, indeed, a purely a posteriori fact. Barring omniscience, there is no way to ascertain the position of the 'margin' until the 'going price' has been established. To say the price of hogs fell because the 'marginal price-offer' for hogs declined is, therefore, to say that price fell because it fell. Hogs sold at $7.53 because they did not sell for more. (Downey, 1910 [1987], p. 55)

Downey combines his analysis with Veblen's to conclude:

The marginal-utility theory aims at showing, not how price is determined in any actual case, but how price would be determined if men were to act in certain ways under certain assumed circumstances. This mode of theorizing is grounded upon the assumption that the behavior of men in any given situation can be predicted from elementary human nature. It appears that adepts of the theory have misconceived human nature, and that the situation in which they assume market price to be worked out never actually occurs. But the decisive objection to this whole line of doctrine goes to the basis upon which it is built up. Elementary human nature may (or may not) be fairly uniform, but it functions through institutions, and these are not uniform. The behavior of men can be neither predicted nor understood apart from their habitual modes of thought and from the institutional situation in which they act. (Downey, 1910 [1987], p. 57)

While one would never guess it from the introductory chapters of the typical principles of microeconomics or intermediate microeconomic theory texts, this theoretical shortcoming is fairly well understood by neoclassical economists who have seriously considered the explanatory power and epistemological status of utility theory in neoclassical economics. Marc Blaug in his highly respected and indisputably mainstream *Economic Theory in Retrospect* discusses at length that marginal utility theory is intended neither as a description of actual human action nor as an explanation for price determination. According to Blaug, 'The fundamental principle of utility theory is that consumers act "as if" they were maximizing utility' (Blaug, 1978, p. 373). Paul Samuelson abandoned the utility concept all together in his theory of revealed preference. (Samuelson, 1938, 1947 [1965]). And, according to Blaug, in 1963 E.J. Mishan commented 'that a budding economist would be just as well off if he accepted the "law of demand" "on trust"' (Blaug, 1978, p. 389). The reason that marginal utility theory has persisted is that it is necessary to provide a theoretical underpinning for the theory of demand. Demand may be observable, if by that you mean that people alter their behavior in response to price changes. But the best these observations can provide is no more than an empirical generalization about what people do.

If marginal utility theory does not explain the motivation for exchange, human behavior or price but, instead, has continued as a mainstay of neoclassical economics because it provides the necessary theoretical foundation for the theory of demand, then where does that leave us in proceeding to understand the relationship between exchange and markets? In the mainstream of economic thought exchange as human behavior is either assumed as an innate capacity or simply asserted to exist. It would be bad enough if no progress since the time of Adam Smith had been made. Alas, the reality is even worse. In addition to assuming all the behavior it purports to explain, the mainstream theory of demand and supply left to us by Alfred Marshall assumes all the necessary institutions exist that are necessary for markets to exist without providing a causal explanation for their development. To make matters worse, the use of differential calculus to derive demand curves requires that the agent engage in behavior whereby they not merely choose things that give them pleasure, but also maximize their utility (which is even more limiting than merely optimizing). This optimizing behavior requires many additional conditions that have serious implications when translated into human behavior: choices must exhibit consistency (transitivity) and completeness (all possible bundles must be comparable). Additionally people cannot be satiable and must have all the information available to make choices that conform to the first two requirements, consistency and completeness. The only real use of this theory is to provide a theoretical foundation to the theory of demand and it can only do that under the highly restrictive assumptions necessitated by the mathematical requirements of optimization theory. The result is a theory of motivation for exchange behavior that strains credulity by the sheer impossibility of the many requirements, conditions and institutional structures it must assume. And that is assuming that the implications of the theory so constructed are well understood, a proposition that is questionable in itself (see Mirowski, 1989).

Another consideration of importance in the classical and neoclassical traditions is an alternative theory of exchange, namely that the division of labor, the other cornerstone of Adam Smith's economics, combined with self-interest (or rationality) and private property create conditions that make the spontaneous emergence of market exchange likely (as in Austrian economics).[2] In the classical framework of Adam Smith, an assumed propensity to exchange is the sufficient cause of exchange behavior, whereas market institutions, private property and the division of labor are the results. For Smith and his predecessors, moral principles were the result of a moral sense parallel to the five senses, thus self-interest (and sympathy) required no explanation. The classical tradition is thus theoretically sufficient to explain exchange *as long as the assumptions are assumed to be correct*.

Everything that classical economics (and Austrian economics) attempt to explain, neoclassical economics assumes. They assume human self-interested behavior – but that does not necessarily imply exchange by itself, so they assume generalized scarcity. This creates the economic problem to be solved. Then they limit themselves to the exploration of how this problem is solved in societies that have already achieved a significant division of labor, created an interdependent economy, developed a legal framework for creating and sustaining fee simple, alienable, private property, and evolved market institutions for all products and services (Friedman, 1976, p. 2). From these assumptions they have developed a theoretical model that purports to explain why a cup of coffee at my local diner costs 80 cents. This model is then applied to other societies with none of these institutions, thereby implicitly asserting that the two assumptions of rational self-interest as the motivation for all human behavior and an objective condition of pervasive generalized scarcity are somehow sufficient to cause this transformation so that their models are then applicable to all societies at all times and all places.

The damage to human lives created as a result of this tautological assertion is incalculable. The new institutionalism is a movement within neoclassical economics that has recognized and attempts to address the structural/institutional aspects of this tautological framework while holding on to the rationality assumptions (in this case that human beings naturally maximize net returns) at the very least. For my purpose it is enough to note from this discussion that neoclassical economics has no theory of exchange or market exchange as mentioned in my first observation.

So after 224 years of mainstream economists' attempts to explain exchange behavior we have moved from the argument that it is natural for people to do so, to the tautology that people engage in exchange to maximize their utility because they would not engage in exchange unless it maximized their utility. Clearly we must move outside the mainstream to address exchange and markets in a meaningful way.

ECONOMIC ANTHROPOLOGY

I have argued elsewhere (Waller, 1984) that a larger framework that encompasses reciprocity is necessary to understand exchange. This argument is based on a long tradition of anthropologists' explication and comparative study of ceremonial forms of exchange, market exchange, barter, and gift exchange. In that work I concluded that employing a comparative method would allow us to consider aspects of our own society that were suppressed by an overly economistic focus on market exchange. But I also found that there was no more satisfactory general categorization of exchange that seemed to provide an alternative framework to unify our understanding or provide a general theory of exchange.

In a 1994 essay that covers much of the same territory (though it is primarily focused on two scholars in particular), Philip Mirowski comes to a similar conclusion. Mirowski also points to but does not discuss in detail some later scholarship that derives this same general observation from a post-structuralist perspective (Mirowski, 1994, p. 339).

In his classic text *Economic Anthropology* (1952), Melville Herskovits devoted Chapter 8 to ceremonial and gift exchange (non-economic exchange) and a separate Chapter 9 to barter and market exchange (economic exchange). This basic division was maintained among early anthropologists and sociologists who have explored exchange. Most have constructed categories of exchanges that they view as qualitatively different, while exploring the commonalities across categories and considering the possibility of universal qualities common to all exchanges. There seem to be a couple of reasons for this general approach. The most important reason for looking at commonalities is the empirical observation that exchanges of all types create new, while maintaining existing, relationships. Ongoing exchange relations tend to reinforce existing relations. These observations seem to suggest that the structure of exchange relations has some commonality.

There have been some sociologists and anthropologists who have continued the formalist approach to exchange. They have embraced a rational choice approach. They will not receive further attention in this chapter because, even as they are modeling on the basis of the behavioral assumption of rational self-interest, understood as constrained optimization, these authors do not for the most part express the view that human beings always and everywhere exclusively behave in this manner. They consider that human beings might be motivated in other and/or a multiplicity of ways. That being the case in sociology and anthropology the rational choice framework is really 'rational choice light' compared to neoclassical economics, although to the extent that it mimics it, it does share the same problems with the neoclassical approach.

Malinowski, Mauss and Lévi-Strauss

Bronislaw Malinowski, though not the first to address the question of types of exchange, begins the modern discussion of exchange in his classic works on the Trobriand Islanders. The circular exchange of armshells and necklaces among the Trobriand Islanders, called *Kula*, draws special attention from Malinowski. In his earliest publications Malinowski adheres to the distinction between economic and non-economic exchange. His earliest publication (1920) on the Trobriand Islanders is on the *Kula* exchange, and is published in *Man*, the premier anthropology journal of the day. It treats

Kula exchange as a non-economic, ceremonial exchange system. His second publication (1921) was on the Trobriand Islanders' economic system and focused on yam growing and agricultural magic; it was published in *The Economic Journal*, the premier economic journal of the day, which was co-edited by J.M. Keynes at the time. In footnotes in each article Malinowski notes that *Kula* seems to have economic aspects, but does not elaborate upon them. When his classic *Argonauts of the Western Pacific* was published (in 1922) he abandoned the strict separation between economic and non-economic exchange and built a taxonomy of exchange.

His taxonomy rejects the strict distinction between *Kula* and *gimwali* (barter). His categories are pure gifts; customary payments, repaid irregularly and without strict equivalence; payments for services rendered; gifts returned in economically equivalent form; exchange of material goods against privileges, titles and non-material possessions; ceremonial barter with deferred payments; trade, pure and simple (Malinowski, 1922, pp. 177–91). In this taxonomy Malinowski is rejecting the distinction between economic and non-economic exchange. Indeed, he is rendering all exchange as a variation on gift giving, thus giving priority to anthropological and sociological theoretical considerations regarding exchange. He cites 'the deep tendency to create social ties through exchange of gifts' (Malinowski, 1922, p. 175). Further, he believes this mechanism 'is a universal feature of all primitive societies' (Malinowski, 1922, p. 175). He elaborates: 'It is easy to see that almost all the categories of gifts which I have classified according to economic principles are also based on some sociological relationship' (Malinowski, 1922, p. 191). He notes: 'If we drew up a scheme of sociological relations, each type of them [gifts] would be defined by a special class of economic duties' (Malinowski, 1922, p. 191).

Malinowski locates the motivation for exchange in custom. Basically, people reciprocate in the appropriate way in social exchanges because of respect for custom. Commenting on this aspect of Malinowski's work, Annette Weiner writes: 'in elevating custom to the motivating force in reciprocity, Malinowski wrote how custom is "obeyed for its own sake" because of the "awe of traditional command and a sentimental attachment to it". For Malinowski, too, reciprocity was imbued with a morality that drew on legal, economic, sociological, magical and supernatural forces and pervaded every aspect of "primitive" life' (Weiner, 1992, p.32).

Marcel Mauss in his classic text, *The Gift* (1954), offers an alternative view of reciprocity as a basis for a theory of sorts of exchange. He defines prestation (gift giving) as a total social phenomenon imbuing all social formations to some degree. As Mauss described it: 'The form usually taken is that of the gift generously offered; but the accompanying behavior is formal pretense and social deception, while the transaction itself is based on obligation and economic self interest' (Mauss, 1954, p. 1). His purpose for looking at this behavior is to answer what underlying principle requires the gift to be repaid and to identify the force in the thing given which compels the recipient to make a return. Mauss is interested in total prestation, not simple gift giving between individuals. He is referring to exchanges and contracts between moral persons, where the moral person is an intermediary representing a larger group. So this is not really individual exchange or contract, it is exchange between groups that confront and oppose one another. These exchanges consist not just of goods, but include 'courtesies, entertainments, rituals, military assistance, women, children, dances, and feasts. Finally although the prestations and counter-prestations take place under a voluntary guise they are in essence strictly obligatory, and their sanction is private or open warfare' (Mauss, 1954, p. 3). For Mauss the motive for exchange is peace. He builds the notion of the gift given embodying the spirit of the person giving it, following Emile Durkheim. Philip Mirowski referred to this as the 'thingification of people and the personification of things' (Mirowski, 1994, p. 326).

Malinowski motivated exchange by custom; Mauss motivated by the spirit of the gift. Claude Lévi-Strauss provided a structural explanation for the motivation of exchange. He argued that gifts and counter gifts could be reduced to 'rigorously defined cycles of reciprocal marriage exchanges, each of which correlates with a particular type of social structure' (Weiner, 1992, p. 27). Weiner notes that while Lévi-Strauss argued that reciprocity did not need external motivation; in fact it was motivated by the desire to control women's sexuality (Weiner, 1992, p. 27).

The Continuing Evolution of Exchange Theory

These three attempts to theorize exchange led to a period of interest in theorizing social reciprocity. To advance our argument we need to discuss several commentators on these classic texts of Malinowski, Mauss and Lévi-Strauss. These commentators include Alvin Gouldner on the norm of reciprocity, Geoffrey MacCormack on the clarity of the reciprocity concept, and Annette Weiner on revisiting the Trobriand Islands, exchange and the role of women. This will be followed by a discussion of the work of Marshall Sahlins on primitive exchange.

Gouldner and the norm of reciprocity

In 1960, Alvin Gouldner published an article entitled, 'The norm of reciprocity'. Gouldner's point was to establish that a universal norm was present in all cultures, as part of his larger argument against the functionalism of Talcott Parsons. He differentiated between particular cases of reciprocal exchange that he views as historically specific and culturally contingent. But he contended that there was a much simpler social norm governing behavior. He wrote:

> Contrary to some cultural relativists, it can be hypothesized that a norm of reciprocity is universal. As Westermarck states, 'To requite a benefit, or to be grateful to him who bestows it is probably everywhere, at least under certain circumstances, regarded as duty.' A norm of reciprocity is, I suspect no less universal and important an element of culture than the incest taboo, although similar, its concrete formulations may vary with time and place.
>
> Specifically I suggest that a norm of reciprocity, in its universal form makes two interrelated, minimal demands: (1) people should help those who have helped them, and (2) people should not injure those who have helped them. Generically, the norm of reciprocity may be conceived of as a dimension to be found in all value systems and, in particular, as one among a *number* of principal components universally present in moral codes. (Gouldner, 1960, p. 171).

Gouldner hypothesized that the generalized norms of reciprocity produced social stability in a number of ways. (1) It set limits on the degree of exploitation that powerful people could engage. (2) The time between the receipt of the initial gift and its reciprocal counter-gift created a period of time of indebtedness where the receiver and the giver were unlikely to engage in hostile behavior. (3) The very indeterminacy of what constitutes an appropriate counter-gift makes it difficult to know when a debt is totally expunged and thus the social obligation of receiver to the giver terminated (Gouldner, 1960, pp. 174–5).

Whether Gouldner was correct about the universality of generalized norms of reciprocity is not of concern here. What is crucial is that discussions of reciprocity as a social norm continued to inform comparative analysis of exchange systems from then on.

Geoffrey MacCormack

In a review article in *Man* (1976), Geoffrey MacCormack cautioned that the term 'reciprocity' had been employed by enough sociologists and ethnographers to describe sufficiently varied types of behavior to suggest a need for real caution with continued use of the term. He noted that all the various authors who used the term used it to identify exchanges that are structurally similar, thus strongly suggesting that various authors meant the same thing. But these same authors were often unclear about the status of the concept. Was the term 'reciprocity' used simply to describe a particular set of behaviors? Did the use of the term 'reciprocity' somehow imply that the behaviors are essential to maintaining the stability of the society? Did the use of the term 'principle of reciprocity' intend to suggest that such behaviors are essential to maintaining the stability of all societies (MacCormack, 1976, p. 101)?

> Where the principle is used as a shorthand description of a state of affairs obtaining within a society it is not always clear from the investigator's account whether the state of affairs is a rule, a standard or ideal, a wish, desire or expectation, or a habit. Or one investigator may use the principle to describe a practice or habit, another to describe a rule or expectation. (MacCormack, 1976, p. 99)

Because of this and other ambiguities he concluded that the term should be avoided.

Annette B. Weiner and Kula revisited

Annette Weiner has done extensive field work in the Trobriand Islands, building on the work of Malinowski. However, her focus on the role of women in the Trobriand Islands both greatly extends and serves as a corrective for omissions and confusions in Malinowski's work. First and foremost for my analysis is the fact that Weiner does not employ the categories of Malinowski. In particular she does not accept Malinowski's distinction between ceremonial goods (the armshells and necklaces of *kula*) that are valuable for their symbolic significance and ordinary goods exchanged in barter (*gimwali*) that are valuable for their use-value. Instead, following Veblen, Weiner argues that all goods have symbolic significance (Weiner, 1992, p. 36). She describes how the various exchanges among different people in Trobriand culture are both a symbolic and a material representation of their social order. For Trobriand Islanders, exchange has (at least) the dual function of both maintaining and representing their social order and culture (Weiner, 1976, pp. 211–12).

In Trobriand culture men's reputation in *kula* affects their status (Weiner, 1988, pp. 143–4), but equally important within their village is the size and contents of their yam house (Weiner 1976, p. 214). Women's power and status are a function of the number and quality of their skirts and their possession of bundles of banana leaves from which the skirts are fabricated. Men's status as measured by *kula* and yam houses is transient. *Kula* reputations are time-consuming to build and maintain and require great skill; moreover it accrues only to the individual man, not his family and heirs. His status as measured by his yam house and yams is dependent on maintaining his intra-villages' social relations and obligations to work in others' gardens and of others to work on his. A social error could result in the loss of his yams and even force the dismantling of his yam house – a tremendous humiliation and loss of status.

Women's wealth, status and power, exclusively put on display during birth and mortuary rituals, are transferable within the matrilineal descent system. For this reason they are a more enduring source of status and represent much more permanent social connections (Weiner, 1988, pp. 125–32).

Weiner's feminist approach to her anthropological research allows her to explicate the overlooked (by Malinowski) role of women's use of their wealth to support men's effort in both trade and *kula*, thereby missing important social connections between inter-village and intra-village social connections and the link between ordinary barter and *kula* that Malinowski speculated must exist.

Weiner demonstrates that considering exchange systems as separate activities will cause us to isolate some forms of exchange from other social activities that may have a tremendous impact on the overall system of exchange (Weiner, 1976, pp. 219–20). Additionally she reinforces the observation that exchange systems not only transfer goods but also serve as symbolic representations of social relations and individuals' status within those social relations (Weiner, 1976, pp. 211–12). Additionally she brings gender into the analysis. Overlooking women's activities has diminished our understanding of the many connections between male-gendered activities and female-gendered activities, and the symbiosis between them in mutually defining social relations and exchange relations (Weiner, 1976, pp. 228–9).

Finally, Weiner's analysis also shows that the *kula* trade is much more strategic than was evident from Malinowski's account. She shows that it is the ability to keep particularly important – meaning valuable, renowned, beautiful – *kula* objects in one's possession for an extended period of time, and to have important items circulating in among one's *kula* partners, that is the goal of *kula* (Weiner, 1992, pp. 144–6, 141–4). Both of these circumstances not only affect one's repute associated with *kula*, but also affect the ordinary exchanges among members of one's own family and village. These ordinary exchanges enhance the ability of *kula* participants, allowing them to draw on the other forms of wealth and valuables to enhance their prospects in *kula*, both by creating social ties through other forms of exchange and possibly by acquiring newly fabricated *kula* items through non-*kula* trade.

Marshall Sahlins and Primitive Exchange

Marshall Sahlins, in his article 'On the sociology of primitive exchange', (1965), made the most comprehensive attempt after Malinowski and Mauss to theorize about social reciprocity and exchange. He distinguished between two types of systems. In redistributive systems items move from individuals to a central authority where they are combined ('pooling' in Sahlins' terminology) and then returned by some social formulae to individuals, and exchange systems where individuals engage in some reciprocal transaction (Sahlins, 1972, p. 188). He also developed a continuum of exchange relations based on the degree of reciprocity ranging from the pure gift (generalized reciprocity, the solidarity extreme) at one end of the continuum to balanced reciprocity in the middle to, essentially, theft (negative reciprocity, the unsociable extreme) at the other extreme end of the continuum (Sahlins, 1972, pp. 193–6). He then connected different obligations based on kinship, power relations, the desire to maintain relations, stabilizing social structure, social and geographical distance (Sahlins, 1972, *passim*). Sahlins sought to combine the moral, social and economic aspects of exchange behavior into a unified theory of exchange.

Sahlins observes that systems of balanced reciprocity lead to self-liquidation, meaning that the mutual obligations are satisfied and consequently the social relationship may end or be extinguished. Sahlins notes that the one-time, temporary, isolated character of these transactions keeps them occasional occurrences and may explain why systems of balanced reciprocity are generally not found in primitive economies. This observation of Sahlins is important when exploring the contribution of institutional economics (Sahlins, 1972, p. 223).

Sahlins' work has been influential in the literature of exchange generally. I suspect that is true because his work is, as Philip Mirowski suggests, a return to theorizing and the first analytic clarification of reciprocity following Malinowski (Mirowski, 1994, p. 330). But Sahlins has been especially influential on institutional economists. In my opinion Mirowski's assessment of Sahlins is the best presentation and critique of Sahlins' contribution to exchange theory for institutional economists interested in the topic. Sahlins was influenced by the work of Thorstein Veblen in two ways. He noted that negative reciprocity, appropriation of items by force or fraud, is connected to relations with social and geographic distance – as did Veblen (Sahlins, 1972, p. 191). He also sees the acquisition of material goods and the control of material flows as being a function of status, emulation and the maintenance of power relations in ways similar to Veblen.

Additionally, Sahlins acknowledges the influence and importance of the work of Karl Polanyi (Sahlins, 1972, p. 189) on his work and views himself as a substantivist rather than a formalist in his analytic approach. Mirowski argues that Sahlins' book *Stone Age Economics* is a sustained (though flawed) critique of neoclassical orthodoxy and the formalist approach to economic anthropology (Mirowski, 1994, pp. 329–30). Sahlins' concluding observation is important in this regard and also points to the direction that institutional economists take to the study of exchange. He writes:

> ... there is a curiosity worth remarking. Here has been given a discourse on economics in which 'economizing' appears mainly as an exogenous factor! The organizing principles of economy have been sought elsewhere. To the extent they have been found outside man's presumed hedonist propensity, a strategy for the study of primitive economics is suggested that is something the reverse

of economic orthodoxy. It may be worth while to see how far this heresy will get us. (Sahlins, 1972, p. 230)

Sahlins also acknowledges the intellectual influence of anthropologist Leslie White on his work (Sahlins, 1972, p. 201). White's emphasis on explaining human behavior at the cultural level of analysis was influential in the formulation of the Ayresian tradition of institutional economics.

The Significance of these Later Contributors

Gouldner, MacCormack, Sahlins and Weiner have each made contributions to exchange theory that have affected the way later scholars approached social exchange theory. Thinking in terms of a norm of reciprocity (Gouldner), economic exchange as fitting on a continuum of social exchange (Sahlins), that exchange systems including economic exchanges are part of an interconnected and gendered system of exchanges that both create and symbolically represent the overall social system (Weiner), and the ambiguity in the use of the term reciprocity among and within the work of anthropologists, ethnographers and sociologists (MacCormack) have all influenced later scholars exploring exchange. Of particular importance for my analysis is that these authors' contributions have significantly influenced economists who have tried to incorporate the work of this interdisciplinary study of exchange into their attempts to construct alternative theories, accounts, typologies and analyses of economic exchange.

As we explore outside of mainstream economics it is important to note that the conceptions of exchange as conceived in neoclassical economics have escaped the confines of the economics discipline. Other social scientists bedazzled (apparently) by the promise of rigor and the allure of mathematization, have employed the modern variant of utility theory in the guise of rational choice theory. Since the above-discussed problems with the approach persist in these adaptations there is no benefit to further discussion of them. So we will proceed to a discussion of economists and other social scientists that might actually help us understand exchange and markets.

THORSTEIN VEBLEN AND THE INSTITUTIONALISTS

In this section of the chapter we will explore the approaches of several institutional economists with regard to markets and exchange. We will start with Thorstein Veblen, as usual, and move on to John R. Commons and Karl Polanyi and then explore the ideas of some other institutionalists who have taken a broader approach to exchange.

Thorstein Veblen

As mentioned in the introduction, Geoffrey Hodgson has commented that Veblen presented little in the way of theory or analysis regarding markets. Additionally, I recall Hodgson indicating that Veblen had little to say on what markets actually do. While surprising me, Hodgson's observations did match my own recollections of Veblen's work, of which I have some familiarity. Fortunately, Malcolm Rutherford has explored Veblen's views on market transactions in some detail: some detail because there is not a great deal said by Veblen (Rutherford, 1994).

Rutherford argues that 'Veblen's discussion of markets proceeds at several levels' (Rutherford, 1994, p. 255). The first level is his critique of the classical and neoclassical views of market exchange. He rejects the natural and normal character of markets and market behavior. He rejects the notion of a tendency in markets toward equilibrium. There is no balancing of natural forces with any ameliorative tendency. Veblen argues that markets operate on the basis of conventional business principles. Rutherford writes:

> Conventional factors, in his analysis, determine the operation of markets, including the valuations placed on goods by consumers, the manner in which firms are operated, and the distribution of income, and call into question the usual connotations of efficiency. Social convention and salesmanship impact on consumption decisions, the utility function of consumers being far from a natural given, while the fact of intangible property (usually ignored in classical and neoclassical discussions of capital) and the possibilities of gain through financial manipulation and other forms of disruption remove any necesssary equivalence between physical and financial capital and between productive efforts and pecuniary reward. (Rutherford, 1994, p. 255)

Rutherford concludes his discussion of Veblen as follows:

> Veblen's discussion of sales promotion, financial manipulation, dislocation, and monopoly power all indicate that he saw market transactions as being far from the orthodox conception of exchange . . . Instead of performing a balancing of natural forces, markets are dynamic social institutions and a matter of haggling and business practice. The predatory competition between businesses produced the manipulation of consumer preferences by advertising, cycles, and excess capacity; the making of financial gains on the basis of inside, or even deliberately misleading, information; and the creation of market power with the intention of damaging rivals, restricting supply, and controlling process. With all of this the concept of goodwill had gradually been transformed from something based on a reputation for honesty and fair dealing to something covering a wide range of monopoly and other advantages, regardless of origin or social consequence. Nevertheless, and despite his frequent use of terms like 'higgling', 'bargaining', 'negotiating', and 'transacting', Veblen did not supply any detailed treatment of how transactions take place. (Rutherford, 1994, pp. 259–60)

Rutherford's careful analysis (which I recommend to the skeptical reader) affirms Hodgson's observation. But we can look at Veblen's writings a little differently. By this I mean considering what a market or exchange or transaction is by focusing exclusively on what Veblen says markets and exchanges do in addition to what they do not do. Specifically these come down to three general themes: (a) classical and neoclassical treatments of market exchange are at least inaccurate and quite possibly completely fanciful mythology at worst, (b) markets, even competitive markets, do not measure value, and (c) markets are social institutions that do a great many things.

First, Veblen's critique of classical and neoclassical economics is extensive. He rejects the underlying Newtonian mechanical metaphor. He rejects the notion that there is any tendency for economic behavior to reach a stable state of rest usually referred to as equilibrium. The forces which are supposedly equilibrated, supply and demand, are explicitly rejected in the alternative theory of the firm presented in *The Theory of Business Enterprise* (Veblen, 1904 [1978]) and the theory of consumption presented in his book *The Theory of the Leisure Class* (1899 [1934]). Human behavior is not motivated by individual self-interest for Veblen, rather, human behavior is motivated by instincts, although these instincts are molded by the social and cultural environment, including language, cultural symbolic systems, social institutions and settled habits of thought, that are present in the society which all human beings are born into and acquire and internalize as they mature. These social characteristics of all societies are different and evolve over time. The markets and transactions that characterize modern industrial capitalism are specific to those societies so organized at a particular time and place. As may be expected from a theorist who is emphasizing the evolutionary character of economic institutions, there are no natural tendencies, natural institutions or natural social processes shared by all societies and cultures at all times and all places.

Second, Veblen's comments on modern industrial markets are few. He rejects the neoclassical accounts. He describes many culturally and historically specific practices drawn from the accounts of the Industrial Commissions. An example is his account of bond and equity markets in *The Theory of Business Enterprise* (Veblen, 1904 [1978]) where he argues explicitly that those markets do not and cannot value these securities on the basis of the discounted value of the future earnings of the enterprises that issue the securities. To Veblen the current quoted price is not the future value of the underlying productive assets, but a financial mechanism through which predatory business activities are exercised. Even in these most competitive of markets, price is neither equal to discounted present value nor is it a measure of any other sort of value. Prices are administered through a variety of describable mechanisms by many different institutions. In this alternative view markets are historically and culturally contingent institutions. And value for Veblen is measured by the contribution an activity or object contributes to the generic ends of life. There is no necessary connection between any of these three concepts: any connection in society is equally contingent. Indeed, one source of ongoing confusion about institutional economics by non-institutional economists is the disconnection of price, markets and value in institutional economics. This observation leads us to our third theme.

Markets transactions are social institutions that do a great many things. Marc Tool makes this clear in his book *The Discretionary Economy* (Tool, 1979). Tool refers to the necessary, ongoing functions of society, those things that any society must do. This is what Veblen means by 'the generic means of life'. The social mechanisms by which we fulfill these necessary ongoing functions Tool calls replaceable structures. Veblen's focus was on the tendency of the predatory instincts of vested interests to sabotage the necessary ongoing social functions. But Veblen recognized that these predatory instincts (and all the other instincts as well) could operate through many different replaceable structures. The importance of the study of economic institutions is to understand how we should organize ourselves to meet the generic means of life of our community, because there are no 'natural' institutions that will insure that the generic means of life are attained and distributed properly. Indeed, human beings probably possess the capacity to turn any replaceable social structure to either humane or predatory purposes.

What these three themes seem to suggest is three conclusions: Veblen has a theory of markets, but since markets are merely replaceable structures in his framework of understanding, that theory is mostly negative (what markets do not do) and rather trivial. The meaning of markets in neoclassical economics is justificatory mythology. Given these conclusions, if markets and exchanges are going to be analyzed seriously it will have to be in terms of the actual workings of these exchanges in a particular historical economy. Put simply, institutionalists will explore what markets and exchanges actually do. This leads us to the work of John R. Commons.

John R. Commons

According to Rutherford, John R. Commons undertook a more critical examination of exchange than Veblen. Commons rejected the category of exchange because of its problematic use in orthodoxy and its common understanding as an uncomplicated and unmediated physical exchange of goods. Instead he put the concept of the transaction in the foreground. For Commons:

Transactions . . . are not the 'exchange of commodities,' in the physical sense of 'deliver.' They are the alienation and acquisition, between individuals, of the rights of future ownership of physical things, as determined by the collective working rules of society. The transfer of these rights must therefore be negotiated between the parties concerned, according to the working rules of society, before labor can produce, or consumers can consume, or commodities be physically delivered to other persons. (Commons, 1934, p. 58)

Commons divided transactions into three types: bargaining, managerial and rationing transactions. Rationing and managerial transactions were typically conducted between parties of differential strength, power and ability to influence the outcome of the transaction. The outcome of these transactions was necessarily the result of the working rules of the society in question. Bargaining transactions are the closest to what we typically think of as market exchange. However, Commons was aware that participants in such exchange were also frequently not on equal footing vis-à-vis their trading partner. Outcomes, it followed, were determined by the combinations of power and adherence to the working rules of society. If society adopted and enforced reasonable working rules then reasonable outcomes could result. Reasonable working rules are those that serve to limit coercion. Bargaining power is the power to withhold consent or decline to participate in a transaction. For Commons the important element that allows for the achievement of reasonable results is the evolution of the working rules for transactions through the courts.

Commons' analysis is specific to modern industrial economies. His method is extremely inductive, focusing on the specific evolution of working rules through particular legislation and court cases. He neither seeks nor is interested in a general theory of transactions, but in specific kinds of transaction and the evolution of working rules to make those transactions more satisfactory to all participants by generating outcomes that put limits on the ability of one actor to coerce another.

When looking at Veblen and Commons together one observes significant similarities. Neither accepts the concept of market prices as either a measure or indicator of value. Neither sees competitive market transactions as particularly important as a social mechanism for determining economic outcomes. Both are more interested in the relative power of economic actors and the role of that power in the determination of outcomes.

The differences in their views may be the result of the different scope of the two economists' overall projects. Veblen begins his evolutionary analysis with the transition from savage to barbarian and then industrial culture (the more modern designation of Paleolithic, Neolithic and Feudal, Handicraft and Modern Industrial culture). He is not focused on the development of institutions in merely the near term. For example, he explores the division of labor as originating out of predatory exploit and the sexual division of work very early in the development of human cultures. Moreover, Veblen is clearly very familiar with the ethnographic literature of his day and is aware of the many particular cultural variants in patterns of trade and exchange. Commons' focus is really on modern industrial capitalism and the development of the working rules or institutions in the near term as a way of understanding how modern capitalism works and how it could be reformed or improved. So, while Commons' discussion of transactions is crucial for understanding how modern capitalism evolves, it is a considerable narrowing of focus relative to Veblen's concerns. However, even though Veblen understood exchange and transactions from a broader perspective, he clearly did not devote much attention to them. That brings us to the next institutionalist to take up exchange from the broader perspective of Veblen, that is, Karl Polanyi.

Karl Polanyi

Karl Polanyi in his contributions to *Trade and Markets in the Early Empires* (1957) draws on an enormous ethnographic and economic history literature to characterize exchange in terms of culture. His approach grows from the rather obvious assumption that has characterized the institutional approach since Veblen (and is clearly not original with him) that economic behavior is embedded within all aspects of human behavior. It follows that the separation and identification of some behavior as specifically economic behavior is a mental abstraction of the economist. It is not an existential or essential difference in the sense that economic behavior is distinguished from non-economic behavior as experienced in the life of people. People live their lives as an integrated whole, not as made up of two distinct aspects, 'the economic' and 'the non-economic'.

Polanyi describes three forms of integration of the economy in society. They are redistribution, reciprocity and markets. Moreover, he differentiates these forms of integration from the distributional mechanisms that give them their names. Redistribution as a mechanism simply describes goods being collected together in some center and then being given out again according to some social formula. Reciprocity describes mechanisms where people give things to one another in a system which includes the requirement that when given something by someone, an obligation to give similarly is incurred. And finally, markets are simply a place where goods and services are bought and sold. Polanyi (and others) argues that most societies use most or all of these mechanisms in one form or another on various occasions. But Polanyi further argues that redistribution and reciprocity can serve as integrating principles in culture, thereby embedding all behavior into a stable system of social relations. He argues that, in societies where market exchange becomes the dominant form of integration, that economic activity becomes disembedded; meaning that the separation between economic activity and non-economic activity ceases to be a merely mental exercise and becomes a genuine existential separation in the lives of people in that society. Reminiscent of Marx and other radical critics of capitalism, Polanyi's disembedded market economy is a jealous and eventually hegemonic social construction that co-opts all other behavior to the purpose of supporting market exchange and organization. It is not that the economy is literally disembedded from society, but rather that there is no part of society not turned to account on behalf of the market economy. The result is disintegrative of other social formations and even necessary social functions, leading potentially to social and even economic disintegration (to be discussed later).

Even within the category of market exchange Polanyi and his followers make a number of distinctions between types of market exchange. Walter Neale extended Polanyi's analysis. Neale distinguished between an actual economy and the use of the concept of market – meaning the particular abstract analytic concept of the self-regulating market employed by neoclassical economics – to describe all economic transactions of any sort. He made a distinction between the economists' analytic concept of the competitive market and actual markets in economic history. Further he emphasized that there is a tangible difference between the presence of market exchange in a society and a society that is organized as a market system. He produces a typology of the different meanings and uses of markets in different societies indicating that the self-regulating market is but one among several possibilities. Indeed, the self-regulating, price-making market system is but one extreme on a continuum that extends to another polar opposite of marketplaces that may or may not involve prices at all (Neale, 1957, *passim*).

The disintegrative character of market exchange comes from the fact that a market purchase and sale is complete. It does not necessarily create any social connection between the buyer and the seller that transcends or extends beyond that particular exchange. Thus market transactions are similar to so-called 'blind barter' where individuals in one social group exchange with members of another social group without ever actually meeting them. They place goods in a prescribed location and leave that place. They return to that place and see if there has been an acceptable return for their initial offering. If so, they take it and the transaction is complete. If the return for their offering is not acceptable, they do not take the counter-offer and their original offering is returned (or the original counter-offer is supplemented). Either way the transactors never meet and no social ties or connections are created. In the abstract neoclassical model of competitive markets this is the ideal as well; indeed, it is a quality that is positively celebrated (Friedman, 1976). It posits so many consumers that no sellers are interested in differentiating among them; so many firms that consumers do not care which firm's homogeneous product they purchase. An offer is made, accepted or rejected, goods and means of payments exchanged, or not, and the transaction is completed. In modern retail sales superstores or warehouse stores, the purchasers pick up the goods they want, pass the items over a sensor, pass an electronic means of purchase over the same sensor along with some membership card and possibly some coupons. A receipt is printed, and the consumers exit the store after showing a guard the receipt. There is no possibility of creating any social ties whatsoever. As market transactions spread to internet purchases, on-line banking, mail order purchases and the rest, the day-to-day economic activity people engage in to secure the income required to make their necessary purchases is increasingly accomplished in complete isolation. This ever-increasing isolation is at least one way that market transactions become disembedded in the sense of being disconnected from the community life of the individuals who are engaged in those transactions.

Wagner, Hamilton and Waller

Three other institutional economists have built on the tradition of the economic anthropologists and Polanyi in an interesting way. Walter Wagner (1953), in an unpublished dissertation, treated the market exchange of neoclassical economic theory as if it were a system of socially reciprocal exchanges. He noted the structural similarities between market exchanges and reciprocal exchanges. There is one party offering an item to another. If the offered item is accepted, the person receiving the item is required to give the person presenting it some other item which is socially defined as being sufficient to satisfy any continuing obligation on behalf of the receiver. Money simply becomes a socially constructed item that is used to fulfill the return obligation of the receiver. Thus in some trivial sense market transactions fulfill the norms of reciprocity identified by Gouldner and reciprocity and market exchange fit nicely on the continuum proposed by Sahlins. Similarly, a failure to meet the social norms associated with reciprocity or market exchange is taboo – negative reciprocity in Sahlins' terminology.

For us, Wagner's analysis concludes two things of interest. First, there are important structural similarities between market exchanges and reciprocal exchanges; second, the meaning or cultural interpretation of the outcome of such exchanges is profoundly different. In both cases individuals are expected to meet their obligations in each of the types of exchange: the norms of reciprocity. However, in the case of socially reciprocal systems, social ties are extended, relationships are deepened and continuity is created. The system of obligations never ends. In the abstract theoretical version of neoclassical theories of markets, the system results in a different outcome, general equilibrium. This is a state where all obligations are simultaneously met and all social ties that are part of the system are terminated. There are no ongoing or continuing obligations that will necessarily cause social or economic interaction to continue. In the market society where all transactions are understood as market or quasi-market transactions governed by individual self-interest, the reaching of equilibrium is the end of social activity.

David Hamilton, in a series of articles written between 1955 and 1984, used the above noted structural similarities between market exchange and reciprocal exchange in another way. He noted, like Wagner, that the structural similarities resulted in not just similar norms for the two types of exchange but, instead, a pretty complete confounding of the norms of reciprocity for both the market and reciprocal forms of social exchange. This provided our market culture with a set of norms and standards for behavior driven by the prevalence of these structural characteristics of the transactions, rather than the social functions or cultural meanings of the transactions.

Hamilton observed that the familiar circular flow diagram used to introduce students to economic principles, the so-called 'Great Wheel of Wealth', was in fact identical to the stylized drawings of systems of social reciprocity employed by anthropologists in their presentation of such systems. The importance of this is that, in this diagram, all transactions are postulated to be of equivalent value. The 'wheel' encompasses product markets, resource markets (including capital) and labor markets in a system of balanced equality that represents not only an interconnected distribution system, but a distribution system that generates the correct values all of the components and processes that produce them, while rewarding individuals on the value of their contributions to the several resources and production activities that the system generates. It is not merely a description or metaphor for a distribution system. It is an argument that the market system is invariantly equitable and just in its distributive results.

As Hamilton argues, there is nothing unusual about a society constructing a collective representation of the rationale and justification for its existing social organization, appropriate behavior and cultural norms. However, these collective representations, the idealized version of society that affirm the moral principles of society, are usually the foundation of religious systems, not descriptions of actual operating economic systems. Moreover, such collective representations not only describe the state of grace – whether heaven, nirvana, or general equilibrium – but they also proscribe the behavior that leads to the road of perdition. Those are the rules that, if broken, cause you to 'go to hell in a hand basket' or some other terrible, end-of-the-world, Armageddon-type, rapture leading to the destruction of our world and all those who have failed to follow the prescripts of the true faith (presumably the faithful depart for the great Bourse in the sky). The road to hell in our collective representation is nicely described by neoclassical orthodoxy: it is the interference or collective intervention in the operations of the 'free-market' system. The source of this evil, then, is collective action that interferes with, substitutes for, or regulates market transactions of individuals.

In my own work in the early 1980s I extended Wagner and Hamilton's ideas. I noted that only transactions that were structurally congruent with reciprocal exchange were considered legitimate in our economy. Thus reciprocal exchanges and market transactions were structurally sound. But non-reciprocal, one-directional transfers were viewed as fundamentally different. For example, a gift from one individual to another was considered a free gift. The gift is a voluntary act of generosity on the part of the giver. There is no obligation to give the gift. The recipient simply receives the gift. It is an act of charity, such as putting coins in a Salvation Army kettle during the holiday season. While the recipient might have a social obligation to be grateful and show gratitude, the giver is not required to give the gift.

Any attempt to force one individual to make a single directional transfer to another individual is a violation of social norms and equated with theft. Voluntary exchanges consistent with the norms of reciprocity are acceptable. I noted that much, if not most, government activity involves unidirectional redistributive acts, usually termed 'transfers'. This necessitates the state requiring the payment of taxes or running deficits to make those transfers to individuals. Most government activity then requires some violation of the norms of reciprocity, some violation of the structure of reciprocal exchange. Therefore government action is often inconsistent with the strong norms of reciprocity that are reinforced by both market transactions and reciprocal exchanges.

In my work I looked at the structure of a number of government activities ranging from transfer programs to macroeconomic policies, noting that the public assessed most government activity by the structural similarity to reciprocal exchange rather than program or policy efficacy. While this suggests that policies that are structurally reciprocal are going to be more politically sustainable, unfortunately they typically are more expensive to operate, and often extremely inefficient when compared to a simple uni-directional transfer. The consequence is that these prior beliefs work to ensure that most government policy, even if effective, will be unpopular because they tend to be in conflict with dominant social norms (Waller 1984, 1987, 1988, 1989).

Wagner's analysis showed that using the concepts of anthropology to interpret neoclassical theory can provide important insights about the implications of that theory. Hamilton's analysis showed that applying the concepts of anthropology to economic activity can bring new light to understanding both the role of economic theory in our society as well. My work took the concepts of anthropology and applied them to economic activity and to the analysis of economic policy bringing to light the problem of the inherent conflict between widely-held social norms and the structure of government programs and government policy in general.

If we add the feminist insights of Weiner and others in anthropology to this project, it yields interesting results. At the very least I would note in passing that the widely-celebrated 'new home economics' of Gary Becker and others recasts family relations in terms of reciprocal exchanges or anticipation of future exchanges. By contrast, feminist accounts of patriarchal family structures focus on the family as a system of power, where power and authority determine the distribution of income within the family. Such an exploration of the impact of different social norms on the understanding of the dynamics of family interaction could certainly be fruitful.

A BRIEF SUMMARY

This chapter has covered a great deal of ground and it seems appropriate to briefly summarize where we have been. We began with two questions: the current status of exchange theory and the seeming neglect of the subject by Veblen. By going back to Smith we were able to highlight some important aspects of the development of exchange theory in economics.

First, for Adam Smith exchange was an expression of human nature; it required no additional explanation. Value was determined through labor. Market processes were institutions that might, by approximation, reveal the ratio of the value of two products. Exchange was natural as was self-interest. With the division of labor and Say's Law the classical system did not need a theory of human behavior that explained exchange or the evolution of markets.

Second, the marginalists and neoclassical economists make all three connections. Human behavior is caused by the pursuit of self-interest. This self-interested behavior causes exchange. Exchange, in a world of ontological scarcity, is both the determinate and measure of value. Market exchange develops as a more efficient form of barter with addition of money, both of which are similarly explained as innovations resulting from the actions of self-interested individuals. It is here that the theoretical connection between exchange, markets and value is made.

The next step was to explore exchange theory in economic anthropology and sociology. In these disciplines serious efforts were made to theorize all exchange, the relationship between non-economic and economic exchange, and to connect the two in some way. These efforts drew upon the extensive ethnographic scholarship on exchange in many different cultures and resulted in a variety of taxonomies, categorization schemes and a plethora of explanatory attempts to develop some theory of exchange. These attempts are of importance to this exploration for two reasons.

First, these efforts greatly influenced the direction of Veblen and later institutionalists because of the grounding of these efforts in historical and cultural analyses. Put simply, these anthropologists shared the substantivists' methodological approach with the institutionalists.

Second, these efforts contributed important conceptual material employed by Veblen and the later institutionalists, specifically, the role of exchange in symbolizing, creating and stabilizing a culture's social structure: the recognition of the complexity and interconnected character of social relations, the evolutionary fluidity of social institutions, the role of social norms and the importance of gender.

When we get to Veblen and the institutionalists we find answers of a sort to our two questions that are important for future theorizing of exchange, markets and value. Veblen's work did examine particular markets at particular times in particular places, just as the ethnographic scholarship did. He explored the role of market exchange within the limited domain of his particular studies, such as equity markets when exploring business enterprise. He seemed to treat market exchange as a particular social mechanism in place for historically and culturally contingent purposes. He did not neglect the symbolic meaning of market transactions any more than he did the symbolic meaning of goods in market societies. Indeed, these were the main matters of his concern. From the subjects he decided to pursue, or not pursue, it is evident that the other non-symbolic consequences of the more general use of the market exchange structure in society was apparently uninteresting to him. This has, in my experience, been a continued source of discomfort for some later readers who are trying to understand Veblen on the subjects of market exchange and value.

Among other institutionalists looking at exchange, Polanyi and Commons each made significant efforts to examine the role of different forms of exchange in both ancient and modern societies. Polanyi employed the substantivist ethnographic tradition in his work. Commons focused on transactions more generally and the legal environment that generated them.

Later institutionalists addressed exchange in markets, employing the later work of the economic anthropologists that explored the broader understanding of the meaning of alternative forms of social exchange. These studies examined the norms of reciprocity of both the societal understanding of exchange and the impact of the use of this structure on social policy.

A GENERAL THEORY OF EXCHANGE AND MARKETS?

Will we create a general theory of exchange? The simple answer is no. That human beings exchange is undeniable. But all of the various forms of exchange discussed in this chapter are mechanisms: for the most part, people exchange to accomplish some functional task. The type of exchange, the motivation for the exchange, the impact of the exchange on provisioning and the impact of the exchange on other human behavior, are all conditioned and structured by the historical, social, cultural, psychological, economic and existential personal contexts in which it occurs.

Every person is born into a community that already has an historical experience with many forms of exchange. For a person to cope with the day-to-day exigencies in that community they must participate in the social activities necessary to be a fully provisioned member of that community. All forms of exchange involve, at a minimum, interaction between two people – this is the very definition of social behavior. In order to engage in this social behavior a person must follow the social norms and routines necessary to make their attempts to achieve an exchange acceptable to other members of that society.

The cultural context of exchange is what gives the social exchanges that a person engages in a social meaning. Each culture will use different forms of exchange and will use them for a variety of purposes. What kind of exchange is appropriate for what occasion will be determined by the purpose of the exchange to its participants, the functionality of the exchange in the society and the symbolic meaning of that exchange within that culture. Of course the people involved in any exchange are, typically, fully acculturated human beings with their own psychological components informing their actions. The unique combinations of the interaction of biology and cultural components to the construction of the psychological self means there will always be a unique element to any exchange.

Of course this sheds a great deal of light on Veblen's so-called omission. Veblen treated exchanges as he treated all other social institutions, as historically and culturally specific. So his failure to theorize more generally about exchange simply anticipates the poststructuralist critique of all exchange theory as both historically and culturally specific (Mirowski, 1994, p. 339). That does not mean that Veblen did not have anything to say about markets or markets exchanges, his comments were simply specific to the larger analysis that he was engaged in at the time. This, however, does not negate in any way Hodgson's observation that Veblen did not have much to say about what markets as a social mechanism do and can do in modern industrial economies.

WHAT CAN WE SAY ABOUT EXCHANGE, MARKETS AND VALUE?

The obvious thing is that there is no necessary connection between these three concepts. Put simply, the fact that neoclassical economics connects all of these concepts does not require that other forms of social theory necessarily do so. In fact, I have shown that in the history of economic thought only neoclassical economics requires a unified theoretical framework for all three concepts. This characteristic of neoclassical economics is central to the theory's meaning, consequently neoclassical economists (and others who take the structure of neoclassical economics to be a reflection of the necessary elements of any economic theory) will not be able to accept or understand a theory of exchange that does not focus on markets and value; or a theory of value that does not encompass markets and exchange prices.

Instead, each of these concepts should be handled carefully and independently until empirical and ethnographic scholarship shows that they are connected in an historic and cultural context. Then the scholar can begin the work of figuring out how these concepts elucidate the relationships among human beings in an actual society.

This study has also shed some light on both the strengths and weaknesses of the comparative method. The comparative method can help us understand a particular institution like market exchange by looking at how this structure works in other historical and cultural contexts. But the way it functions in other societies does not necessarily tell us how it will function in the next society in which we encounter it.

I have found the above perspectives to be very helpful in understanding Polanyi's notion that societies that employ market systems disembed the economy from society. For me his insight always seemed puzzling, but once one understands that exchange usually creates, extends and maintains social relationships it becomes possible to see how it is that market exchanges minimize this role by creating impersonal, one-time exchange relations. Then, as the system of market exchanges grows and encompasses more and more of social relations, it is evident that these other characteristics of social exchange, those that create, extend and maintain relationships, diminish. This analysis gives a dynamic meaning to Polanyi's analysis that I find very helpful.

This also allows us to escape the poststructuralist alternative (which I have not discussed in this chapter). The fact that exchange is always historically and culturally contingent, and as a consequence a general theory of exchange, or a general theory of markets, or a general theory of value are an impossibility, does not paralyze theorizing about these matters or employing these concepts. It does mean we will have to exercise caution.

Studying Exchange

In studying exchange behavior, we will have to be cognizant of (at least) four things:

1. Exchange mechanisms are social structures. We will have to carefully describe and characterize the particular exchange structure, emphasizing both its commonalities with other forms of exchange we know about and even more carefully documenting its unique elements and how they differ from other forms.
2. Exchange mechanisms, and markets as a special case, are merely replaceable social structures. Human beings may structure their behavior in many ways: the only limit is the human imagination. In our scholarship we must explore the ongoing social functions that are being met by this particular social structure. We must remain aware that often a structure may carry out a number of interconnected functions, or be part of a larger interrelated set of structures carrying out a multitude of functions. Cultures are extraordinarily complex.
3. This complexity means we must explore all the effects of a particular cultural form: not just the intended effects, but also the unintended effects, the synergistic effects and the unaccounted for effects, of the use of a type of institution by a particular culture.
4. Social systems in all their complexity come to become part of a culture's larger symbolic system. Institutions take on metaphorical and framing significance in the way a group of people understand themselves, their behavior, the world they live in, and what it all means.

There is certainly more to be considered. But at least these four elements will be necessary.

A final Veblenian note: the list of elements of exchange (or other social institutions) to be considered suggests to me that Veblen focused almost exclusively on (2) and (4) in the above list. This suggests that there is still much work to be done in institutional economics, though the efforts of Commons and Polanyi have helped a great deal in addressing (1) above.

NOTES

1. International Conference on Thorstein Veblen as a Systematic Thinker, Bevangna, Italy, November 2003, sponsored by the University of Rome.
2. Indeed, this is the theory of market exchange proposed in Ludwig von Mises' treatise, *Human Action* (1949 [1966]). In the Austrian tradition individual rationality is the fundamental premise from which all theory is derived. In this case some version of individual rationality is assumed and from individual purposeful behavior the division of labor, private property, and the institutions necessary for market exchange spontaneously emerge. So in this case market exchange is an effect, assumed rationality is the cause.

BIBLIOGRAPHY

Blaug, Mark (1978), *Economic Theory in Retrospect*, 3rd edn, Cambridge: Cambridge University Press.

Commons, John R. (1934), *Institutional Economics*, New York: Macmillan.

Downey, Ezekial H. (1910), 'The futility of marginal utility', reprinted in Randy Albelda, Christopher Gunn and William Waller (eds) (1978), *Alternatives to Economic Orthodoxy*, Armonk, NY: M.E. Sharpe, Inc., pp. 48–59.

Friedman, Milton (1976), *Price Theory*, New York: Aldine de Gruyter.

Gouldner, Alvin W. (1960), 'The norm of reciprocity: a preliminary statement', *American Sociological Review*, **25**(2), 161–78.

Hamilton, David (1955), 'A theory of the social origins of the factors of production', *American Journal of Economics and Sociology*, **15**(1), 73–82.

Hamilton, David (1965), 'The great wheel of wealth: a reflection of social reciprocity', *American Journal of Economics and Sociology*, **24**(4), 241–8.

Hamilton, David (1970), 'Reciprocity, productivity, and poverty', *Journal of Economic Issues*, **2**(4), 35–42.

Herskovits, Melville J. (1952), *Economic Anthropology*, 2nd edn, New York: Alfred A. Knopf.

Hicks, John R. (1939), *Value and Capital*, 2nd edn, New York: Oxford University Press.

Lévi-Strauss, Claude (1969), *The Elementary Structures of Kinship*, Boston: Beacon Press.

Levine, David (1975), 'The theory of the growth of the capitalist economy', *Economic Development and Cultural Change*, **24**(1), October, 47–74.

MacCormack, Geoffrey (1976), 'Reciprocity', *Man: The Journal of the Royal Anthropological Institute*, new series **11**(1), 89–103.

Malinowski, Bronislaw (1920), 'Kula: The circulating exchange of valuables in the archipelagoes of eastern New Guinea', *Man: The Journal of the Royal Anthropological Institute*, old series, **20**(51), 97–105.

Malinowski, Bronislaw (1921), 'The primitive economics of the Trobriand Islanders', *The Economic Journal*, **31**(121), 1–16.

Malinowski, Bronislaw (1922), *Argonauts of the Western Pacific*, London: George Routledge and Sons, Ltd.

Malinowski, Bronislaw (1926), *Crime and Custom in Savage Society*, London: Routledge and Kegan Paul, Ltd.

Mauss, Marcel (1954), *The Gift: Forms and Functions of Exchange in Archaic Societies*, London: Cohen and West, Ltd.

Mirowski, Philip (1989), *More Heat than Light*, New York: Cambridge University Press.

Mirowski, Philip (1994), 'Tit for tat: concepts of exchange, higgling and barter in two episodes in the history of economic anthropology', in Neil De Marchi and Mary S. Morgan (eds), *Higgling: Transactors and Their Markets in the History of Economics*, annual supplement to vol. 26 *History of Political Economy*, Durham: Duke University Press, pp. 313–42.

Mitchell, Wesley Clair (1948), *Types of Economic Theory: From Mercantilism to Institutionalism*, vol. 2, reprinted in Joseph Dorfman (ed.) (1967), *Types of Economic Theory: From Mercantilism to Institutionalism by Wesley Clair Mitchell*, New York: Augustus M. Kelley.

Neale, Walter C. (1957), 'The market in theory and history', in Karl Polanyi, Conrad M. Arensburg and Harry W. Pearson (eds), *Trade and Market in the Early Empires: Economies in History and Theory*, Glencoe, Illinois: The Free Press and The Falcon's Wing Press, pp. 357–72.

Plattner, Stuart (1985), 'Introduction', in Stuart Plattner (ed.), *Markets and Marketing,* Monographs in Economic Anthropology, no. 4, New York: University Press of America and Society for Economic Anthropology, pp. vii–xx.

Polanyi, Karl (1957), 'The economy as an instituted process', in Karl Polanyi, Conrad M. Arensburg and Harry W. Pearson (eds), *Trade and Markets in the Early Empires: Economies in History and Theory*, Glencoe, Illinois: The Free Press and The Falcon's Wing Press, pp. 243–69.

Routh, Guy (1975), *The History of Economic Ideas*, White Plains, NY: M.E. Sharpe.

Rutherford, Malcolm (1994), 'Predatory practices or reasonable values?' in Neil De Marchi and Mary S. Morgan (eds), *Higgling: Transactors and Their Markets in the History of Economics*, annual supplement to vol. 26 *History of Political Economy*, Durham: Duke University Press, pp. 253–75.

Sahlins, Marshall (1965), 'On the sociology of primitive exchange', in M. Banton (ed.), *The Relevance of Models for Social Anthropology*, American Sociological Association Monograph 1, New York: Praeger.

Sahlins, Marshall (1972), *Stone Age Economics*, Chicago: Aldine-Atherton.

Samuelson, Paul (1938), 'A note on the pure theory of consumer behavior', *Economica*, new series **5**(17), 61–71.

Samuelson, Paul A. (1965), *Foundations of Economic Analysis* (originally published by Harvard University Press, 1947), New York: Atheneum.

Smith, Adam (1759), *The Theory of Moral Sentiments*, reprinted 1982, Indianapolis: Liberty Press.

Smith, Adam (1776), *An Inquiry into the Nature and Causes of the Wealth of Nations*, reprinted 1937, The Cannan Edition, New York: Modern Library.

Tool, Marc R. (1979), *The Discretionary Economy*, Santa Monica, CA: Goodyear Publishing.

Tronto, Joan C. (1993), *Moral Boundaries*, New York: Routledge.

Veblen, Thorstein B. (1899), *The Theory of the Leisure Class*, reprinted 1934, New York: Modern Library.

Veblen, Thorstein B. (1904), *The Theory of Business Enterprise*, reprinted 1978, New Brunswick: Transactions Publishers.

Veblen, Thorstein B. (1909), 'The limitations of marginal utility', *The Place of Science in Modern Civilization*, reprinted 1990, New Brunswick: Transactions Publishers, pp. 231–51.

Veblen, Thorstein B. (1914), *The Instinct of Workmanship*, reprinted 1990, New Brunswick: Transactions Publishers.

Von Mises, Ludwig (1949), *Human Action: A Treatise on Economics*, reprinted 1966, Chicago: Contemporary Books.

Wagner, Walter Charles (1953), 'The theory of economic equilibrium: a reflection of social reciprocity', unpublished PhD dissertation, University of Texas, Austin, Texas.

Waller, William (1984), 'Social reciprocity in market economies', unpublished PhD dissertation, University of New Mexico, Albuquerque, New Mexico.

Waller, William (1987), 'Transfer program structure and effectiveness', *Journal of Economic Issues*, **21**(2), 775–84.

Waller, William (1988), 'Creating legitimacy, reciprocity, and transfer programs', *Journal of Economic Issues*, **22**(4), 1143–51.

Waller, William (1989), 'The impossibility of fiscal policy', *Journal of Economic Issues*, **23**(4), 1047–58.

Weiner, Annette B. (1976), *Women of Value, Men of Renown*, Austin: University of Texas Press.

Weiner, Annette B. (1988), *The Trobrianders of Papua New Guinea*, Orlando FL: Harcourt Brace Jovanovich.

Weiner, Annette B. (1992), *Inalienable Possessions: The Paradox of Keeping-While-Giving,* Berkeley: University of California.

6. Some myths of Veblenian institutionalism

Geoffrey M. Hodgson

During his lifetime Thorstein Veblen was widely hailed as a leading intellect.[1] After some ups and downs in the past, his reputation is growing today. But, as with all icons, there is always the danger that their views are distorted, and their presumed ideas are reproduced by repetition, rather than by renewed authentication. A longer analysis of Veblen's fundamental philosophical and psychological standpoint is presented elsewhere (Hodgson, 2004). To get to the true fundamentals of Veblen's position, we have to remove the layers of later misinterpretation. In this chapter I consider the following four myths of Veblenian institutionalism and show why they are false: (a) Veblen's psychology was behaviorist, (b) Veblen saw individual behavior as being almost entirely explained by culture or institutions, (c) Veblen upheld a 'dichotomy' between institutions and technology, (d) the work of Clarence Ayres represents a direct continuation and development of Veblenian precepts.

These myths appear in innumerable discussions of Veblen's works.[2] The first and second myths emanate from major changes in American social science in the inter-war period (Stocking, 1968; Cravens, 1978; Degler, 1991; Weingart et al., 1997; Hodgson, 2004). The earlier, instinct–habit psychology of William James was eclipsed by the rising behaviorism of John B. Watson (1914). The pragmatist philosophy of Charles Sanders Peirce, William James and John Dewey was gradually swamped by the rising tide of positivism. The use of evolutionary ideas from biology became highly unfashionable. Anthropology moved towards explanations that were entirely cultural, rejecting a priori any biological determination of behavior.

The third and fourth myths result from the emergence after 1945 of Clarence Ayres as the de facto leader of the American institutionalists, and the claim that his views were a continuation of the Veblenian tradition. Ayres has had an enormous direct and indirect influence on successive generations of American institutionalists (Sturgeon, 1981). Accordingly, the interpretation that he and his followers gave of the Veblenian legacy became pre-eminent. I address each of these four myths in turn. I will conclude by arguing that this reinterpretation of Veblen's ideas shows his economic and social analysis to be strikingly modern and in keeping with many ideas being promoted as 'new' today.

VEBLEN AND BEHAVIORIST PSYCHOLOGY

James was the foremost psychological influence on Veblen. James (1890) developed what came to be known as a version of instinct–habit psychology, which was strongly influenced by Charles Darwin. Instinct, habit and reason formed three interacting layers of personality, and were related sequentially in terms of human evolution and individual development. While it was also acknowledged that culture and institutions had an effect on individual personality, the role of the individual was maintained by focusing on biologically inherited instincts and habits acquired in particular individual circumstances.

Veblen referred only episodically to his intellectual mentors. but James's influence is clear in Veblen's most extensive excursion into psychological territory, in his *Instinct of Workmanship* (1914). Veblen adhered to this Jamesian outlook throughout his life, and never abandoned the view that instinct and habit played a foundational role in helping to influence the deliberations and actions of humankind.

Behaviorist psychology emerged relatively late in Veblen's life, and consequently there are no major direct references to behaviorism in his writings. Thus we have to surmise his attitude toward behaviorism by comparing his psychology with that of the behaviorists, and by considering some indirect references to behaviorism.

John Watson (1914) announced the new behaviorist psychology, arguing on the basis of animal experiments that environmental conditioning was primary and instinct a secondary concept. But the behaviorist standpoint was not confined to a radical belief in the possibilities of environmental influence over behavior. Behaviorists such as Watson eschewed consciousness and intentionality as 'unscientific' concepts because they could not be observed directly. Although several American psychologists resisted the behaviorist elimination of mind from their science (Samelson, 1981), the behaviorist ethos of experimentation swept over the discipline. Eventually, Watson and other early behaviorists also entirely abandoned the concept of instinct. By 1919, 'what had been ... a sort of rebellious sideshow among the academic psychologists took on the dimensions of an intellectual revolution' (Kallen, 1930, p. 497). Behaviorism reached a climax in the postwar work of B.F. Skinner.

Behaviorists promoted a positivist vision of science and concentrated on empirically manifest behavior. This reflected a growing general adherence to (first Comtean and later logical) positivism amongst social and natural scientists (O'Donnell, 1985; Taylor, 1985; Lewin, 1996). Considerations of intent, consciousness and cognition were scornfully dismissed as 'metaphysical'. As Floyd Matson (1964, p. 174) wrote, at a time when behaviorism was still influential: 'Merely to mention these pariah words in scientific discourse is to risk immediate loss of attention and audience.'

Although it had several variants, behaviorism was a distinctive movement and approach. In general, behaviorism focuses on the role of psychological conditioning, but it does not simply mean a psychology in which the influential roles of culture or institutions are paramount. In addition, behaviorism had some other key differences from the instinctual theory. First, it adopted a positivist conception of science that proscribed all discussion of metaphysical precepts and unobservable entities such as intent and consciousness. Second, it meant the relegation and eventually banishment of the concept of instinct from psychology. Third, it meant the treatment of habit as behavior rather than a disposition, and its less frequent use as more of a descriptive rather than an explanatory term.[3] Fourth, it meant a supreme focus on the conditioning mechanism of stimulus and response. Its positivist epistemological outlook relegated discussion of the conceptual and cognitive frameworks through which sensory stimuli are interpreted or prioritized.

Let us compare Veblen's views in turn with each of these four features of behaviorism. First, Veblen rejected the positivist view that science could be founded on experience or experiment alone. Veblen (1900 [1919], p. 241) thus rejected the Comtean attack on metaphysics, asserting instead that the 'ultimate term or ground of knowledge is always of a metaphysical character'. For Veblen (1900 [1919], p. 253), 'a point of view must be chosen' and consequently the 'endeavor to avoid all metaphysical premises fails here as everywhere'. Veblen understood that experience alone could not be the foundation of knowledge, as all knowledge also depends on preconceptions, some of which are unavoidably 'metaphysical'. For Veblen, unlike the positivists, 'metaphysical' was not a term of abuse. Veblen rightly held that some 'metaphysical presuppositions' were necessary and unavoidable for science.[4]

One of Veblen's principal criticisms of Comtean positivism concerned the need in science to impute causal relations, and especially unilinear causation. As David Hume had rightly pointed out in the eighteenth century, no causal connection can itself be observed. Moreover, in the practice of social science, the imputation of causal connections must always involve preconceptions by the analyst, and such imputations cannot be derived from experience or data alone. Influentially, Comte had argued that any search after causes would be futile, because they cannot be discerned directly in experience. Veblen did not endorse this argument. Against positivism, Veblen (1906 [1919], p. 597) appropriately identified the 'preconception of causation' as necessary for 'the actual work of scientific enquiry'. Veblen (1908a [1919], p. 398 n.) elaborated: 'Causal sequence ... is of course a matter of metaphysical imputation. It is not a fact of observation, and cannot be asserted of the facts of observation except as a trait imputed to them.' Veblen (1914, p. 260) repeated, in a similar vein: 'The principle, or "law", of causation is a metaphysical postulate, in the sense that such a fact as causation is unproved and unprovable. No man has ever observed a case of causation.' Veblen (1904, p. 371) asserted that 'the endeavor of the Positivists ... to reduce scientific theory to a system of accountancy has failed'. Overall, then, Veblen clearly distanced himself from positivism.

The second feature of behaviorism is its dismissal of the concept of instinct. Malcolm Rutherford (1984, p. 333) has proposed that Veblen's 'use of instinct theory declined markedly in his later work'. Clearly and uncontroversially, Veblen's most elaborated use of instinct–habit psychology was in his 1914 book. He died 15 years after its publication. Accordingly, any evidence for such a decline in usage must come from the last 15 years of his life. Sure enough, there is a much less frequent discussion of instinct–habit psychology in his works in the later period from 1915 to 1929 than there is in the earlier years from 1898 to 1914. But there is also less discussion generally of philosophical and psychological fundamentals in the later rather than the earlier period. His later works are more topical and political, in part reflecting his decision to leave academia in 1918. After his resignation from the University of Missouri in 1918, he resolved to play a more active role in debates concerning the future of America and the world after the end of World War I. Given the less foundational character of his later works, there is no clear evidence of any shift in fundamental view from one school of psychology or philosophy to another.

Third, in contrast to behaviorism, it can be readily demonstrated that Veblen continued to employ the concept of habit throughout his writings. Treating habit as a disposition, Veblen (1898 [1919], p. 390) early on wrote of 'a coherent structure of propensities and habits which seeks realization and expression in an unfolding activity'. True to his earlier viewpoint, Veblen (1923, p. 101 n.) wrote in his last book: 'An institution is of the nature of a usage which has become axiomatic and indispensable by habituation and general acceptance.' Similarly, in his last published essay, 'Economic theory in the calculable future', Veblen (1925 [1934]) makes significant use of the concept of habit.

Fourth, there is indirect evidence of a critical attitude by Veblen to an exclusive or pre-eminent focus on the mechanism of stimulus and response. In his famous essay on 'the reflex arc concept', John Dewey (1896) provided a critique of assumptions concerning the stimulus–response mechanism that would later be central to behaviorist psychology. For Dewey, the stimulus–response mechanism was flawed because stimuli are not given data. The actions and dispositions of the agent are necessary to perceive the stimulus. Stimulus and response cannot be separated, because action is necessary to obtain a stimulus, and the response invokes further stimuli. Hence 'the distinction of sensation and movement as stimulus and response respectively is not a distinction which can be regarded as descriptive of anything which holds of psychical events or existences as such' (Dewey, 1896, p. 369).

Veblen (1900 [1919], pp. 246–7) replicated part of this argument with approval, but without mentioning Dewey by name. Under the influence of Dewey, Veblen (1900 [1919], pp. 246–7) noted the 'modern catchword' of 'response to stimulus' and pointed out that 'the reaction to stimulus' is conditioned also by 'the constitution of the organism' which 'in greater part decides what will serve as a stimulus, as well as what the manner and direction of the response will be'. This passage clearly demarcates Veblen from behaviorist psychology, where the stimulus itself is seen as sufficient to condition a response. In contrast, Veblen saw the human agent as discretionary, with 'a self-directing and selective attention in meeting the complex of forces that make up its environment'. For Veblen, as with James, part of this discretionary and selective capacity was molded by habits and instincts. While Dewey made some partial accommodations to behaviorism in the inter-war period, Veblen never abandoned instinct–habit psychology and he showed no enthusiasm for behaviorism.

VEBLEN, CULTURE AND INSTITUTIONS

Throughout Veblen's work there is frequent reference to the influence of culture and institutions on human dispositions and behavior. Furthermore, Veblen upheld that the persistence of cultural traits had little to do with racial features or biological inheritance. These elements of interpretation should be uncontroversial to anyone with at minimal familiarity with Veblen's work.[5]

It would be a mistake, however, to suggest that Veblen endorsed explanations of individual behavior entirely in terms of cultural or institutional circumstances. Throughout his writings, Veblen attempted to steer a distinct middle course between, on the one hand, the view that individuals were entirely determined by cultural and institutional settings, and on the other hand, the assumption of an individual with given preferences or purposes beyond the purview of social science. We can observe this middle course in a number of his works, but three exhibits are worthy of brief discussion here.

The first exhibit is a review of a critique of Marxism by Max Lorenz, *Die Marxistische Socialdemokratie* (1896). In his review, Veblen (1897, p. 137) criticized Marxism as supporting the view that individuals were largely determined by their social circumstances. Such doctrines lacked an explanation of 'the operative force at work in the process'. Moreover, these doctrines did not explain how social forces impel individual actors to think and act. Veblen explicitly rejected the proposition that the individual is '*exclusively* a social being, who counts in the process *solely* as a medium for the transmission and expression of social laws and changes' (emphasis added). In other words, Veblen dismissed the idea that the individual's actions are formed entirely by his or her socio-economic circumstances.

However, although Veblen rejected explanations exclusively in terms of systemic wholes, he did not replace this doctrine with explanations of socio-economic phenomena exclusively in terms of individuals. Hence Veblen did not deny that a human is 'a social being' or 'a medium for the transmission of social laws and changes'. He simply rejected an exclusive stress on social determination, and asserted that the human agent is '*also* an individual, acting out his own life as such' (emphasis added). This suggests that humans mold their circumstances just as they are molded by them. For Veblen, explanations of socio-economic evolution must involve individual agents as well as institutions and structures.

Nevertheless, the evolution of individuality must itself be explained, as Veblen put it, in terms of 'a theory of social process considered as a substantial unfolding of life as well'. This need for an explanation of origin led Veblen to conceive the individual in both biological and socio-economic terms. Humans are biotic as well as social beings, so their biology cannot be ignored. However, Veblen did not see socio-economic phenomena as reducible to their biotic substratum. The 'theory of the social process' had to be compatible with, but also more than, the theory of the evolution of human life.

The second exhibit is Veblen's extended review of the first volume of Gustav Schmoller's *Grundriss der allgemeinen Volkswirtschaftslehre* (1900). Here Veblen sees Schmoller's work as being a significant advance on that of earlier members of the historical school. This interpretation relied on a Hegelian view of historical development, in which the 'life process is essentially active, self-determining, and unfolds by inner necessity, – by necessity of its own substantially active nature. The course of culture, in this view, is an unfolding (exfoliation) of the human spirit; and the task which economic science has in hand is to determine the laws of this cultural exfoliation in its economic aspect' (Veblen, 1901 [1919], p. 76). Veblen also categorized Marxism as 'a theory of self-determining cultural exfoliation'. In contrast to notions of the human agent as a mere receptacle of culture, and theories with supreme explanatory emphasis on cultural determination, Veblen emphasized that individuals created institutions and culture, just as individuals were molded by them.

The third exhibit is a key passage in Veblen's article, 'The limitations of marginal utility'. Veblen (1909b [1919], pp. 628–9) started by criticizing the assumption of given individuals. The assumption of 'consistent, elemental human nature under given, stable institutional conditions – such as is the case with the current hedonistic economics – can reach statical results alone; since it makes abstraction from those elements that make for anything but a statical result'. Veblen then made it clear that institutions serve not merely as constraints, but that they also affect the very wants and preferences of individuals themselves:

> Not only is the individual's conduct hedged about and directed by his habitual relations to his fellows in the group, but these relations, being of an institutional character, vary as the institutional scene varies. The wants and desires, the end and the aim, the ways and the means, the amplitude and drift of the individual's conduct are functions of an institutional variable that is of a highly complex and wholly unstable character. (Veblen, 1909b [1919], p. 629)

This statement amounts to a strong assertion of the reconstitutive power of institutions over individuals. Institutional changes affect individual 'wants and desires'. Preferences are endogenous, rather than exogenously given. Nevertheless, Veblen acted immediately to forestall any misunderstanding that this amounted to a view that the social wholes entirely determine the individual parts. Veblen made it absolutely clear that the individual was still causally effective, that institutions were a product of individuals in a group, and institutions could not exist without individuals.

> The growth and mutations of the institutional fabric are an outcome of the conduct of the individual members of the group, since it is out of the experience of the individuals, through the habituation of individuals, that institutions arise; and it is in this same experience that these institutions act to direct and define the aims and end of conduct. It is, of course, on individuals that the system of institutions imposes those conventional standards, ideals, and canons of conduct that make up the community's scheme of life. Scientific inquiry in this field,

therefore, must deal with individual conduct and must formulate its theoretical results in terms of individual conduct. (Veblen, 1909b [1919], p. 629).[6]

However, it must be noted that the above passage does not amount to an assertion of methodological individualism.[7] Instead, Veblen upheld that individuals could not be removed from the bigger social and cultural environment within which they lived, and therefore he always placed the individual in its social context. Veblen (1909b [1919], pp. 629–30) insisted that a complete and detailed causal explanation means an explanation of how the individual acquires relevant habits of thought and behavior.

Veblen (1909b [1919], p. 630) then went on to criticize those mainstream economists who 'disregard or abstract from the causal sequence of propensity and habituation in economic life and exclude from theoretical inquiry all such interest in the facts of cultural growth'. By emphasizing 'cumulative causation' and 'continuity of cause and effect', Veblen broke from any idea that explanations could ultimately be reduced to one type of entity or level.

In sum, although he did not use the modern terminology, Veblen simultaneously rejected a methodological individualism (where social phenomena have to be explained entirely in terms of individuals) and a methodological collectivism (where individuals have to be explained entirely in terms of culture or institutions). Veblen's position therefore does not give solace to any form of (biological, cultural, structuralist or individualist) reductionism.[8]

Concerning the anthropological use of the concept of culture, all the evidence suggests that Veblen's views were very close to those of the leading American anthropologist Franz Boas, who was with Veblen in Chicago in the 1890s. Veblen knew Boas and occasionally referred to his work. It is likely that Boas (1894) influenced Veblen with his insistence that the evolution of culture and civilization did not simply track the biological evolution of the human mind and body. Boas did not deny that there were natural and genetic influences on human characteristics and behavior. He just saw social culture as far more important. Boas's views on such matters were similar to Veblen's: together they stressed the causal roles of both culture and instinct.

Largely under the influence of Boas's research, a number of leading American sociologists and anthropologists became convinced of the importance of nurture over nature. Like Veblen, they rejected the prevalent idea that human culture was largely determined by biology. But, during the 1920s, many went much further than Boas and Veblen, to argue that culture alone explained human behavior. This shift in thinking, in the last decade of Veblen's life, reflected the growing view that biology could add nothing to the explanation of human behavior. For example, Alfred Kroeber

(1923) declared that social science should be separated, in both method and substance, from biology. In Kroeber's view, biological inheritance had no significant part in the history of humankind. Margaret Mead continued Kroeber's line of argument. In 1928, she published a classic plea for the supremacy of culture over biology in her *Coming of Age in Samoa*.[9] The views of Kroeber and Mead were widely accepted by American social scientists. Ruth Benedict, a former student of Boas, consolidated the victory with the publication in 1934 of the equally influential work *Patterns of Culture*.

Yet there is no evidence that Veblen endorsed this shift within anthropology and sociology. On the contrary, he retained the view that biologically inherited instincts were a significant influence on human behavior. He also saw individuals as interacting with culture and institutions, which were irreducible to biology. All the evidence suggests that his anthropological views remain close to those of Boas, rather than the generation of anthropologists that followed.

THE 'VEBLENIAN DICHOTOMY'

Ayres repeatedly asserted that his dichotomy between technology and ceremony was derived from the writings of Veblen. For instance, Ayres (1973, p. v) wrote: 'Veblen made the dichotomy of technology and ceremonialism his master principle.' Ayres (1944, p. 99) also proposed that Veblen was the first 'to make this analytical distinction between technology and ceremony the point of departure of all further economic analysis'. On the contrary, there is no evidence that Veblen used a 'distinction between technology and ceremony' as an analytical 'point of departure' of any kind. Veblen did not see institutions as wholly non-instrumental, nor did he define them essentially in terms of ceremony. Furthermore, Veblen saw strong institutional elements within technology itself.

Ayres (1961, p. 30) referred to 'the institutional process (or ceremonialism, as Veblen often called it)'. But I have found no use by Veblen of the word 'ceremonialism', although he occasionally used words such as 'ceremony' and 'ceremonial'. Contrary to Ayres, Veblen *never* described 'the institutional process' as 'ceremonialism'. Moreover, Ayres failed to provide an adequate analysis of the alleged origins of the 'Veblenian dichotomy'. In one passage Ayres (1944, p. 176) quoted Veblen's (1914, p. 25) depiction of a 'triumph of imbecile institutions over life and culture' from *The Instinct of Workmanship*. Other authors have claimed that the 'Veblenian dichotomy' is to be found in *The Theory of the Leisure Class*, *The Theory of Business Enterprise*, *The Place of Science in Modern Civilization* or in *Imperial Germany*. But there or elsewhere in Veblen's writings, a general dichotomy between institutions and technology cannot be found, but rather a dichotomy between certain kind of institutions and certain kinds of progressive elements, for example, business and industry in *Theory of Business Enterprises*, or leisure and menial classes, in *Theory of Leisure Class*, as will be explored below.

It is however true that Veblen highlighted the conservative facets of *some* institutions. An important and frequently quoted passage is the following:

> It is to be noted then, although it may be a tedious truism, that the institutions of to-day – the present accepted scheme of life – do not entirely fit the situation of to-day. At the same time, men's present habits of thought tend to persist indefinitely, except as circumstances enforce a change. These institutions which have so been handed down, these habits of thought, points of view, mental attitudes and aptitudes, or what not, are therefore themselves a conservative factor. This is the factor of social inertia, psychological inertia, conservatism. (Veblen, 1899, p. 191)

With no mention of science or technology in this quotation, Veblen noted a mismatch between the inherited 'institutions of to-day' and the general 'situation of to-day', and that some institutions may resist change. Veblen went on to consider how institutions may in fact be changed.

> Social structure changes, develops, adapts itself to an altered situation, only through a change in the habits of thought of the several classes of the community; or in the last analysis, through a change in the habits of thought of the individuals which make up the community. The evolution of society is substantially a process of mental adaptation on the part of individuals under the stress of circumstances which will no longer tolerate habits of thought formed under and conforming to a different set of circumstances in the past. (Veblen, 1899, p. 192)

Again there is mention of neither science nor technology here. Instead, Veblen vaguely identified the causes of social change in an 'altered situation' or the 'stress of circumstances'. For Veblen, such 'circumstances' included *other institutions* as well as technological practices. Veblen alluded to processes by which one particular institution may adapt to the others, each institution thus interacting with the rest. He depicted several jostling institutions, themselves changing and impelling change in others. Veblen's theory of institutional change was much more a process of sifting, selection and rivalry between different institutions, rather than institutions generally succumbing to the autonomous forces of technology. Contrary to many of his interpreters, Veblen did not see technology as the only important factor causing institutional evolution.

Turning to *The Theory of Business Enterprise*, Veblen (1904, p. 303) remarked: 'The factor in the modern situation that is alien to the ancient régime is the machine technology, with its many and wide ramifications.' This is not evidence of a general dichotomy between institutions and technology but between a specific (machine) technology and specific institutions. In the same work Veblen wrote of a 'concomitant differentiation and specialization of occupations ... resulting in an ever weakening sense of conviction, allegiance, or piety toward the received institutions' (p. 324). Again there is no universal theory or dichotomy here. The conflict is not between technology and institutions writ large but rather between the 'differentiation and specialization of occupations' and 'the received institutions' currently in effect.

Therefore, Ayres's claim to find a general dichotomy between institutions and technology in *The Instinct of Workmanship* turns out to be invalid. The relevant and often-quoted passage refers to the possibility that instincts such as 'the parental bent or the sense of workmanship' may overturn 'institutional elements at variance with the continued life-interests of the community' and 'the bonds of custom, prescription, principles, precedent' may be broken. Veblen then goes on to state, 'But history records more spectacular instances of the triumph of imbecile institutions over life and culture' (Veblen, 1914, p. 25). Here Veblen simply asserted that workmanship and other instincts *could* come into conflict with some institutions, and with different possible outcomes. In some cases 'imbecile' institutions block these instinctive drives. In other cases institutions prove more accommodating. Emphatically, Veblen did *not* suggest that *all* institutions are 'imbecile'. Hence this passage does not give us the general dichotomy associated with Ayres.

Another passage in the same work might seem at first sight to give Ayres's claim more support. There Veblen (1914, p. 148) wrote of changes in 'the technological scheme' and advances in 'workmanlike mastery' being potentially hindered owing to 'limitations' including 'the institutional situation'. Veblen clearly admitted that 'institutional factors have doubtless retarded the advance in most cases'. But this statement was in the context of a discussion of 'lower cultures' and even in this case Veblen gave priority to other constraints: for example, 'the insurmountable obstacles to such an advance appear to be those imposed by the material circumstances'. Hence, for Veblen, institutional inhibitions were neither foremost nor universal. Veblen asserted no general dichotomy between all institutions and all technology.

Furthermore, Veblen frequently suggested that technology might come into conflict with specific institutions or habits of thought. For example, Veblen (1934, p. 26) wrote: 'In many of the lower cultures ... the workday routine of getting a living is encumbered with a ubiquitous and pervasive scheme of such magical or superstitious conceits and observances.' He also considered several cases where technological change had helped to promote or encourage institutional change. What he did not explicitly propose, however, was a notion that technology *always and everywhere* conflicted with *all institutions*. The reason for the absence of such an idea is simple: for Veblen technology itself was also institutional in character.

A passage from *The Instinct of Workmanship* made this last point in decisive fashion. Veblen (1914, p. 176) wrote: 'the body of knowledge (facts) turned to account in workmanship, the facts made use of in devising technological processes and applications, are of the nature of habits of thought'. Recollecting Veblen's own descriptions of institutions in terms of habits, this was tantamount to a statement that *technology itself has institutional features*. This was suggested in other places in Veblen's writing. For example, in *The Theory of Business Enterprise* Veblen (1904, p. 312) asserted: 'The discipline exercised by the mechanical occupations ... is a discipline of the habits of thought.' A similar idea is found in *Absentee Ownership*, where Veblen wrote:

> The technological system is an organisation of intelligence, a structure of intangibles and imponderables, in the nature of habits of thought. It resides in the habits of thoughts of the community and comes to a head in the habits of thought of the technicians. (Veblen, 1923, p. 280)

Science and technology depend on facts, and for Veblen (1914, p. 53) the perception of the facts depends on habits of thought. It again follows that both science and technology are, according to Veblen, of an institutional nature. Both institutions and technology are based on habits of thought. Not only is a general 'Veblenian dichotomy' absent from Veblen's writings, but also some passages in his other writings are inconsistent with this idea. For example, in *Theory of the Leisure Class,* Veblen (1899, p. 193) wrote of 'economic institutions' as 'habitual methods of carrying on the life process of the community'. This suggests that Veblen saw some institutions were instrumental. Moreover, Veblen (1899, p. 206) considered 'the leisure class as an exponent and vehicle of conservatism or reversion in social structure. The inhibition which it exercises may be salutary or the reverse'. Here Veblen accepted the possibility that 'conservatism ... in social structure' *may* be considered as 'salutary' – a formulation that would grate on Ayres. Two pages later, Veblen (1899, p. 208) addressed 'pecuniary or industrial institutions ... institutions serving either the invidious or the non-invidious economic interest'. This passage undermines the Ayresian dichotomy, by recognizing that some institutions can serve acceptable economic interests.

Veblen (1899, p. 266) also wrote of 'the institutional structure required by the economic situation of the collectivity'. This contradicts the Ayresian dichotomy by acknowledging that an 'institutional structure' could be positively 'required' and not necessarily a drag on the economic dynamic. In a similar vein, Veblen (1899, p. 363) wrote that 'habits of thought which are so formed under the guidance of teachers and scholastic traditions have an economic value'. Bearing in mind Veblen's own view of an institution as a vehicle for conveying and reinforcing common habits, this passage suggests that institutions can sometimes have a positive role.

Passages in Veblen's other works support an equivalent verdict. One of the clearest and most dramatic is the following. In an amazingly prescient analysis of the Japanese socio-economic system, Veblen (1934, p. 251) remarked: 'It is in this unique combination of a high-wrought spirit of feudalistic fealty and chivalric honor with the material efficiency given by the modern technology that the strength of the Japanese nation lies.'

Such an observation is commonplace in the recent literature on the 1945–90 Japanese economic miracle, but Veblen made it well before the rise of modern Japan, and nevertheless saw the root of Japan's future strength. This strength does not lie in technology alone but in its *combination* with conservative and ceremonial institutions 'of feudalistic fealty and chivalric honor'. This assertion does not simply contradict the Ayresian dichotomy; it turns it upside down. In sum, Ayres's notion of a conflict between institutions and technology is not only absent in Veblen's writings but it is contradicted by Veblen's own words and conceptions.

VEBLEN AND AYRES

We now turn to the proposition that the work of Ayres is essentially a continuation of the Veblenian tradition. At a more superficial level there are obvious similarities in the writings of Ayres and Veblen. The authors shared a distaste for waste and useless ceremony; both applauded technology and functional efficiency. But these similarities are at the level of attitudes, and do not necessarily connote deeper similarities in their philosophical and psychological presumptions.

The standard view of Ayres today is that he synthesized the thought of Veblen and Dewey. Without doubt, Ayres was strongly influenced by both writers, but this influence is not evident in Ayres's early works and there is no evidence in his writings of a scholarly treatment of their texts. Ayres's earliest two books, *Science: The False Messiah* (1927) and *Holier Than Thou* (1929) bear no more than slight possible traces of the influence of Veblen or Dewey. Moreover, Ayres himself (1973, p. iii) later admitted: 'When I was writing these two books, I had no thought of contributing to the literature of Institutionalism.' There is no quotation from either Veblen or Dewey in these works. Ayres did not begin by building on a bedrock of ideas from Veblen or Dewey.

It is possible that Ayres's early reluctance to take on the Veblenian mantle was partly a result of Ayres's adoption of behaviorist psychology and his strong opposition to the concept of instinct. Ayres (1921a, p. 561) believed that the literature on instincts was 'largely self-refuting. ... When instincts fall out, institutions get their due'. As a result, he believed that: 'The social scientist has no need of instincts; he has institutions' (p. 565). Much later, Ayres (1958, pp. 25–9) wrote that 'the very notion of instincts is now scientifically obsolete. ... It is now quite conclusively established that no such complex behavior patterns are in a literal sense "inborn". We now know that such patterns are wholly cultural'. Indeed, between the 1920s and the 1960s, this became the view of the overwhelming majority of social scientists (cf. Stocking, 1968; Cravens, 1978; Degler, 1991). Ayres was an early opinion former in this respect.

There is a related difference between Ayres and Veblen on the normative inferences they drew from their discussions of technology. Ayres (1944, p. 220) argued that science and technology provided the normative means of valuation by which economic developments and policies can be assessed: 'It is the technological continuum which is, and has always been, the locus of value; and it has this meaning because of its continuity.' In contrast to Ayres, Veblen rejected the idea that technology was intrinsically worthwhile. Veblen (1908b [1919], p. 109) wrote that 'technological proficiency is not of itself and intrinsically serviceable or disserviceable to mankind, – it is only a means of efficiency for good or ill'. For Veblen (1899, p. 99) the 'instinct of workmanship' was 'the court of final appeal in any question of economic truth or adequacy'. But Ayres wanted nothing to do with instincts. Veblen and Ayres differed on the intrinsic merits or demerits of technology and on the evaluative use of instincts in this context.

As with instinct, the Veblenian concept of habit plays an insignificant part in Ayres's work. Very occasionally, Ayres (1944, p. 84) referred to 'social habits'. But this was a metaphor for social custom, acknowledging that the habits of an individual were entirely (and somewhat mysteriously) a product of 'the mores of his community'. Ayres (1923) reviewed Dewey's (1922) *Human Nature and Conduct* and expressed regret that Dewey had not adopted the behaviorist schema of stimulus and response. In short, both Veblen's and Dewey's adoption of the concept of habit contrasted greatly with Ayres's behaviorism.

Veblen saw institutions as both constraining and enabling human action, but Ayres concentrated on their conservative and constraining aspects. Veblen emphasized the role of the individual alongside institutions and culture; but for Ayres the individual was subordinate to culture. Ayres

(1921b, p. 606) approvingly quoted the words of the sociologist Charles Cooley (1902, p. 1): 'A separate individual is an abstraction unknown to experience.' But Ayres ignored the rest of Cooley's sentence: 'and so likewise is society when regarded as something apart from individuals'. While Cooley saw the individual and society as equally and symmetrically implicated in social explanation, Ayres in contrast put almost the entire explanatory weight on institutional structures, cultural pressures or the forces of technology.

Indeed, Ayres (1918, p. 57; 1961, p. 175) went so far as to repeat his exact statement: 'there is no such thing as an individual', after a gap of over 40 years. In each case, Ayres went on to attempt to qualify and explain this proposition, but his qualifications cannot undo the damage already done. To put us in little doubt about his extreme position, Ayres (1936, p. 235) wrote that orthodox economists 'conceive the institutions to be an expression of human nature. The institutionalists ... hold precisely the opposite view of human nature, to wit, that it is an expression of institutions'. Much later, and in similar vein, Ayres (1951, p. 49) wrote: 'Social patterns are not the logical consequents of individual acts; individuals, and all their actions, are the logical consequents of social patterns.' Ayres (1952, p. 41) proposed 'a universe of discourse to which the concept "individual" is simply irrelevant.' Overall, Ayres inverted the methodological individualism of neoclassical economics to propose a predominantly 'top down' methodological collectivism. From his youth until his death, Ayres did not waver from this methodological view.

This extreme version of methodological collectivism was not the position adopted by Veblen. While Veblen always emphasized that the individual was molded by cultural and institutional circumstances, he insisted that the individual had to remain as part of the causal explanation. For Veblen (1909b [1919], p. 629), as quoted above, scientific inquiry 'must deal with individual conduct and must formulate its theoretical results in terms of individual conduct'.

As explained above, Veblen insisted that ontological or 'metaphysical' presuppositions that could not be validated by evidence were necessary for any theory; but Ayres – like all positivists – eschewed metaphysics. In contrast to Veblen, Ayres (1942, p. 343) believed 'science must establish its ascendancy over the thought and action of the community at every point, leaving nothing whatever to metaphysics'.

Veblen attempted to apply Darwinian principles to social evolution, but Ayres underplayed the significance of Darwinism for the social sciences and ignored Veblen's Darwinian agenda. In an early work Ayres (1932, p. 95) regarded Darwin's theory as 'outmoded'. Although he later adjusted this view of Darwinism, he never promoted the Veblenian project of turning economics into a 'post-Darwinian' science. The Veblenian emphasis on the Darwinian selection of habits and institutions is absent from Ayres's work.

Overall, and especially at the fundamental levels of philosophy and psychology, there are huge differences between the approaches of Ayres and Veblen, only some of which have been visited here. However, the contribution of Ayres should be acknowledged, not only for its intrinsic value, but also for the way that Ayres led the dwindling institutionalist movement through the difficulties of the post-Veblen era. Rather than for their fidelity to Veblen, his additions to institutionalist doctrine should be recognized as adaptations to the intellectual climate of his time. These adaptations helped institutionalism to survive in the period from the 1920s to the 1960s, when positivism and behaviorism were dominant.

CONCLUSION

The importance of these arguments is not simply to get the record straight concerning Veblen's views. When we remove the layers of misinterpretation, it is evident that Veblen's true position is strikingly modern in the context of recent developments in philosophy, psychology, sociology, anthropology and economics. Consider philosophy. As noted above, Veblen was influenced by the pragmatist philosophy of Peirce, James and Dewey. After being eclipsed for much of the twentieth century, pragmatism has recently re-emerged to become 'if not the most influential, at least one of the fastest growing philosophical frameworks on the intellectual landscape' (Hands, 2001, p. 214).[10]

Next, consider psychology, where Veblen (1914) embraced the instinct–habit approach of James and likewise insisted that psychological assumptions had to be consistent with a Darwinian understanding of human evolution. After the hegemony of behaviorism from the 1920s to the 1960s, Jamesian and other evolutionary approaches are now enjoying a renaissance in psychology (Degler, 1991; Plotkin, 1994, 1997). The key Veblenian concept of habit has also re-emerged in modern psychology (Ouellette and Wood, 1998; Wood et al., 2002).

In other scholarly pursuits as well, as Darwinian ideas are making a comeback in contexts outside biology, again Veblen's ideas appear strikingly modern. While embracing Darwinism, Veblen (1909a [1934], p. 300) emphatically discarded the idea that explanations of phenomena can or should be reduced exclusively to biological terms. Instead, Veblen (1899, p. 188) suggested a multiple-level selection theory where, in addition to the natural selection of individuals in terms of their fitness, there was a 'natural selection of institutions' as well. Veblen used the concept of selection in a social context on numerous occasions: I have counted over one hundred instances. Veblen thus foreshadowed modern anthropological theories of 'dual inheritance' where selection and information transmission operate at the cultural as well as the biological level (Boyd and Richerson, 1985; Durham, 1991).

Veblen argued that conceptions concerning the economic agent and individual psychology must be consistent with a Darwinian understanding of human evolution, and that general Darwinian principles can be fruitfully applied to the evolution of human society. It is striking, however, that these themes almost disappeared from the institutionalist movement for much of the twentieth century. With notable exceptions such as Morris Copeland (1931) and David Hamilton (1953), leading institutionalists including Clarence Ayres, John Commons and Wesley Mitchell saw little economic relevance for Darwinian ideas, and abandoned their expressions in Jamesian psychology and evolutionary theory (Hodgson, 2004). The word 'evolution' was embraced by institutionalists in broad terms, but with little employment of its Darwinian and Veblenian meaning.

Consequently, the restoration of Veblen's original outlook and research program offers a line of development that is not only in accord with movements in philosophy, psychology and the social sciences in the twenty-first century, but also may help to enhance the vitality of the original institutionalist movement by returning it to its Veblenian course, which was largely abandoned by institutionalists in the 1920s.

NOTES

1. This essay makes use of some material from Hodgson (2004).
2. There are so many as to undermine any attempt at a representative listing. Some examples are found in Hodgson (2004). Others can be provided on request.
3. When Clark Hull (1943) attempted to reinstate the concept of habit in a behaviorist framework, he had to make a case for including unobservable variables, thus relaxing one of the original behaviorist precepts.
4. See Veblen (1900 [1919], pp. 241, 253; 1904, pp. 311, 314, 344; 1906 [1919], pp. 596–7; 1914, pp. 260, 336). The unavoidability of some 'metaphysical presuppositions' is now the consensus view among modern philosophers of science. See Popper (1972), Caldwell (1982) and many others.
5. See, for example, Veblen (1899, p. 241; 1901 [1919], p. 76; 1906 [1919], p. 598; 1909a [1934], p. 300; 1909b [1919], pp. 628–30; 1914, pp. 18, 180; 1917, p. 55; 1919, pp. 98, 103–4, 473).
6. As a representative critic, Khalil (1995, pp. 555–6) asserted: 'Inspired by Veblen's legacy, old institutional economists generally tend to view the preferences of agents as, in the final analysis, determined by cultural norms.' This may be true of some old institutionalists, but it was not true of Veblen who insisted that social science must 'formulate its theoretical results in terms of individual conduct'. From an evolutionary perspective, as

Veblen understood well, there is no 'final analysis'. Despite its subtitle, Khalil's (1995) article is essentially about neither Veblen nor his true legacy, but about versions of institutionalism that became prominent in America after Veblen's death.

7. In contrast, Rutherford (1984, p. 345) quoted two of the above three sentences in isolation and concluded that Veblen was a methodological individualist. However, Veblen does not state that explanations must *exclusively* be in terms of individuals. An appreciation of Veblen's broader methodological position is gained by placing the above statement in the context of the passages that precede, succeed and qualify it.

8. Whether Veblen was a 'holist' depends on the definition of the term. If it connotes explanation entirely in terms of collectives or social wholes then Veblen was not a holist. But that term is used in many other different ways. Its usage has become so widespread and wide-ranging, and generally at variance from that of Smuts (1926) who originated the term, that it is best not used at all.

9. See the powerful critiques of Mead's work by Freeman (1983, 1992).

10. See, for example, Joas (1993).

REFERENCES

Ayres, Clarence E. (1918), *The Nature of the Relationship Between Ethics and Economics*, Chicago: University of Chicago Press.

Ayres, Clarence E. (1921a), 'Instinct and capacity – I: the instinct of belief-in-instincts', *Journal of Philosophy*, **18**(21), 561–5.

Ayres, Clarence E. (1921b), 'Instinct and capacity – II: homo domesticus', *Journal of Philosophy*, **18**(22), 600–606.

Ayres, Clarence E. (1923), 'John Dewey: naturalist', *The New Republic*, 4 April, pp. 158–60.

Ayres, Clarence E. (1927), *Science: The False Messiah*, Indianapolis, IN: Bobbs-Merrill.

Ayres, Clarence E. (1929), *Holier Than Thou: The Way of the Righteous*, Indianapolis: Bobbs-Merrill.

Ayres, Clarence E. (1932), *Huxley*, New York: Norton.

Ayres, Clarence E. (1936), 'Fifty years' developments in ideas of human nature and motivation', *American Economic Review (Papers and Proceedings)*, **26**(1), 224–36.

Ayres, Clarence E. (1942), 'Economic value and scientific synthesis', *American Journal of Economics and Sociology*, **1**(4), 343–60.

Ayres, Clarence E. (1944), *The Theory of Economic Progress*, Chapel Hill, North Carolina: University of North Carolina Press.

Ayres, Clarence E. (1951), 'The co-ordinates of institutionalism', *American Economic Review (Papers and Proceedings)*, **41**(2), 47–55.

Ayres, Clarence E. (1952), *The Industrial Economy: Its Technological Basis and Institutional Destiny*, Cambridge, MA: Houghton Mifflin.

Ayres, Clarence E. (1958), 'Veblen's theory of instincts reconsidered', in Douglas F. Dowd (ed.), *Thorstein Veblen: A Critical Appraisal*, Ithaca, NY: Cornell University Press, pp. 25–37.

Ayres, Clarence E. (1961), *Toward a Reasonable Society: The Values of Industrial Civilization*, Austin: University of Texas Press.

Ayres, Clarence E. (1973), 'Prolegomenon to institutionalism', introduction to the combined reprint of Clarence E. Ayres (1927), *Science: The False Messiah* and

Clarence E. Ayres (1929), *Holier Than Thou: The Way of the Righteous*, New York: Augustus Kelley.

Benedict, Ruth (1934), *Patterns of Culture*, New York: New American Library.

Boas, Franz (1894), 'Human faculty as determined by race', *Proceedings of the American Association for the Advancement of Science*, **43**, 301–27.

Boyd, Robert and Peter J. Richerson (1985), *Culture and the Evolutionary Process*, Chicago: University of Chicago Press.

Caldwell, Bruce J. (1982), *Beyond Positivism: Economic Methodology in the Twentieth Century*, London: Allen and Unwin.

Cooley, Charles Horton (1902), *Human Nature and the Social Order*, New York: Scribner's.

Copeland, Morris A. (1931), 'Economic theory and the natural science point of view', *American Economic Review*, **21**(1), 67–79.

Cravens, Hamilton (1978), *The Triumph of Evolution: American Scientists and the Hereditary–Environment Controversy, 1900–1941*, Philadelphia: University of Pennsylvania Press.

Degler, Carl N. (1991), *In Search of Human Nature: The Decline and Revival of Darwinism in American Social Thought*, Oxford and New York: Oxford University Press.

Dewey, John (1896), 'The reflex arc concept in psychology', *Psychological Review*, **3**, 357–70.

Dewey, John (1922), *Human Nature and Conduct: An Introduction to Social Psychology*, New York: Holt.

Durham, William H. (1991), *Coevolution: Genes, Culture, and Human Diversity*, Stanford, CA: Stanford University Press.

Freeman, Derek (1983), *Margaret Mead and Samoa: The Making and Unmaking of an Anthropological Myth*, Cambridge, MA: Harvard University Press.

Freeman, Derek (1992), *Paradigms in Collision: The Far-Reaching Controversy over the Samoan Researches of Margaret Mead and its Significance for the Human Sciences*, Canberra: Research School of Pacific Studies.

Hamilton, David B. (1953), *Newtonian Classicism and Darwinian Institutionalism*, Albuquerque: University of New Mexico Press.

Hands, D. Wade (2001), *Reflection Without Rules: Economic Methodology and Contemporary Science Theory*, Cambridge and New York: Cambridge University Press.

Hodgson, Geoffrey M. (2004), *The Evolution of Institutional Economics: Agency, Structure and Darwinism in American Institutionalism*, London and New York: Routledge.

Hull, Clark L. (1943), *Principles of Behavior: An Introduction to Behavior Theory*, New York: Appleton-Century.

James, William (1890), *The Principles of Psychology*, 2 vols, New York and London: Holt and Macmillan.

Joas, Hans (1993), *Pragmatism and Social Theory*, Chicago: University of Chicago Press.

Kallen, Horace M. (1930), 'Behaviorism', in Edwin R.A. Seligman and Alvin Johnson (eds), *Encyclopaedia of the Social Sciences*, vol. 2, New York: Macmillan, pp. 495–8.

Khalil, Elias L. (1995), 'The socioculturalist agenda in economics: critical remarks on Thorstein Veblen's legacy', *Journal of Socio-Economics*, **24**(4), 545–69.

Kroeber, Alfred L. (1923), *Anthropology*, New York: Harcourt Brace Jovanovich.

Lewin, Shira B. (1996), 'Economics and psychology: lessons for our own day from the early twentieth century', *Journal of Economic Literature*, **34**(3),1293–1323.

Lorenz, Max (1896), *Die Marxistische Socialdemokratie*, Leipzig: George M. Wigand.

Matson, Floyd W. (1964), *The Broken Image*, New York: Doubleday.

Mead, Margaret (1928), *Coming of Age in Samoa: A Psychological Study of Primitive Youth for Western Civilization*, New York: William Morrow.

O'Donnell, John M. (1985), *The Origins of Behaviorism: American Psychology, 1870–1920*, New York: New York University Press.

Ouellette, Judith A. and Wendy Wood (1998), 'Habit and intention in everyday life: the multiple processes by which past behavior predicts future behavior', *Psychological Bulletin*, **124**, 54–74.

Plotkin, Henry C. (1994), *Darwin Machines and the Nature of Knowledge: Concerning Adaptations, Instinct and the Evolution of Intelligence*, Harmondsworth: Penguin.

Plotkin, Henry C. (1997), *Evolution in Mind: An Introduction to Evolutionary Psychology*, Harmondsworth: Penguin.

Popper, Karl R. (1972), *The Logic of Scientific Discovery*, 3rd edn, translated and revised from the German edition of 1935, London: Hutchinson.

Rutherford, Malcolm H. (1984), 'Thorstein Veblen and the processes of institutional change', *History of Political Economy*, **16**(3), 331–48.

Samelson, Franz (1981), 'Struggle for scientific authority: the reception of Watson's behaviorism, 1913–1920', *Journal of the History of the Behavioral Sciences*, **17**, 399–425.

Schmoller, Gustav (1900), *Grundriss der allgemeinen Volkswirtschaftslehre, Erster Teil*, Munich and Leipzig: Duncker und Humblot.

Smuts, Jan Christiaan (1926), *Holism and Evolution,* London and New York: Macmillan.

Stocking, George W. Jr (1968), *Race, Culture, and Evolution: Essays in the History of Anthropology,* New York: Free Press.

Sturgeon, James I. (1981), 'The history of the Association for Institutionalist Thought', *Review of Institutionalist Thought*, **1**, 40–53.

Taylor, Charles (1985), *Human Agency and Language: Philosophical Papers 1*, Cambridge and New York: Cambridge University Press.

Veblen, Thorstein B. (1897), 'Review of *Die Marxistische Socialdemokratie* by Max Lorenz', *Journal of Political Economy*, **6**(1), 136–7.

Veblen, Thorstein B. (1898), 'Why is economics not an evolutionary science?', *Quarterly Journal of Economics*, **12**(3), 373–97; reprinted in Veblen (1919).

Veblen, Thorstein B. (1899), *The Theory of the Leisure Class: An Economic Study in the Evolution of Institutions*, New York: Macmillan.

Veblen, Thorstein B. (1900), 'The preconceptions of economic science: III', *Quarterly Journal of Economics*, **14**(2), 240–69; reprinted in Veblen (1919).

Veblen, Thorstein B. (1901), 'Gustav Schmoller's economics', *Quarterly Journal of Economics*, **16**, 69–93, reprinted in Veblen (1919).

Veblen, Thorstein B. (1904), *The Theory of Business Enterprise*, New York: Charles Scribners.

Veblen, Thorstein B. (1906), 'The place of science in modern civilisation', *American Journal of Sociology*, **11**(1), 585–609; reprinted in Veblen (1919).

Veblen, Thorstein B. (1908a), 'The evolution of the scientific point of view', *University of California Chronicle*, **10**(4), 396–416, reprinted in Veblen (1919).

Veblen, Thorstein B. (1908b), 'On the nature of capital II: investment, intangible assets, and the pecuniary magnate', *Quarterly Journal of Economics*, **23**(4), 104–36; reprinted in Veblen (1919).

Veblen, Thorstein B. (1909a), 'Fisher's rate of interest', *Political Science Quarterly*, **24**(2), 296–303; reprinted in Veblen (1934).

Veblen, Thorstein B. (1909b), 'The limitations of marginal utility', *Journal of Political Economy*, **17**(9), 620–36; reprinted in Veblen (1919).

Veblen, Thorstein B. (1914), *The Instinct of Workmanship, and the State of the Industrial Arts*, New York: Macmillan.

Veblen, Thorstein B. (1915), *Imperial Germany and the Industrial Revolution*, reprinted 1964, New York: Augustus Kelley.

Veblen, Thorstein B. (1917), *An Inquiry into the Nature of Peace and the Terms of its Perpetuation*, New York: Huebsch.

Veblen, Thorstein B. (1919), *The Place of Science in Modern Civilization and Other Essays*, New York: Huebsch.

Veblen, Thorstein B. (1923), *Absentee Ownership and Business Enterprise in Recent Times*, New York: Huebsch.

Veblen, Thorstein B. (1925), 'Economic theory in the calculable future', *American Economic Review (Papers and Proceedings)*, **15**(1), 48–55, reprinted in Veblen (1934).

Veblen, Thorstein B. (1934), *Essays on Our Changing Order*, ed. Leon Ardzrooni, New York: Viking Press.

Watson, John B. (1914), *Behavior: A Textbook of Comparative Psychology*, New York: Henry Holt.

Weingart, Peter, Sandra D. Mitchell, Peter J. Richerson and Sabine Maasen (eds) (1997), *Human By Nature: Between Biology and the Social Sciences*, Mahwah, NJ: Lawrence Erlbaum Associates.

Wood, Wendy, Jeffrey M. Quinn and D. Kashy, (2002), 'Habits in everday life: thought, emotion, and action', *Journal of Personality and Social Psychology*, **83**, 1281–97.

7. Veblen: economics raised to the cultural level

David Hamilton

To the conventional economic mind the ideas of Thorstein Veblen are perplexing indeed. Surely this is not meant to be economic analysis. Sociology, perhaps? Maybe social commentary and satire! But surely, not economics. This consternation is augmented when reference is had to some of the footnotes. Jane Ellen Harrison on Greek religion and myth? A Bureau of Ethnology (US) report on Zuni religion? Franklin Frazier on ancient myth? Spencer and Gillen on the Arunta in central Australia? Just how does this relate to economics? How could it relate to the 'modern' world of business and industry?

To the conventional economist the modern economy is thought to be subject to laws of nature that govern the social universe somewhat analogously to the way in which the physical universe is supposedly governed. This preconception of contemporary political economy has its roots in eighteenth-century economics as formalized by the Physiocrats and Classical Political Economy. But, as Guy Routh in his *Origin of Economic Ideas* insisted, the basic elements of the economics being expounded consisted of ideas concerning the social virtues of buying and selling as envisioned by late Medieval merchants, at least two and perhaps three hundred years before Adam Smith (Routh, 1977). In seeking their own gain merchants had not the welfare of the commonweal in mind. Nevertheless the outcome was the same had this been their intent. What the Physiocrats and the Classical school of economists did with these self-serving notions was to recast them with a seeming Newtonian rigor.

The eighteenth century within which Smith did his work has often been referred to as the 'Age of Newton'. Most certainly even the leading savants and philosophes of that era did not exactly carry around copies of Newton's *Principia* with which to while away the time; nevertheless, Newtonian ideas and Newtonian metaphors were in the air, a part of common discourse. Just as vague Darwinian notions and Freudian notions infused the social and political theorizing of the subsequent two centuries, so did those of

Newton in the eighteenth. This is evident in Smith, who was fond of using Newtonian metaphors as, for example, in his discussion of market price 'gravitating' around natural price.

Social and political theorists of that period were under the delusion that they were doing for our understanding of the social universe no less than what Newton had done to the understanding of the physical universe. In pursuing this end the political economists of the time, now the classical economists, made several simplifying assumptions concerning human nature and the social and political order. Their intellectual descendants continue to do so to the present time. These trends are evident even in what are alleged to be some of the more advanced areas of thought such as behavioral economics.

To the classicist as well as to the present day the economics presented by the conventional theorist begins with a stable and narrowly defined human being. All economic behavior is an expression of the personality of a pre-programmed individual bent on securing something referred to as self-interest. All behavior is then explained as a venture to maximize whatever is in the self-interest of these sterile individuals. The social is no more than the sum total of these atomistic individuals. Of course that means that the present social order is almost sacred in nature because it is the uninhibited expression of a primal human nature, which expresses the inner yearnings of a pre-programmed human heart.

The social order is a mirror reflection of these stable individuals. Thus a social order made up of laborers, landlords and capitalists is presented as 'natural', one to be found in a rudimentary form even in so-called 'primitive' society. To the classicist this order reflects the elements of which the economic universe is composed, land, labor and capital, much as the early Greek philosophers viewed the physical universe as being composed of earth, air, fire and water. Perhaps the two views differ in that the Greek view was drawn from physical phenomena and processes while that of the classicist was drawn from a set of social practices among people acting in the roles of landlords, laborers and capitalists. In any event the classic preconceptions almost drive the inquiry to a concern over social balance or equilibrium, to give it a Newtonian flavor, a concern never stronger than it is today when nothing is prized more than a formal mathematical model of what is thought to be the economic process.

The economics offered is one in which solitary individuals express themselves in market activity, either as producers or consumers. But a critical condition is that each 'agent' is autonomous and independent of the others. The expression of individual preferences in the market is what constitutes society. But this remains a one-dimensional analysis. What society exists is no more than a simple aggregation of these individual actors. As one recent writer put it:

> And the story it tells is a marvelous one. In it an enormous multitude of strangers, all individuals, all striving alone, are nevertheless all bound together in a beautiful and natural pattern of existence: the market. This understanding of markets – not as artifacts of human civilization but as phenomena of nature – now serves as the unquestioned foundation of nearly all political and social debate. (Bigelow, 2005)

This way of analyzing economic affairs, by design, minimizes the social dimension. If, on the other hand, one begins by considering economic phenomena to be cultural phenomena the whole analysis becomes two-, or if one considers time as a dimension, three-dimensional. This was Veblen's approach and fundamental contribution to economics. Additionally, it is what provokes consternation on the part of the conventional mind when the latter encounters Veblenian analysis. The significance of this shift in perspective to an understanding of today's economy was never more clearly stated than it was by Anne Mayhew two decades ago (Mayhew, 1987).

The conventional view of the economy is rooted in the preconceptions of the eighteenth-century social and political philosophy, that of a solitary individual who bands together with similarly isolated individuals to form some rules which define acceptable behavior and which enable the individuals to secure their 'self-interests' in relative harmony. To Adam Smith man once lived in an 'original state of nature', one that predated the appropriation of land and the accumulation of capital, by which he meant tools. This view of matters was indeed Lockean and Hobbesian as one would have expected before the work of anthropologists had observed the vast variety in human behavior among the so-called primitive peoples and before the archaeologists had dug through the trash left by Adam's ancestors. Knowledge of the superorganic level of generalization, as Leslie White and Alfred L. Kroeber before him put it, awaited these events. In other words conventional thinking in economics was myopic on the most important matter concerning human behavior. It remains pretty much so even today.

This myopia was never more apparent than in the collection of essays in honor of Clarence Ayres put together by William Breit and William P. Culbertson, some three decades ago. The authors of the collected essays expressed the same kind of consternation over Ayres's work as that expressed one hundred years ago by conventional economists over the work of Veblen. Although the book was entitled *Science and Ceremony*, which would of course have alerted the knowledgeable reader to the fact that Ayres' work was on the cultural level of generalization, to most of the writers it was merely confusing (Breit and Culbertson, 1976; Hamilton, 1977).

In one of his last publications, Ayres insisted that the uninvolved observer of any culture could not help note its two aspects of rationality and irrationality. As he went on to write, '... ancient mythologies persist in juxtaposition to the most advanced technology, such as a manned spacecraft hurtling back to earth from a landing on the moon' (Ayres, 1973, p. iv). And it might well be noted in support of this statement that, while gathering rocks on the moon and performing other matter-of-fact exercises, the participants took time to plant an American flag on the moon surface.

In these same passages Ayres notes that the existence of these two behavioral aspects is what differentiated Veblen's economics from that of his predecessors. The dichotomy was never clearer in Veblen's writings than in *The Theory of Business Enterprise* within which he distinguished between business and industry. He saw clearly that the making of money was one endeavor while the making of goods was still another (Veblen, 1904 [1935]; Hamilton, 1956).

To the conventional economist the making of money and the making of goods are much the same. No sharp distinction is made between the two actions. By 'investing', businessmen create hotels, factories, office buildings, retail stores and all the other physical aspects of modern technology. The making of goods and the making of money exist side-by-side in a symbiotic relationship. One, the money making, simulates the other, the matter-of-fact activity by virtue of which human beings successfully secure their livelihood. What is ignored or repressed is the money manipulation by virtue of which ownership is conveyed and removed. This latter is a process within which mysterious forces give to the technological ceremonial adequacy, to use a Veblenian term.

While mankind is engrossed in tool behavior, at the same time it is involved in a world of make believe within which mysterious forces are manipulated in such a fashion as to assure success in the matter-of-fact activity. Meticulous adherence to the crafting of seaworthy canoes in the Trobriand Islands is alone insufficient in the eyes of those involved. Rather, it is the efforts of the bullroarer that assure success.

This duality of behavior among so-called primitive people is apparent to Ayres' uninvolved observer, but not to the involved participants. Bull roaring and adze manipulation are both essential to success in the endeavor. So be it with the work of the skilled iron worker in the construction of a skyscraper along with that of the entrepreneur who sees to the punctilios of finance and the bestowal of ownership. To those involved, the participants, all the activity is of equal social worth, although some, such as that of manipulation of money funds and the transference of ownership, is more equal than more mundane activity, that is, iron working.

At this point of the analysis, the conventional mind balks. So it would be in the Trobriands had the uninvolved observer (Malinowski, 1948) suggested that the bullroaring was not essential to effective sailing ships. And that Veblen's work suggests the non-essentiality of some of the financial legerdemain is what suggests to the conventional thinker that he is unworthy of attention. Funny and fun, perhaps, but serious? Never.

By relegating the drama of making money to the ceremonial realm Veblen seems to be divesting economic activity of all its deeper meaning as well as the excitement of the chase. And in so doing he appears to be denigrating capitalism, allegedly from whence all blessings come. In the eyes of conventional beholders, it was presumably by virtue of frenzied buying and selling in an active market, even initially with frenzied trading in flint futures, that mankind's long trek from Olduvai Wash to today's Silicon Valley was made possible.

To the conventional mind the ultimate cause of technological activity is the ex ante quest for profit. If circumstances are for the moment such that profitable opportunities are perceived to be slight or non-existent, then all effort must be directed toward restoring confidence in the minds of those primarily concerned with profit making, who are presumed to be the entrepreneurs (of course, this conflates the entrepreneur, the engineer and the capitalist, a mistake that neither Thorstein Veblen, nor one of the more astute of mainstream economists such as Joseph Schumpeter, would make). At no time in the history of the United States and perhaps that of the Western industrial world was this mind set more evident than during the early days of the Great Depression.

Within the United States, at least, the notion prevailed that business confidence could be restored by balancing the federal budget. Just as good business practice insisted that, in times of adversity, corporations could save themselves by cutting back, so it was held must the federal government. Budget balancing, although elusive by virtue of its very nature, was by common consent on the part of the leading minds of the day, the proper government policy. It was an almost fatal prescription. For at a time when investment expenditure and consumption expenditure were in retreat, balancing the federal budget meant that government expenditure was also put into the retreat mode. Nothing could have contributed more to the decline. Since government revenue was already declining, the only possibility for balancing the budget was to cut federal expenditure. Some likened it to prescribing blood-letting for those suffering from anemia. The results were everywhere to be seen by those who could see. The chiefs, the holy men and the wise men of Wall Street were inflicting mass unemployment on the natives while assuring them that 'prosperity was just around the corner'.

At no time in US history were the ideas of Veblen more appropriate. Technological activity was primary, pecuniary activity was permissive at best. To those of a Veblenian frame of mind, and many of the New Deal leading lights were so minded, direct action was in order. Post offices were built and artists were employed painting murals in their lobbies; the arts and the crafts truly joined hands. Shelter belts were in order on the wind-eroded plains and young men were put to work creating them. Unemployed musicians were put together in the form of the Newark Symphony Orchestra, an orchestra that was non-existent before. Central station-generated electricity was extended to the rural population where none had been before. Floods were reduced, hydro-electric power generated, and river valleys were made navigable to tug-pulled barges in the Tennessee River Valley. Hiking trails and campsites were created in the Appalachians and in the Rockies employing young men off the urban streets where only unemployment awaited. Farm to market roads were constructed, getting the farmers and rural population out of muddy impassable roads. Hospitals for children with disabilities were constructed, university buildings constructed by the Public Works Administration (PWA) and the Works Progress Administration (WPA) paid labor. Reforestation was undertaken where forests had been depleted by profit-driven lumbering companies.

All of these activities could not be ascribed to Veblen, of course. In fact, any specific program could not be assigned to his authorship. But it was said at the time that many institutionalists were involved in the economics of the New Deal, and they could be said to have been influenced, if not inspired, by Veblen.[1] These policies were clearly the products of minds freed from notions that the economy and economic activity were bound by laws of natural origin. If one raised his/her sights to the cultural level, then actions were made here on earth. Our economic life was a cultural construct and not something made in heaven. The economy was man-made, not one of divine creation.

Of course to those of the old frame of mind, all of these activities were fraught with unforeseen consequences if not inherently evil. One hears today the argument against direct action framed in terms of the inexorable 'law of unintended consequences', a very old ploy used to stop social change. That any action may well have unforeseen consequences, the so-called law is a stricture designed to stop all conscious social and economic action (Hirschman, 1991). If one adhered to it in daily life one would never cross a street, for if one did so a hurtling automobile just might strike and put you in the hospital rather than on the other side of the street. Life is a series of unforeseen consequences for it is a string of possibilities enmeshed in uncertainty and probability. As a condemnation of the direct action of the New Deal it is indeed a weak piece of intellectual obfuscation contrived to stop any progressive social action. As such it is a contrivance to uphold the status quo.

The New Deal, as was true of Veblen, rested on high hopes and a spirit of experimentalism. To those of the eighteenth-century thought ways it was a violation of some natural order guided by natural law. But if one does raise one's economic perspective to the cultural level, the 'naturalization' of matters once perceived as a reflection of holy writ is retired from one's purview, and economic matters become amenable to human intelligence. To those who have a low estimate of the latter, one can only ask, what else have we got? To that low estimate of human intelligence Veblen might well have responded, to what would you suggest we turn? This pragmatic outlook is what is positive in Veblen. When one raises the level of generalization from the individual to the cultural level, this is most certainly the outcome.

NOTE

1. See for example, William J. Barber (1996), *Designs within Disorder: Franklin D. Roosevelt, the Economists, and the Shaping of American Economic Policy, 1933–1945*, Cambridge: Cambridge University Press.

REFERENCES

Ayres, C.E. (1973), 'Prolegomenon to Institutionalism', 1 vol. edn of *Science: The False Messiah & Holier than Thou*, Clifton, NJ: Augustus Kelley Publishers.
Barber, William J. (1996), *Designs within Disorder: Franklin D. Roosevelt, the Economists, and the Shaping of American Economic Policy, 1933–1945*, Cambridge: Cambridge University Press.
Bigelow, Gordon (2005), 'Let there be markets: the evangelical roots of economics', *Harpers*, **310** (May), 33–9.
Breit, William and W. Patton Culbertson, Jr (eds) (1976), *Science and Ceremony: The Institutional Economics of C.E. Ayres*, Austin, TX: University of Texas Press.
Hamilton, David (1956), 'What is positive in Veblen', *The New Mexico Quarterly*, **26**(1), 147–55.
Hamilton, David (1977), 'Review of Breit and Culbertson (eds), Science and Ceremony: The Institutional Economics of C.E. Ayres', *Journal of Economic Issues*, **11** (3), 635–9.
Hirschman, Albert O. (1991), *The Rhetoric of Reaction*, Cambridge, MA: Harvard University Press.
Malinowski, Bronislaw (1948), *Magic, Science and Religion*, Glencoe, IL: The Free Press.
Mayhew, Anne (1987), 'Culture: core concept under attack', *Journal of Economic Issues*, **21**(2), 587–604.
Routh, Guy (1977), *The Origin of Economic Ideas*, New York: Vintage Books (Random House).
Veblen, Thorstein (1904), *The Theory of Business Enterprise*, reprinted 1935, New York: Scribner.

8. Veblen on higher education

Anne Mayhew

INTRODUCTION

Veblen's *The Higher Learning in America: A Memorandum on the Conduct of Universities by Business Men* (1918 [1954]), continues to have appeal, especially to academics. In the 90 years since the book was published, college and university faculties have continued to fret about boards of trustees constituted of businessmen who know little about academic subject matter, about often indifferent students who enroll in search of vocational training rather than wider knowledge, about curricula that allow wide choice of electives, some without great academic merit, from which students are not well equipped to choose. Veblen's disdain for the American universities of his era was clear:

> The greater number of these state schools are not, or are not yet, universities except in name. These establishments have been founded, commonly, with a professed utilitarian purpose, and have started out with professional training as their chief avowed aim. The purpose made most of in their establishment has commonly been to train young men for proficiency in some gainful occupation; along with this have gone many half-articulate professions of solicitude for cultural interests to be taken care of by the same means. They have been installed by politicians looking for popular acclaim, rather than by men of scholarly or scientific insight, and their management has not infrequently been entrusted to political masters of intrigue, with scant academic qualifications. (Veblen, 1918 [1954], p. 31)

Veblen did not reserve harsh judgment for state schools, for he also wrote of 'two instances, in the Middle West and in the Far West' where large endowments and high ideals had nevertheless failed to produce 'an effectual university'. Instead, said Veblen, these two, which are obviously the private University of Chicago and Stanford University, 'have come substantially to surrender the university ideal . . . and so have found themselves running substantially the same course of insidious compromise with "vocational" aims, undergraduate methods, and the counsels of the Philistines' (Veblen, 1918 [1954], p. 265).

Is Veblen's work a good guide to the higher education of his day? Is it possible that the continued appeal of Veblen's words is due more to a nostalgia shared by Veblen and his modern readers for a world of higher education that may, or may not, have existed before the twentieth century? Is the continued appeal a superficial one based, as suggested by David Riesman in his introduction to the 1954 edition of *The Higher Learning in America*, upon a 'somewhat snobbish view that gives the highest status to research and the lowest to "bureaucracy" and "politics"' (Veblen, 1954, p. xv)? Or does Veblen's analysis continue to have some relevance in spite of the many changes that have occurred in American higher education over the past century?

AN INITIAL CRITIQUE

Most of the *The Higher Learning* was written while Veblen was still at the University of Chicago (he left in 1906) and was, as he says in the 'Preface', an attack on the president of that new institution, William Rainey Harper, and only slightly less directly on John D. Rockefeller, who had provided much of the funding for the creation of the university. By the time of publication Veblen had been on the faculty of Stanford University (another new institution founded by yet another newly rich businessman) and then at the University of Missouri and so had had years to observe higher education in practice. In spite of this the book reads more as an attack by a highly frustrated academic than as a reasoned analysis of practice, and it shares some of the less fortunate traits of Veblen's later work. By 1918 he was living in New York, writing for *The Dial* and by all accounts was an embittered and difficult person. The work that he did during this period was more vitriolic than his previous work and was often repetitive of earlier work, and not always to great advantage. According to Joseph Dorfman, former students and sympathizers thought the articles written for *The Dial* during the later period (and collected as *The Vested Interests*) showed that 'the agitator and phrase maker was taking precedence over the thinker' (Dorfman, 1934 [1972], p. 422). That is a good summary of much that is wrong with *The Higher Learning.*

Veblen's great strength as an analyst, and particularly so in parts of *The Theory of the Leisure Class* and in all of *The Theory of Business Enterprise* (1904 [1975]), derived from his ability to describe at a high level of abstraction the patterns of actual socioeconomic evolution. It was clear throughout these works that his Spartan sensibilities, his abhorrence of ostentatious display and his sense of fairness were often offended by what he described as happening. However, this offense did not interfere with his ability to describe, and the relationship of what he was describing and his development of abstractions is clear. The same cannot be said of *The Higher Learning.*

Throughout this work Veblen talks of 'the higher learning' as the goal that higher education in America is failing to achieve. To interpret this assertion it is vitally important to understand the difference between the two, but Veblen does not make this easy. He begins Chapter 1 by saying that 'in any known civilization there will be found something in the way of esoteric knowledge . . .' that is held '. . . in the keeping of a select body of adepts or specialists' (Veblen, 1918 [1954], p. 1). Given that Veblen includes 'scientists, scholars, savants, clerks, priests, shamans, medicinemen' in his list of the keepers of such 'higher' knowledge, the reader who goes on to read his denunciations of schools of divinity and commerce as 'seminaries for training a vocational kind' rather than institutions of higher learning should be confused. Does not the training of clerics and of clerks involve esoteric knowledge both valued by society and passed on to those being trained in the vocations of church and commerce?

The key to understanding Veblen's argument comes quickly for readers who have understood his arguments in *The Instinct of Workmanship,* 'The place of science in modern civilisation' (1906 [1990]) and 'The evolution of the scientific point of view' (1908 [1990]). To be fair to Veblen he does cite these works on the second page of the book and he then summarizes the arguments made there. However, he does not make it entirely clear for readers not familiar with that earlier work that he is resting his entire argument on what he perceives to have been a shift in the last part of the nineteenth century in the United States (and elsewhere in the Western world) to a new kind of 'esoteric knowledge', knowledge derived largely from 'non-purposive' idle curiosity, and knowledge that was, therefore, relatively uncontaminated by culturally specific myth.[1]

Here is Veblen's account of how this happened, and it is worth quoting at length in order to grasp Veblen's core idea in *The Higher Learning.*

> In point of historical pedigree the American universities are of another derivation than their European counterpart; although the difference in this respect is not so sharp a matter of contrast as might be assumed at first sight. The European (Continental) universities appear to have been founded, originally, to meet the needs of professional training, more particularly theological (and philosophical) training in the earlier times. The American universities are, historically, an outgrowth of the American college; and the latter was installed, in its beginnings, largely as a means of professional training; chiefly training for Divinity, secondarily for the calling of the schoolmaster. But in neither case, neither in that of the European university nor in that of the American College, was this early vocational aim of the schools allowed to decide their character in the long run, nor to circumscribe the lines of their later group. *In both cases, somewhat alike, the two groups of schools came to their mature development, in the nineteenth century, as establishments occupied*

with disinterested learning, given over to the pursuit of intellectual enterprise, rather than as seminaries for training of a vocational kind . . . from the era of the Civil War and the Reconstruction . . . the American college was, or was at least presumed to be, given over to disinterested instruction, not specialized with a vocational, or even a denominational, bias. (p. 22, italics added)

How Veblen came to this conclusion about the history of American higher education in the last part of the nineteenth century is not clear. Perhaps his move from Carlton, which was denominational, to Johns Hopkins, a graduate institution patterned on the scientific learning that was being championed in Germany, continued to color his understanding.[2] He may also have been heavily influenced by President Rainey's goal to have the new University of Chicago join Johns Hopkins as the only other 'institution [in America] doing real university work' (Rucker, 1969, p. 7). In any event, Veblen clearly had the notion that, in the absence of business influence, and the 'autocratic' direction by those imbued with business principles, institutions devoted to the modern disinterested learning might have come into existence as a consequence of competition among universities engendered by the influences then becoming evident at Chicago and Johns Hopkins.

For Veblen this would have meant universities devoted solely to graduate study, without any of the 'undergraduate methods' of course credit and fixed degree requirements, and with an unspecified but beneficent form of management of the pecuniary flows necessary in a commercially organized society. Whatever the faults of administration and organization that existed at the University of Chicago and Stanford University during Veblen's tenure there, there was surely little likelihood that they could have been run in this manner.

In *The Theory of Business Enterprise*, Veblen, for all his disapproval of many aspects of the new form, described with a high degree of accuracy the amalgamation of small-scale commercial establishments of trade and handicraft with the requirements of large scale industrial production techniques. His description, though much more abstract, is very like that which emerged from the detailed descriptive analysis of Alfred Chandler many decades later (Mayhew and Carroll, 1993). However, in the case of *The Higher Learning,* no descriptive work at any level of abstraction could produce an account whereby the land-grant institutions created in the years after the Civil War, and their privately funded but comprehensive competitors (Chicago, Duke and Stanford, to name three), could have followed the evolutionary path that Veblen imagines to have been possible. Nor does Veblen attempt to give specific examples of the existence of actual institutions along such a path.

What actually happened, of course, is that scientific endeavor of the sort that so interested Veblen in 'The place of science', and to which the new

Johns Hopkins was dedicated, did take firm root in the new universities. Even after private industry began to fund its own laboratories (Mowery and Rosenberg, 1998), universities continued to be centers for the kind of higher learning that Veblen envisioned. And, somewhat ironically, this higher learning extended even into the social sciences where dispassion is harder to achieve, and did so with particular strength at the University of Chicago. It was, after all, at the University of Chicago that John Dewey taught philosophy and education, Albion Small founded the first graduate department in Sociology and the philosophy/psychology pioneers George Herbert Mead, James Rowland Angell and James Tuft all gathered. They came not so much for salaries as for a promise of academic freedom which they apparently had even though the university had been founded by the American Baptist Education Society.[3] However, these same universities, and particularly those founded as a result of the Morrill (Land Grant College) Act, also became powerful engines for upward mobility of the 'industrial classes' as that act directed. Scientific agriculture, engineering and domestic science all flourished alongside 'purer' scientific endeavors and continued study of the classics. And, as the bureaucracies that large-scale business firms necessarily entailed grew in size and number, so too did advanced training in accounting, in the organization and management of bureaucratically hired and managed personnel, and so on.

The new universities were on their way to becoming multi-purpose institutions. In such institutions, even in the earliest days, there were already tensions between the goal of passing on received wisdom to those eager to land jobs and succeed in the world that was, and the goal of revising received wisdom in the hope of changing that world. The new universities were also places that clothed themselves in old proprieties and rituals just as Veblen, in his chapter on 'The higher learning as an expression of the pecuniary culture' in *The Theory of the Leisure Class* had said they would (1899 [1975], p. 371). Had Veblen written *The Higher Learning* in the same spirit and manner in which he wrote *The Theory of Business Enterprise*, this is the story that he might have told. It would have been a story of the amalgamation of inherited forms and new possibilities. Instead, he wrote a diatribe of unhappiness that does not seem particularly well grounded in reality.

AN APPRECIATION NONETHELESS

There is, however, another way to read *The Higher Learning*. Instead of seeing it as a somewhat odd and amusing juxtaposition of a jaundiced account of what was wrong with what never could have been, we could ask instead how useful Veblen's analysis is for understanding the effects of fundamental tensions that have indeed existed in American higher education. To what extent has higher learning been sabotaged by historically inevitable, but possibly regrettable, aspects of higher education? In order to answer this question it is necessary to recognize that much has changed in higher education since Veblen wrote. A combination of the land-grant universities, the GI Bill of World War II and its extensions, financial aid and tuition discounting have dramatically increased access to higher education. This trend has continued with the growth in community colleges and now with distance education, especially as the credentials of higher education have become increasingly important as keys to job entry and advancement. At the same time, the federal government, with its deep pockets, has become the source of funding for expensive research in both laboratories and libraries. Colleges and universities are widely regarded as major drivers of economic development both as consequence of research and because of an educated work force. All of this has produced great and growing conflict between a rhetorical commitment to universal access to higher education, pressures to limit government expenditures and public demand for accountability in management of those expenditures. Add to this mixture the growth of athletic/entertainment enterprises as part of universities and colleges, and you have a complex of activities and issues that lie well beyond the scope of this chapter. What we can do, however, is consider several of Veblen's major complaints and suggest some of the advantages and disadvantages of using *The Higher Learning in America* as a guide to the several complex problems of early twenty-first century higher education in the United States.

Veblen began his assault with a chapter on 'the governing boards', noting that control of institutions of higher education had only recently passed from the hands of clergymen to 'businessmen and politicians; which amounts to saying that it is a substitution of businessmen' (1918 [1954], p. 64). Successful businessmen were appointed, Veblen observed, in some hope that they would share their own wealth with the institution, and because 'the modern civilized community is reluctant to trust its serious interests to others than men of pecuniary substance' (ibid. pp. 67–8). There is irony in this situation for, as Veblen noted, it is widely held in the business community that business success is not predicated upon higher learning and, indeed, that such learning may be detrimental to pecuniary achievement. On the other hand, such is the sway of commitment to the soundness of business principles that those who have achieved business success are held to be in the best position to guide that of which they should not know too much. Although Veblen points out that the businessmen appointed to governing boards have little to do with the day-to-day management of institutions of higher education, their position on governing boards would, he said, lead to interference with academic policy and to budgetary decisions that are not consistent with the goals of higher learning.

These issues continue to be a major source of tension across all of higher education in America. The history of higher education is littered with dramatic instances in which boards have tried, with greater or less success, to change the direction of academic policy, and the drive to develop the current system of tenure grew out of concern with intrusions on academic freedom. [4] Today, governing boards of most colleges and universities are more cautious about direct interference than they once were, but the influence of money and its possessors is surely not absent. When those with money want different curricula they are more likely to create their own new institutions that exist somewhat out of the mainstream of higher education and advertise this fact proudly.[5] And within mainstream institutions the ability of some to endow chairs and fund selected activities certainly plays a role in directing activity.

Veblen also worried about the faculty who would and could be hired into institutions run by businessmen, and feared a selection process inconsistent with higher learning. Access to faculty membership has been considerably democratized since Veblen wrote, so that his concerns that 'preference [in hiring] is shown for teachers with sound pecuniary connections, whether by inheritance or marriage' (ibid. p. 153) seems entirely dated. Additionally, he was clearly writing about a world almost exclusively constituted of white males, which, thanks to the effects of affirmative action and the empowerment of women and of racial minorities, universities and colleges no longer are. However, his observation that the 'conventional requirement' that 'university men live on a scale comparable to that of well-to-do businessmen' often serves as an incentive 'to take on supernumerary work' still rings true (ibid. p. 165), with a variety of schemes for 'extra pay' common among most faculties. This is especially true among business faculty and those most able to improve the profitability of supporting firms. The effects on higher learning and especially upon scholarly objectivity are, most would agree, deleterious.

While the battles over academic freedom have in fact resulted in considerable (and widely admired) academic freedom in American colleges and universities, Veblen's concern about the power of governing boards to make budgetary decisions contrary to the best interests of higher education remains a matter of concern. Consider the continued relevance of these passages:

> Imbued with an alert sense of those tangible pecuniary values which they are by habit and temperament in a position to appreciate, a sagacious governing board

> may, for instance, determine to expend the greater proportion of the available income of the university in improving and decorating its real estate.

and

> There is, indeed, a visible reluctance on the part of these businesslike boards to expend the corporation's income for those intangible, immaterial uses for which the university is established. . . . [and when such expenditures are made] . . . the boards unavoidably incline to apportion the funds assigned for current expenses in such a way as to favour those 'practical' or quasi-practical lines of instruction and academic propaganda that are presumed to heighten the business acumen of the students or to yield immediate returns in the way of a creditable publicity. (Ibid., pp. 80–81)

Almost all faculty members can understand Veblen's frustration over decisions to build expensive buildings and sports facilities for use of alumni and perhaps students, even when those same students may have been penalized by the results of inadequate funds for instruction. And there is reason to worry that current fads and competitive fashions in learning and education may create academic priorities that are not consistent with scholarly imperatives.

And yet Veblen's complaints seem slightly out-of-focus because of the importance of other major players in the decision-making processes of modern higher education: educational bureaucrats and administrators, governments and large-scale athletic/entertainment complexes. Actually, Veblen did recognize the importance of the administrators and devoted an entire chapter to their often pernicious influence. And Veblen's words do remain those which, in a thousand variations, can be heard from faculty today:

> Yet, when all . . . sophistications of practical wisdom are duly allowed for, the fact remains that the university is, in usage, precedent, and commonsense preconception, an establishment for the conservation and advancement of the higher learning, devoted to a disinterested pursuit of knowledge. As such, it consists of a body of scholars and scientists, each and several of whom necessarily goes to his work on his own initiative and pursues it in his own way. . . . the system and order that so govern the work . . . are the logical system and order of intellectual enterprise, not the mechanical or statistical systematization that goes into effect in the management of an industrial plant or the financiering of a business corporation. . . . In order to their best efficiency, and indeed in the degree in which efficiency in this field of activity is to be attained at all, the executive officers of the university must stand in the relation of assistants serving the needs and catering to the idiosyncrasies of the body of scholars and scientists that make up the university. (Ibid., pp. 85–6)

Veblen gave greatest attention to the dilemma that this goal of administrator-as-servant model created for university presidents, and clearly this remains a source of tension. However, the more important issues today have to do with the necessarily bureaucratic processes that control college and university governance. The fact of the matter is that university presidents stay in office at any given institution for relatively short periods of time, with the average tenure in recent years being somewhat less than five years (Martin, Samels and associates, 2004). In large institutions especially rapid turnover in the presidential suite can go largely unnoticed among both faculty and students. What this says is not so much that all university and college presidents are cut from the same mold, for they are not; rather it is the case that management is by bureaucracy and even the decisions of governing boards are largely dictated by bureaucratic routines and imperatives.

Veblen was scornful of the need for bureaucratic process, for he attributed it to the importance given to undergraduate education. From the twenty-first century perspective, however, the growth of administrative bureaucracy appears to have been largely a consequence of the growth in size of institutions of higher education, the importance of funding provided by governments at various levels and the growth of federal funding for research.

It is important in considering this growth to recognize that *accountability* need not mean, as Veblen seems at times to suggest, management according to business principles. Private sector business firms in a commercial society are always governed (though perhaps only loosely so in the case of very large corporations that may be deemed too large to be allowed to fail) by the commercial logic that requires that revenues at least equal expenses. This is the logic that was both created by and gave importance to double-entry bookkeeping and the modern accounting that has developed from it. Governmental and non-profit organizations, on the other hand, need not operate according to this same logic. Indeed it may be that an increase in expenses will be the cause for an increase in funding in a way that is unlikely in a purely commercial organization. However, in a society in which most inputs are purchased, even by governmental and non-profit entities, some form of commercial accountability is required, and the language is usually that of double-entry bookkeeping.

The use of this language does produce difficulties. In the absence of products produced for sale, there is often a question of how to value outputs. The same difficulties arise, of course, in many other areas of government-provided services and have tempted analysts to make a variety of efforts to estimate 'benefits'. In higher education there are continued pressures for 'assessment' and more precise measures of 'value added' and these pressures are a form of verification that would have worried Veblen.

The tasks of the bureaucrats of higher education, as it is for all who work with accounting practices designed for not-for-profit organizations, are also made difficult because of the intractability of the measurement of unit costs. Because most of the costs of colleges and universities are labor costs, and because a large share of these costs are paid to faculty who do not keep regular hours, much less account for those hours, it becomes very difficult to say what the 'cost' of an academic course actually is. To a considerable extent the problem is one of allocating fixed costs, a problem common to all large establishments, whether profit-seeking or not. However, within universities and colleges where faculty do insist, as did Veblen, that '. . . the executive officers of the university must stand in the relation of assistants serving the needs and catering to the idiosyncrasies of the body of scholars and scientists that make up the university' (1918 [1954], p. 86), the problem is even more complicated. It is very difficult to get agreement about a standard measure of the cost of a unit of instruction, and especially when a faculty (or faculty member) may want to argue simultaneously that a graduate course with only three students 'costs little' because the faculty member is already on the faculty, and that 'extra pay' would be required for the same faculty member to take on an additional undergraduate course. The bureaucrat may well wonder how to calculate cost of a credit hour of instruction under such circumstances.

At the same time, it is understandable and reasonable that legislators and citizens should want to have information about the salaries paid to those employed in government agencies, and quite reasonable that there should be some assurance that these salaries are being paid for the kind of work that citizens and their legislators deem important. At the beginning of the twentieth century all of government accounting was relatively rudimentary, for it was only in wartime that major expenditures had been required. With the growth of local, state and federal government responsibilities over the course of the century, much more complicated processes were devised. This was the case for public colleges and universities as well, with private institutions adopting similar procedures.

Organizations such as NACUBO (the National Association of College and University Business Officers) today have membership of more than two-thirds of the higher education institutions in the United States. A visit to the NACUBO website will convince the reader of the complexity of the task. Should colleges and universities be required to verify attendance in all courses in order to assure that students receiving Title IV financial aid are actually in attendance? (NACUBO argued no.) What expenditures may colleges and universities include when they calculate overhead costs to be charged to federally funded grants and contracts? The answer is tediously complex. How should 'instructional expenses' be defined? Many papers could be and have been written on these and related questions and the discussions go well beyond the organizational boundaries of NACUBO. The point here is that, for better, and sometimes for worse, critical administrative decisions are made in consequence of complex systems of accountability that share elements with business firms and business principles, but are in many other ways designed to accommodate the special processes of Veblen's higher learning. Although there are recurring calls, often from new trustees, and from frustrated legislators, for some way to reduce the academic processes to more uniform inputs and outputs so that a narrowly conceived commercial logic can be applied, the existence of specialized accounting protocols guarantees against this. Presidents, governing boards, administrative staff and faculty are all part of the community that has created modern educational accounting. Veblen's concerns remain reasonable, but his conclusions would surely need to be substantially modified.

Although Veblen takes swipes at (mis)management of the physical plant and other perennial faculty concerns along the way, he devotes much more attention to another complaint that will strike most, though certainly not all, of today's faculty as odd. Over and over he returns to the theme that it is undergraduate education that substantially undermines the higher learning in institutions of higher education. It is certainly true that the importance of a college degree for entry into many kinds of employment means that vocational training is most often uppermost in the minds of students, their parents and the legislators and donors who provide funding. This does make dispassionate learning and instruction difficult. The same emphasis on getting ahead not only breeds insistence on quick and vocationally focused courses but also renders the students conservative in their pursuit of knowledge lest they learn something that might tempt them to change paths or question the vocations that promise greatest pecuniary reward.[6]

At the same time, and contrary to what Veblen claimed, the broadening of opportunities for undergraduate students to study, even if often in willy-nilly fashion, with scholars who are engaged in relatively uncorrupted higher learning has recruited many to similar pursuits. It is hard to know how many scientists and scholars have pursued the 'higher learning' because of exposure as undergraduates to a first-rate scholar, but the number is surely not insignificant. How to account, then, for Veblen's aversion to undergraduates? In some part this probably stemmed from his own unhappy experiences in teaching and from his own refusal to assign grades in the normal manner or to comply with any of the other requirements of academic life (Dorfman, 1934 [1972], pp. 248–52, 307–18). Because graduate education had not yet become the bureaucratized process that it is today, Veblen held to a dream that somehow graduate, though not undergraduate, education could be a matter of purely scholarly interchange.

More interesting, however, than Veblen's dreamy academic bohemianism (to borrow a phrase from David Riesman[7]) is that in some ways its partial achievement in our time has been a consequence of the growth of graduate education and higher learning. It is ironic that he did miss this trend, for his argument in 'The place of science', which serves as the foundation for *The Higher Learning in America*, provides a basis for understanding what was to come.

Recall that Veblen argued that the 'higher learning of the modern world', the dispassionate pursuit of modern scientific inquiry, was a consequence of the use of machines, of technology. Science was no longer speculative but rather a matter of using machines to manipulate things which resulted in the ability to use machines to manipulate more things. When Veblen wrote *The Higher Learning* the consequences of this development for higher education were only beginning to be felt, and it was not until after World War II that the requirements for laboratory space and equipment became a driving force in higher education. When computers became important in the 1960s and beyond, this only added to the costs of scientific inquiry, so that it quickly became impossible for most institutions of higher education to pay for modern research out of their traditional sources of revenue. In part because of the competition with the Soviet Union, but also because of the growth of a science and technology lobby, federal funding grew rapidly. Today, defense remains an important argument for such funding but international economic competitiveness and the desire for state and regional economic growth have also emerged as funding imperatives.

Without doubt 'scholarly learning' in the physical and natural sciences has been greatly enhanced because of this funding. However, it is also possible to wonder whether or not the increasingly pragmatic focus of such learning will stifle the idle curiosity that was the original impetus. Veblen argued that investigation undertaken to solve a recognized purpose would be less 'idle', less free, and therefore less productive of truly new knowledge. On the other hand, he did suggest that technologically driven investigation could take on a logic of its own. Another, and more familiar, way of putting the issue is to ask whether or not the emphasis on 'applied' science, especially where funding is required, is consistent with 'basic' science. This is a question to which Veblen gave little attention.

There are other complexities as well. Graduate education has expanded enormously with the growth of funded science. Today almost all graduate students in the physical and natural sciences are supported financially while they study and are, in fact, essential to the completion of faculty work.

This growth has bureaucratized graduate education in ways that Veblen would deplore, but it has also resulted in a larger and larger cadre of young scientists who are trained in the use of the equipment of science and for this reason are able to carry out dispassionate inquiries into the world of matter of fact. It is hard not to be impressed by how much humans have learned, and stand ready to learn, about themselves and their habitat in the decades of 'big science'.

Again there are ironies. It is often the case that today's most successful scientists look very much like Veblen's ideal scholar, largely free from teaching, with their own group of post-doctoral students, and well funded. At the same time these individuals are often de facto administrators who spend most of their time in pursuit of more grants and contracts. These are people who may never teach undergraduates and who may do little in their own labs. Instead, they move from acquisition of one grant to completion of proposals for the next. In many ways this leads to highly productive science but it is also a process that is not easily placed in Veblen's scheme for either good or ill.

Surely Veblen would have found good reason for scornful satire in the emulation of 'big science' that pervades so much of today's social science and related disciplines. Under pretext of doing 'science' in the truly scientific ways of the physicist, economists in particular have become theologians for the business schools through manipulation of the symbols of mathematics and have largely abandoned the descriptive (and more truly scientific work) that Veblen's former colleagues (such as Wesley Clair Mitchell, Edith Abbott or Edward Bemis) were doing, or beginning to do, at Chicago and Stanford. In Colleges of Education as well as of Business, scientists, who generate great numbers of multiple-authored reports through what are essentially industrial processes of investigation, are models for emulation by faculty whose papers and publications are meant to rival in form and number those of the natural scientists.

CONCLUSION

Veblen's words in *The Higher Learning* remain amusing and many of the tensions that he identified in higher education remain. Still, it is hard to see it as a guide to critical thinking about either the higher learning or higher education in the twenty-first century. Too much has changed. It is ironic indeed that what is arguably the most important of these changes is a consequence of the higher learning having become an industrial process, and not, as Veblen feared, of sabotage by business principles.

NOTES

1. See Mayhew (this volume) for more on this point.
2. John M. Barry provides a nice description of the kind of fanfare that surrounded the creation of Johns Hopkins: 'On September 12, 1876, the crowd overflowing the auditorium of Baltimore's Academic of Music was in a mood of hopeful excitement, but excitement without frivolity. Indeed, despite an unusual number of women in attendance, many of them from the uppermost reaches of local society, a reporter noted, "There was no display of dress or fashion." For this occasion had serious purpose. It was to mark the launching of the Johns Hopkins University, an institution whose leaders intended not simply to found a new university but to change all of American education; indeed they sought considerably more than that. They planned to change the way in which Americans tried to understand and grapple with nature' (Barry, 2004, p. 11).
3. For an excellent account of all of this and much more about the University of Chicago of Veblen's time, see Darnell Rucker (1969).
4. One of the early and notorious firings was that of Edward A. Ross at Stanford as a consequence of his investigations into labor conditions on railroads, which were offensive to the widow of Leland Stanford, railroad magnate and the founder of the University. Ross's firing was also the consequence of his advocacy of 'free silver' in the fight over the gold standard – an issue that led to the firing of Benjamin Andrews at Brown University. Alexander Meikeljohn, who had been Andrew's student, was subsequently fired at Amherst, in 1922, as a result of disputes over the curriculum, athletics and other issues (Brown, 1981). As a response to the turmoil caused by these and other dismissals the American Association of University Professors was organized in 1915. The statement of tenure adopted by that group and still in widespread use among American colleges and universities, dates back to 1940, so that reasonably effective protection of academic freedom came well after Veblen wrote.
5. Bob Jones and Liberty Universities, both religious institutions, are examples of this phenomenon.
6. Without doubt the frustrations of those devoted to some form of 'higher learning' and questioning of the status quo are greater in the many institutions of higher education that operate apart from graduate education and as part of the system of community colleges, or in some cases, as purely teaching-oriented four-year institutions within state systems. It is interesting, and fits with Veblen's own perception of the probability of quasi-scholarship, that in some of these institutions there is a growing effort to develop 'research agendas', but the necessary support to do so is absent.
7. Riesman wrote: 'All in all, it is my impression that the Veblen legend and the Veblen book have helped give us many guardedly inefficient academic Bohemians, proud of their inability to preside at a meeting, or to turn in grade lists on time, or to remember appointments and the names of students, or to write memoranda not tainted by irrelevance' (Veblen, 1918 [1954], p. xv). We doubt that all of this highly recognizable type owe their existence to Veblen, but he surely has served many as a justificatory model.

REFERENCES

Barry, John M. (2004), *The Great Influenza*, New York: Viking Penguin.
Brown, Cynthia (1981), *Alexander Meiklejohn: Teacher of Freedom*, Berkeley, CA: Meiklejohn Civil Liberties Institute.
Dorfman, Joseph (1934), *Thorstein Veblen and His America*; reprinted 1972, Clifton, NJ: Augustus M. Kelley Publishers.

Martin, James, James E. Samels and associates (2004), *Presidential Transition in Higher Education: Managing Leadership Change*, Baltimore, MD: Johns Hopkins University Press.

Mayhew, Anne and Sidney L. Carroll (1993), 'Alfred Chandler's speed: monetary transformation', *Business and Economic History*, **22**(1), 105–13.

Mowery, David. C. and Nathan Rosenberg (1998), *Paths of Innovation: Technological Change in 20th-century America*, Cambridge, UK and New York: Cambridge University Press.

Rucker, Darnell (1969), *The Chicago Pragmatists*, Minneapolis, MN: University of Minnesota Press.

Veblen, Thorstein (1899), *The Theory of the Leisure Class*, reprinted 1975, New York: Augustus M. Kelley.

Veblen, Thorstein (1904), *The Theory of Business Enterprise*, reprinted 1975, Clifton, NJ: Augustus M. Kelley Publishers.

Veblen, Thorstein (1906), 'The place of science in modern civilisation', *The American Journal of Sociology*, **XI** (March), reprinted 1990 in *The Place of Science in Modern Civilization*, New Brunswick and London: Transaction Publishers.

Veblen, Thorstein (1908), 'The evolution of the scientific point of view', reprinted 1990 in *The Place of Science in Modern Civilization*, New Brunswick and London: Transaction Publishers.

Veblen, Thorstein (1918), *The Higher Learning in America*, reprinted 1954, Stanford, CA: Academic Reprints.

9. Thorstein Veblen and the sabotage of democracy

Sidney Plotkin

'Only he can conquer who knows his prey better than it knows himself.'
(Bruno Bauer)[1]

In the aftermath of the 2004 election, liberals were angry, frustrated and disheartened. Many were downright astonished. In spite of a war gone awry in Iraq, corporate scandals, sour job markets and sagging incomes, millions of working class Americans opted to stay the course, joining their votes to those of the affluent to re-elect the most conservative president in a generation.[2] Liberal critic Thomas Frank tells of a conversation that he had with a friend. 'She was perplexed', he reports. 'How can anyone who has ever worked for someone else vote Republican?' she asked. Frank's answer, one echoed by many observers, is that working people allowed themselves to be misled (Frank, 2004, p. 1). Republicans, he argued, successfully manipulated workers into voting on the basis of trumped up moral and religious issues that distracted attention from more tangible questions of economic justice and war. As Frank lamented, 'People getting their fundamental interests wrong is what American political life is all about.' Thorstein Veblen would have agreed. Political misperceptions can end up producing a world of hurt for members of 'the underlying population' – not only low wages, unemployment and high prices, but thousands of dead and injured young people of the working class, sent off by the state to fight wars over which the underlying population has little control, and from which they draw no benefit. But Veblen went deeper: after years of studying American culture, he concluded that the 'common man does not know himself' (Veblen, 1919, pp. 174–5).

Of course, Veblen was not writing about the last third of the twentieth century. His works span the calamitous years between 1892 and 1923, a period during which the nation felt the full sweep of industrial revolution, saw a vast concentration of business power, endured a series of assaults against the rights of working people, and fought two wars far from home,

170

having only recently torn itself apart in a Civil War. Veblen's account of these years is, in part, a running commentary on the injustice, irrationality and absurdity of the nation's ruling class and the tragic folly of mass support for leaders and institutions that are inimical to popular interests.[3] His first two books, *The Theory of the Leisure Class* (1899b) and *The Theory of Business Enterprise* (1904) speak directly to these themes. Veblen saw in ruling class behavior and the underlying population's tolerance for it, enduring patterns of ancient barbarism, themes that he would explore in such later works as *The Instinct of Workmanship* (1914 [1990]), *The Nature of Peace* (1917), *The Higher Learning in America* (1918 [1957]), *The Vested Interests and the Common Man* (1919) and his last book, *Absentee Ownership* (1923 [1997]). Throughout his writings it is clear that, although Veblen sympathized with radical critics of capitalism and the warfare state, he doubted that impassioned appeals to reasoned interests would do much to change conservative habits of mind.[4]

Veblen brought an unusual dose of radical realism to his analysis of American democracy and the warfare state. Like Marx and his followers in America, Veblen exposed the waste, destructiveness and amorality of business enterprise, imperialism and war. But in ways different than Marx, Veblen insisted that capitalism was only part of the problem. The warfare state served the imperial interests of absentee owners, but it had reasons and interests of its own to make war and engage in predatory politics. Far from reducing the state to an economic tool, as many of his critics suggest, Veblen's analysis of the state points to his realist preoccupation with power as a motivating factor in political and economic life. As we shall explore below, Veblen's distinction between the emulative aspirations of power and its exploitative methods is crucial to understanding how his critical analysis both parallels and diverges from Marxism. From this analytical root Veblen examines how institutions organize power, emulation and exploit, and how habits of popular deference to elite powers and ruling classes continue to influence democratic society.

This deference shows itself in two basic ways. In the social and economic realms, the system of absentee ownership transformed traditional forms of class deference and subordination into a new ethos of opportunism, an often-cynical opportunism at that, whose effect is to underpin popular faith and hope in the system. But even as capitalism encourages dreams of personal success through free markets and private property, democracy also reinforces traditional habits of political deference and civic subordination; not only in the way that the underlying population looks up to the rich as models of success, glamour and celebrity, but in the more ominous way that the democratic state remains a warfare state, with all that implies for the willingness of people to trust their leaders, honor their claims to secrecy and to look with loyal suspicion upon those who question the sanity of official policy.

In short, Veblen brought to radical criticism an appreciation for the human enchantment with power and an understanding of how that fascination is institutionalized in forms of state and class rule. Not that Veblen was completely without hope. Although his own political sympathies ran toward anarchism, Veblen saw progressive possibilities in the insubordinate traditions of democracy (Hodder, 1956; Dugger, 1984; Patsouras, 2004). Most important, he thought the main drift of technological modernization spurred workers toward dispassionate, matter-of-fact ways of thinking. Intellectual sobriety would lead people to be increasingly hostile to 'coercion, personal dominion, self-abasement, subjection, loyalty' and 'suspicion'. These attitudinal changes might slowly subvert the venerable habits that turn free and insubordinate citizens into willing and compliant followers (Veblen, 1915 [1954], pp. 268–9). Citizens might yet come to know themselves and their generic needs as human beings.

But Veblen was not a wishful thinker. He recognized that other factors than technical rationality affected human thinking, and many of these had powerfully counter-rational, conservative impacts. In one of his clearest statements on the subject of political consciousness, he wrote that human 'reasoning is largely controlled by other than logical, intellectual forces … the conclusion reached by public or class opinion is as much, or more, a matter of sentiment than of logical inference; and … the sentiment which animates men, singly or collectively, is as much, or more, an outcome of habit and native propensity as of calculated material interest' (Veblen, 1898 [1969], p. 441, 1899a [1964], p. 436).

Veblen's comments on the relation between sobriety and sentiment in popular thought take us well beyond conventional observations about Republican manipulators of popular consciousness. Veblen's probing of social forces suggests that democratic politics unfolds under the constraint of a fundamental tension between rationalization and habit, between sober insight into the present and a vigorous, reactionary pull of illiberal habits, institutions and sentiments, such as patriotism, religion and the warfare state. At the more visible level of institutions, democracy develops as a product of concrete struggles, the political forces of popular autonomy, insubordination and struggles for satisfaction of human needs arrayed against claims of society's major institutions for subordination and compliance. In a sense, then, every contemporary political system is, at bottom, its own peculiar blend of irresponsible powers and democratic institutions, a 'distinctive form of the current compromise between the irresponsible autocracy of the mediaeval state and the autonomy of popular self-government' (Veblen, 1915a [1954], p. 230). The great problem of political analysis, for Veblen, then, is how to come to terms with the ambiguities of popular consciousness, the pull and tug between sobriety and sentiment.

Many scholars of Thorstein Veblen might be surprised by this formulation of his political significance. A common view is that Veblen was preoccupied with economics and technology, and paid too little attention to politics (Diggins, 2000; Baran, 1957; Dobrianksi, 1957). There is much truth in these observations. Throughout his writings, Veblen did stress forces of technological change, and his theory of business enterprise offers rich insights into the workings of corporate capitalism. But above all, I think, Veblen worked to understand relationships between culture, economics and technology, relationships in which, more often than not, predatory cultural institutions sabotaged the potential of economic forces, turning industrial promise to the advantage of the few at the expense of the many.

To the extent that Veblen identified exploit with political activity, he understood the relation of predatory culture to economics and technology to be fundamentally political and undemocratic. Veblen associated barbaric aspects of culture with power relationships, with institutions that endow ruling classes with authority to exploit economic means for their own self-indulgent purposes. In this respect, the relationship between power and exploit lies at the heart of Veblen's under-appreciated contribution to radical theories of politics, including democratic politics. It is important to understand how this relationship works in Veblen's thought. Once we do, it becomes easier to grasp why he thinks that contemporary versions of democracy that promise popular sovereignty in fact deliver irresponsible power and tolerate exploitation.

EXPLOIT, POWER AND EMULATION

The fundamental distinction underlying Veblen's social theory is that between industry and exploit. Industry refers to work, to peaceable, quiet, creative activity, in which people labor to convert inanimate objects into useful things. It embraces the whole realm of human technical ingenuity, including all the technical knowledge and tools that humans have developed to help themselves survive in the material world. Exploit entails a very different kind of human action, the effort to induce or to compel other animate or living forces to work for the exploiter rather than for themselves or their community. Veblen offered an anthropological theory of exploit. Exploit, he argued, stems from humanity's earliest struggles to deal with peculiarly baffling or recalcitrant aspects of their environment, parts of their world that seem alive with antagonism. In trying to pacify wild animals and ghostly spirits, for example, Veblen hypothesized that primitive humans tended to project their own strong sense of purpose and will onto that of their unruly neighbors.[5]

To prevail over equally purposeful spirits, primitive humans developed military or sportsmanlike strategies of conquest, which depended on shrewd applications of force and cunning. To prevail against other living spirits meant something quite other than invention. Whether by force or by fraud, it meant turning the animated spirits of others to the exploiter's own purposes, transforming their will into a tool of one's own. In Veblen's words, 'exploit, so far as it results in an outcome useful to the agent, is the conversion to his own ends of energies previously directed to some other end by another agent' (Veblen, 1899b [1979], p. 13).

A crucial evolutionary point follows. Gradually, the experience of exploit built on itself, contributing, however haltingly, to foundation of an unmistakably different human experience of the world than was to be found in quiet inventive work. Industry is uneventful; it lacks the challenging dare to compete. Industry has no drumbeat of excitement created by challenging encounters with clever rivals. Industry is productive, fruitful, peaceable and dull. In exploit, by contrast, humans discovered the attention-grabbing dynamic of conflict.

Exploit cast human experience into dramatic, tension-ridden contexts, political situations of intense conflict.[6] Experientially, Veblen suggests, exploit seemed to touch human beings in an especially stimulating way, to enliven them in a more directly human way, because it put humans face to face with something both like and yet opposed to themselves. In exploit more than industry, Veblen suggests, people came to feel a sense of novel, even magical strength and power, a capacity to govern and control living things that demanded talents and virtues of a wholly different order than those required of work with inanimate materials. Exploit came to be culturally valued, because it signaled man's capacity, not only to understand the other, but to anticipate its oppositional strategies and then to master them.[7] Life could become a game, a sport, a contest or struggle, and there was a whole new order of militant, competitive values and habits to be derived from that novel understanding.

Here was a vindication of more than mere workmanship; this was vindication of human power over other beings bold enough to challenge humanity's position in the world. Exploit illuminated the potential for man to stand astride the other creatures in his world and to make himself lord of their fate. Here was a basis for social distinction and honor truly worthy of humanity's highest strategic intellect and most formidable potential for command. In other words, the evolution of exploit deeply affected the way people valued and distinguished their relations with one another.

In savage societies, which survived by industry, the evidence of a successful contribution to the community was a person's material output. People honored and distinguished each other on the basis of the tangible evidence of their work. But mastery or exploit (political skill) is not a thing; it is an imputed inner quality of strength and cunning. It is an aspect of a person, not the person's public product. A key to Veblen's theory of power, then, is his belief that exploiters aggressively seek ways to confirm their inner prowess by regularly exhibiting those qualities in relationships with other people.[8] Among the first and most graphic displays of exploitative potency, Veblen suggests, was the capture and enslavement of women, whose subordinate relation to their captor was a living trophy of male power.[9]

In certain respects, Veblen's critique of exploit, as described above, seems similar to Marx's theory of exploitation. But Veblen was not convinced by Marx's claim that economic motivations explained capitalist behavior.[10] Veblen's more cogent explanation was that endless capital accumulation was the modern, legitimate economic expression of power's ceaseless desire to prove its mastery. Before capitalism, barbaric aristocrats used leisure with its many rituals of sport, culture and war to display their potency. Once capitalism developed, ruling classes turned more and more to material possessions and business conquests to evidence their prowess. Just like the barbarians of old, capitalists struggle and compete to materialize the immateriality of their personal and institutional claims to power. Capital and its perquisites can only signify power; they can never match the elusive quality of power itself, which remains, as it was in the earliest days of barbarism, an imputation of immaterial inner strength. In other words, Veblen held that, because of the intangible character of their claim to power, the powerful are doomed to feelings of perpetual uncertainty and insecurity, a chronic dissatisfaction that is in constant need of re-certification through relations and icons of mastery and predation.

As a psycho-political relationship that thrives on dominance and subordination, prowess depends profoundly on how the parties to the relationship perceive it. What drives the powerful in capitalist society, then, is the same ever-receding goal that drove the first warriors, to be compared favorably with other powerful figures, to be perceived by others as indomitable, as willful, assertive, even menacing individuals, who are precisely capable of converting others' energies and purposes to their own.[11]

In sum, for Veblen, power is really an invidious competitive relationship, but one whose objective reality is determined by class control of institutions and resources. The special gratification of power lies perversely in the chronic uncertainty of its relationship with others; it is the uncertainty of this social relationship of power that drives rulers' struggle to accumulate ever more signs of its inner possession, including control of the political and economic institutions of mastery. What makes Veblen's account of our social life so strange, and yet so familiar, is that he untangles the perverse relationship that exists between the motivations and mechanisms of power, the confusion between an elusive quest for a sense of inner superiority and the need this generates for an objective capacity to exploit others, which depends on command of institutions and resources.

In pre-capitalist societies, exhibition of prowess for its own sake was much more transparent and more assured than it is in capitalist and democratic societies. Rulers in barbaric cultures, feudal society, for example, were usually overtly military leaders: warlords, fighters, conquerors and commanders. Pre-capitalist barbarism could directly and explicitly assume 'the congenital unworthiness of the common man'. Conventional wisdom embraced the idea that people of low social rank are insubstantial in respect to power, which explains why 'the common man has in the nature of things no claims which his god or his masters are bound to respect' (Veblen, 1915b, pp. viii–ix). Early capitalism and democracy dramatically changed the form and much of the substance of those relationships. But not all of the old ways disappeared.

DEMOCRACY AND OPINION

Veblen traced modern democracy back to institutions that developed during 'the handicraft era' in Europe, when industry revived itself at the expense of exploit. A long and consequential period of change, stretching roughly from the fourteenth to the late eighteenth centuries, the handicraft era comprised the decline of feudalism, growth of urban commercial towns, early industrialism and appearance of the modern state system. For Veblen, this period inaugurated a great onrush of freedom and technological progress, developments embodied by its leading figure, 'the masterless man'. The 'masterless man' was Veblen's term for the serfs and peasants who rejected the grip of feudal control, people who hit the open road in search of a better life in the emerging commercial and industrial towns of Western Europe.

Masterless men, like the earliest savages, occupied themselves with industry. Claiming natural rights of labor and property, the masterless men were unruly, insubordinate citizens, a nascent middle class of small craftsmen and petty shop-keepers, who were repelled by feudal forms of allegiance and violence, and the demands of absolute monarchs. The kind of liberal capitalist social order for which they fought challenged the predatory political relationships and militarized values of feudal society. The very fact that masterless men threw off their shackles symbolized how much 'the spirit of insubordination' lay at the heart of their increasingly free institutions. Yet, for Veblen, the scope of their liberation was limited. Masterless men did not wholly forgo opportunities to be masters themselves. They dominated their wives, for example, treating them as property; they had few misgivings about confiscating the lands of native peoples; and one class among them became slave-masters themselves. Most important, they found it hard to give up old emulative habits and sentiments. 'The ever-insistent need of some intoxicating make-believe' led these newly democratic citizens to find novel bases for imputation in accumulations of wealth and fortune. In this regard, large accumulations of wealth did 'very nicely as a base on which to erect a colorable personage, sufficient to carry a decently full charge of imputed merit' (Veblen, 1923 [1997], p. 117).

By the mid-nineteenth century, the modern democratic die were cast, and America led the way. There, white males enjoyed equal political rights that their leaders were bound to respect; public opinion had gained a leading position in society and politics; law circumscribed the state's use of force; the principle of equality supplanted aristocratic claims to deference; and the constitution placed military power under civilian control. Overall, energized by the combined force of impersonal law, public opinion and the creativity of handicraft production, liberal democracy in the US seemed poised to rid society of its ancient abuses – the crimes of exploit and of irresponsible, predatory power – at least in regard to white men. Veblen noted the contradictions of patriarchy, class, slavery and conquest, but he also saw potential for wider patterns of equality and democratization. After all, respect for popular will gradually settled in as a basic political expectation among all classes. The days were over when arrogant warlords and absolute monarchs could push white men around; democratic citizens would no longer tolerate overt predation, at least domestically (foreign policy was another matter) for equality and accountability had become prevalent themes of modern democratic life.

The unmistakable power of public opinion offered new measures for judging conformity of elite institutions with popular aspirations. 'Elder statesmen continued to direct' society from above, Veblen wrote in 1919, yet 'it is the frame of mind of the common man that makes the foundation of society in the modern world' (Veblen, 1919, p. 16).

To be sure, Veblen thought the legal theory of popular sovereignty was ludicrous: the idea that 'democratic citizens, each and several, by Grace of God hold sovereign dominion over the underlying population of which they each and several are abjectly servile components' (Veblen, 1923 [1997], pp. 26–7). But he took the political consequence of popular sovereignty more seriously. Democratic political leaders had to acknowledge that their power was but the reflected glory of popular power, a power delivered unto the leadership only with the consent of the governed. This meant that the people now held an 'eventual power of veto' over their leaders. In form, at least, democratic citizens seemed substantial and their opinion carried weight. At the very least, democracy made it 'ceremonially necessary for the gentlemanly classes to consult the wishes of ... their sovereign'. The vital political power to say 'what may be safely done or left undone in society' depended on the 'frame of mind of the common man' (Veblen, 1919, p. 126). If any principle signaled the arrival of democracy, it was this one. Reinforcing such tendencies, an impersonal system of constitutional law promised to channel the new power of public opinion and to keep its representatives responsible. Law, not the personal whim of rulers, defined conditions under which emerging democratic power would have effect. This law also had definite industrial implications, for it embraced powerful levers of economic policy, such as taxation and eminent domain, which, in theory, could harness the forces of industry to satisfy popular needs.[12] Now, Veblen was by no means a liberal democrat, but he had unmistakable sympathies for democracy. In this sense, Max Lerner (1948, p. 36) surely overstated the case when he asserted, 'Veblen carefully avoids any reference to democratic ideals.' To the contrary, democratic ideals permeate his critique of democracy as it really worked.

OSTENSIBLE DEMOCRACY

In one sense, though, Lerner was correct: Veblen was no idealist; he never confused what ought to be, or what society claims about it itself, with what really is. What he brought to social analysis was not idealism, but a radical sense of realism. Veblen's analysis of democracy exemplifies this radical realist stance. It is conveniently expressed in a term that he introduced in one of his later books, *The Nature of Peace,* to describe the working democracies of his day. 'Ostensible democracies' he called them. Consider the linguistic roots of this term, 'ostensible'. It comes from the Latin, 'ostensibilis', which has dual roots, 'ostendere', which means, 'to show ... against;' and 'tendere', which means, 'to stretch' (Webster, 1968, p. 1037). As usual, Veblen chose his words carefully. To say that a democracy is 'ostensible' is to say that such a democracy makes a show of its forms, in the process 'stretching' its showy appearances to convey impressions that obscure darker truths. It is a matter of 'what the older logicians ... called *suppressio veri* and *suggestio falsi*': Suppress the truth and suggest the false (Veblen, 1923 [1997], p. 159). That this logic also served as 'the rule of country town salesmanship' in America, is revealing, for Veblen conceived of 'the country town' as the single American institution that has had the greatest influence 'in shaping public sentiment and giving character to public opinion' (ibid., p. 142).

In part, Veblen's theory of ostensible democracy is about the chasm between ideals that American democracy proclaims for itself and the way this 'ostensible democracy' really works. But it is also a term that refers more subtly to contradictory guises that power assumes in democratic society.

As we have seen, Veblen argued that aspirations to power, the emulative quest for deference and subordination, provide ulterior motives of business expansion and accumulation. In this sense, the newer power holders of capital sought to display the old predatory virtues of mastery and dominance, to parade their prowess, to preen, show off and boast. We can see this aspect of emulative power today in the indulgent life styles of the corporate rich, the astronomical salaries, the fleets of sleek corporate jets, the giant corporate towers that arch over urban skylines, and in the televised celebrity longings of such businessmen as Donald Trump, Robert Welch or George Steinbrenner. We can see it too in struggles among corporations to seize control of one another's assets, to defeat one another in business competition, to outdo one another's stock valuations. Economic power holders in America carefully prune their displays of power to pecuniary, monetary economic and social forms, forms of display that seem to be about wealth, status and hard-earned economic success, not raw political power. This is understandable, for in American democracy the people reserve power to themselves; power, in American terms, is distinctively political, democratic and dangerous, and much in need of strict oversight and balance. The prevailing marketplace ideology holds that, in contrast to the state, there is no real economic power in the marketplace; competition, the invisible hand and anti-trust laws see to that (Hayek, 1945; Friedman, 1962; Kristol, 1978; Gilder, 1981).

'Americans have gloried in the conspicuous consumption of wealth,' writes Samuel P. Huntington, an author who has moved smoothly between the higher academic world and that of the national security state. But those same Americans, egalitarian and democratic to the core, 'never' gloried 'in the conspicuous employment of power' (Huntington, 1981, p. 75). Note Huntington's meticulous distinction between wealth as display and elite reticence concerning the 'employment', or uses of power. Americans want to be known for their wealth, but they do not wish to be seen as using power to obtain it. Power, an unholy predatory goal, must be washed clean by the purifying gloss of money earned 'the old fashioned way'. Or, in the related words of John Kenneth Galbraith, 'power obviously presents awkward problems for a community which abhors its existence, disavows its possession, but values its exercise' (quoted in Lynd, 1956, p. 7).

In a similar vein, Veblen recognized a difference between the emulative motivations of self-promotion that lie behind power and the actual exploitative methods of power itself, which, especially in a democratic society, demand due discretion, privacy and concealment. Power desires emulation, but its methods remain those of an exploit best kept hidden. Especially in democracy, the processes by which absentee owners and statesmen convert the people's purposes, energies and resources to elite ends must be spared the limelight. No one likes to be reminded that she is being abused, especially not in a democracy, where the people are supposed to rule. Thus, as Huntington advised, 'The architects of power in the United States must create a force that can be felt but not seen. Power remains strong when it remains in the dark; exposed to the sunlight it begins to evaporate' (Huntington, 1981, p. 75).[13] For Veblen, that 'dark ... force' arises from the pooled institutional effects of absentee ownership and its chief institutional ally, 'ostensible', or absentee democracy.

THE CLOAKING OF POWER

First, the privacy of corporate operations constitutes an abstract but effective Berlin Wall that screens vast quantities of socially relevant economic information from public view. Much of private business activity is a 'dark ... force'; at least it is opaque to the light of democratic inquiry. 'The system of free private business enterprise is not merely a system of private ownership of property; it depends even more for its survival on the privacy of information. It is probably true that the business system could not survive a full public disclosure of its internal transactions, because publicity would lead to the discovery and development of so many conflicts that large-scale public intervention would be inescapable' (Schattschneider, 1960, p. 12).[14]

On the other side of this informational Berlin Wall, key operations of the democratic state have themselves grown less visible. For the US, 'much of the structure of secrecy' currently in place settled in during the early days of World War I, only to be strengthened by World War II, the Cold War and now a global 'War on Terror'. 'A record 15.6 million documents were classified' in 2004 alone, 'nearly double the number in 2001, according to the federal Information Security Oversight Office.' This secretive habit 'shows no sign of receding', having 'become our characteristic mode of governance in the executive branch' (*New York Times*, 3 July 2005; Moynihan, 1998, pp. 2, 84, 214).[15]

Not only has secrecy become a predictable feature of bureaucracies in all spheres of the state; a continuous sales effort by elected officials, from the president on down, exhausts media coverage of politics with official statements and staged events, obscuring the inner workings of power. The vast preponderance of daily news coverage, for example, 'is directly attributable to such official propaganda efforts', while 'less than 1 percent of all news stories' is 'based on the reporter's own analysis' (Bennett, 2001, pp. 142–3). In effect, for a Veblenian analysis of democracy, the complicity of media in the secrecy and stagecraft of politics is a central mechanism of the American variant of exploit. But most fundamentally, the very design of 'ostensible democracy' is, at bottom, that of an absentee democracy, an ostensibly representative government from which most citizens voluntarily remove themselves for all purposes except to cast a vote, and about half the citizenry does not even bother to do that much, even in presidential elections.

Veblen's idea of 'ostensible democracy' points to the fact that the most important distinction in US politics is between the tiny class of those Veblen called 'substantial citizens', who dominate the immediate circles of influence in the state with their class prestige and wealth, and the rest of the population of insubstantial citizens, who depend on virtual representation for such muted voice as they have in the political system. In effect, the relationship between absentee ownership and absentee democracy forms a system of dual citizenship, which serves two political systems that really function in entirely different ways: an absentee public democracy, based on media, for insubstantial citizens, and a highly responsive quasi-private oligarchy, heavily but by no means exclusively based on cash contributions, for the substantial ones. In this way, Veblen's model clearly anticipated a central conclusion of Murray Edelman's classic formulation: the 'distinction between politics as a spectator sport and political activity as utilized by organized groups to get quite specific, tangible benefits for themselves' (Edelman, 1964, p. 5). In short, the phenomenon of absenteeism has radically different implications in economy and state.

In the economy, Veblen emphasized, absentee owners disengage themselves from personal contact with industry and tangible property, invoking paper claims to draw real profits. Absentee ownership defines the legitimate economic power to exploit labor and technology. But remoteness has completely opposite implications in democracy. There it reflects weakness, not strength. When the institutions of representative democracy effectively exclude working-class people from interior operations of the state, citizens relinquish their place in political space to two much narrower circles. There are the lobbyists, lawyers and advocates of the absentee owners, the party officials and political cadres of 'the substantial citizens', who occupy the corridors of power in Washington, as well as locales near every state capitol and town hall. There these 'bailiffs' of business join the formally elected public officials, establishing relationships with politicians whose campaigns and careers they fund, and whose deepest values the politicians hold dear. Through lobbying, organized political representation and the party system, absentee owners use their class-based political power to establish permanent residence in the halls of government, where the vast economic majority of citizens have no comparable address. Absenteeism in the public sphere implies the status of an insubstantial citizenship, a kind of make-believe, virtual, pretended citizenship. An insubstantial citizen is an ordinary member of the ostensibly sovereign people, someone who lacks the high economic standing and economic power, the pecuniary respectability Veblen might say, that gives substance to citizenship, that automatically commands respect and acknowledgement in government, just as it does nearly everywhere else in a capitalist society.

In the words of one orthodox political scientist, Charles Lindblom, 'Any government official who understands the requirements of his position and the responsibilities that market-oriented systems throw on businessmen will therefore grant them a privileged position. He does not have to be bribed, duped or pressured to do so. He simply understands … that, to make the system work, government leadership must often defer to business leadership … Businessmen can not be left knocking at the doors of the political systems, they must be invited in' (Lindblom, 1977, p. 175; cf. also Lindblom, 1984, Block, 1984).

Insubstantial citizens are people who can be left 'knocking at the doors' of the state, who enjoy no 'privileged position' and whose exclusion from the inner-workings of government amounts to the political equivalent of the privacy of business enterprise.[16] Insubstantial citizens are connected to power vicariously, by the whole remarkable technology of democratic ostensibility. And through the symbolic politics of television screens, computer monitors, opinion polls and political advertising, they doubtless receive ample increments of intangible, psychic income. Political theorist Sheldon Wolin offers a modern rendition of Veblen's basic theme:

> Democracy as we know it in the self-styled 'advanced industrial democracies' has been constituted, that is, given forms, structure, boundaries. Constitutional democracy is fitted to a constitution. It is not democratic or democratized constitutionalism because it is democracy without the demos (the people) as actor. Its politics is based not, as its defenders allege, upon 'representative democracy' but on various representations of democracy: democracy as represented as public opinion polls, electronic town meetings and phone-ins and as votes. (Wolin, 1996, p. 34)

For Wolin, as for Veblen, the democratic states have become 'standard containers' of political life, 'each' according to 'its distinctive cultural tincture' (Wolin, 1996, pp. 33–5; Veblen, 1923 [1997], p. 440). Wherever it may be found, from the US to Britain, France, Germany or Japan, absentee democracy closely 'regulates the amount of democratic politics that is let in' (Wolin, 1996, p. 34). In these ways, as Veblen concluded a century ago, political power is decisively concentrated: 'a numerical minority – under ten percent of the population – constitutes a conclusive pecuniary majority' (Veblen, 1917, p. 154). The end result is that 'constitutional government has, in the main, become a department of the business organization ... guided by the advice of the business men ... Representative government means, chiefly, representation of business interests' (Veblen, 1904 [1978], pp. 287, 286).

Veblen acknowledges, as most political scientists would insist, that government does more than see to business needs; but whatever else government does, he immediately adds, tends to happen within an ideological framework that rarely, or with only the greatest difficulty, goes beyond what is acceptable to the substantial citizens. 'In most of its work, even in what is not ostensibly directed to business ends, it is under the surveillance of the business interests.'[17] Thus 'it seldom happens, if at all, that the government of a civilized nation will persist in a course of action detrimental or not ostensibly subservient to the interests of the more conspicuous body of the community's business men' (Veblen, 1904 [1978], pp. 286–7).[18] To gain public compliance with these implicit boundaries of democratic power, it helps greatly to have a constitutional system that faithfully embraces them.

LAW AND THE SABOTAGE OF DEMOCRATIC OPINION

Veblen heavily emphasized the conservative cast of the American constitutional framework. The constitution, he argued, not only establishes a regime of absentee democracy, which we like to call representative government, it also affects how people think about economic life and institutions and the proper purposes of democratic power. Much of this effect is obvious, support for private property, for example; but the constitution's silence on other economic matters also has major political and ideological consequences. It is of more than passing interest, for example, that the Constitution ignores the subject of economic need, turns a blind eye to basic facts of industry and work, and effectively legitimates private economic coercion. For Veblen, the Constitution's indifference to human needs, blindness to industry and tolerance for monetary coercion radically limits the people's chance to use law as a means of economic change.

Before we explore this theme in a little more detail, it is important to stress one point. In Veblen's perspective, it is not the Constitution as a legal document that is so very important. He anticipated that business and state powers would find whatever legal affirmations they needed in compliant courts and responsive legislatures. He is more interested in how the Constitution gets into people's way of thinking about things. What matters is that the underlying population learns to venerate the constitution, imputing to it a kind of divine sanction that speaks to the way a good society is properly organized. Law helps to solidify connections in people's minds between absentee ownership and the seemingly eternal verities of economic life. Thus many people believe that what the Framers took to be natural, right and acceptable in 1787 is the beginning of wisdom for what ought to be done today. Two hundred-year-old pre-conceptions become today's eternal convictions. As Veblen put it, our 'principles of law and morals' are '"immemorially ancient" and "eternally right and good"', and have been 'ever since they became ingrained by habit and presently reduced to documentary statement in modern times ... from A.D. 1776 or 1787, according as one may prefer to see it' (Veblen, 1923 [1997], p. 15). After all, even liberals, who insist that judges should interpret the constitution in response to evolving needs and conditions, think in terms of sacred constitutional principles that emanate from what Veblen liked to call 'the day before yesterday' (Tribe, 1978, 1990). In short, the importance of the Constitution is that its once-upon-a-time historical norms and ideas enter into public consciousness as universal, natural norms, establishing what most people take to be the legitimate legal boundaries of respectable economic thought. Consider industry first.

As far as the economy is concerned, the Constitution elaborates rules that protect the conduct of private business and financial relations, but it says next to nothing about labor, work or the technological factors and resources whose control by business is the core of its power in society. Business can legitimately and freely sabotage production – under-utilize capacity, shut plants, postpone the introduction of socially useful technologies, prolong social dependence on dangerous or inefficient industrial processes, abuse the environment, fire workers – in part because the Constitution envisions economic life as a set of business and property relationships, not as the control of society's industrial resources. The basic law's focus on securing private property and 'the obligations of contract' subordinates the task of how to make sure that industry is used to promote 'the general welfare'.[19] It is worth emphasizing that the concept of human labor is nowhere even mentioned in the Constitution, except to sanction the slave trade until 1808, and to give southern states rights to count their slaves as three-fifths of a person for purposes of 'representation' (Wills, 2003).

Then again, the Constitution does not mention business corporations or absentee ownership. But once corporations became major economic actors in the post-Civil War era, lawyers, legislators and judges carved out special, highly protected niches for corporate enterprise, endowing the new business institution with artificial personhood, including an array of rights and privileges that allowed corporations to swing their economic powers with far greater force than any biological person ever could. That American law saw fit to create a category of fractional personhood for a whole class of real human beings, only later to endow a whole category of impersonal institutions with full artificial personhood, speaks volumes about political connections between law and power.[20]

Much the same can be said about relations between the basic law and economic needs. That 'no person may be deprived of life, liberty or property without due process of law' is a familiar and sacred constitutional rule. But the principle carries the defect of its virtue. The Constitution may prohibit physical coercion between persons, but it does not forbid some people from keeping others from use of resources they may need to survive. That is, it nowhere addresses itself to the problem of economic power, the 'power to withhold from others what they need' (Commons, 1924 [1968], p. 52). To the contrary, its security for private property protects precisely the power to deprive and exclude. The Constitution recognizes rights to claim ownership of the means to satisfy others' economic needs, but it does not even broach the question of those economic needs as a matter worthy of legal notice or protection. Business ownership has standing in the eyes of the law; economic needs do not. Like technology, human economic needs are not 'a legal metaphysically competent reality' (Veblen, 1904 [1978], p. 276). They are bracketed by the constitutional system, their satisfaction, like control of the industrial system, essentially sub-contracted to the corporate persons that control industry (ibid. p. 278).[21]

Veblen wants us to appreciate the law for what it teaches us to ignore. But this is not only an ideological question. Coercion is involved too. Constitutional and statutory law place limits on physical coercion in democratic society; but the law deploys its limits very selectively. State officials may not use force against individuals without a showing of 'due process of law'. And individuals may not use force against each other, except in self-defense. But that same law protects the freedom and power of absentee owners routinely to charge people whatever the traffic will bear to meet their elemental economic needs. In effect, when it comes to basic human needs, the power to deprive is the power to compel.

Coercion here is not expressed at gunpoint, but in the experience of hunger, homelessness or lack of health care that drives people to work for whatever wages the traffic will bear to assure that they and their families survive. In this sense, the law supports economic power to coerce and deprive much more than it protects people from the pressure of economic coercion, especially poorer people, who find it difficult at best to meet their needs through the price system. Indeed, 'such coercion' is 'in point of legal reality, no coercion' at all, even in 'cases where the pressure is severe enough to result in insolvency, sickness, or death' (ibid., p. 276). In American law, violence is prohibited, but 'pecuniary pressure can not be barred' (ibid., p. 274).

As powerful as the democratic state is, Veblen wants to remind us of how much coercive power society tolerates through the normal workings of market institutions. In fact, most of the coercion organized into domestic life is exerted by business, outside the state, legally displaced to a price system, whose obligations must never be taken lightly, especially not in pecuniary America.[22] It rarely occurs to most people to question how the legal presumptions of business enterprise govern everyday life, or how 'the life process taken impersonally' is affected or thwarted by the law's 'pecuniary bias' (Veblen, 1899b [1979], p. 99; Veblen, 1904 [1978], pp. 269–84). In this view, which can seem virtually natural to a people who have learned to believe it, it is proper to treat coercion as a political, not an economic, fact. In contrast with the governmental realm, where law and force control us, the economy and marketplace are veritable free fire zones. But as much as the market's opportunistic freedom invites optimism, its real workings can also invite cynicism, hard-boiled attitudes toward life that are no less a vital piece of the American democratic sentiment.

OPPORTUNISM AND THE SENTIMENT OF EVASION

Americans believe in business, but Veblen did not think they were completely naïve, for their belief in business is stiffened by cynical appreciation of the way they think the world really works.[23] Americans' belief in the system can be tough-minded, to a fault. Veblen sensed that Americans are much less captivated by economic theories than by hopes to make a fast buck, feeling there is little wrong in cutting a few corners to get something for nothing. It is not that the work ethic, patriotic loyalty and religious and moral feeling do not have solid foundations in the culture. They do. It is just that the prevailing norms of civic virtue and religious righteousness do not necessarily inhibit other less flattering forms of behavior. For Veblen, the sense of tolerance of evasion lends a kind of amoral uplift to popular endurance of business and state power.

Cynicism and opportunism were, for Veblen, peculiarly important factors in the American case. In an economy dominated by giant corporations, whose connections to the state confer access and advantages unavailable to small business and workers, 'the little guy' often understands that the roots of inequality lie less in hard-earned moral virtues than in questionable patterns of influence. 'It's not what you know,' after all, 'it's who you know'.

In that context, then, if big business buys influence and reaps the rewards, if politicians live high on the hog, then average folks deserve chances to seize their own advantages in their own way. Civility and honesty are all right as far as they go, but 'nice guys finish last' and 'you do what you have to do'. In the classic phrase of machine politician George Washington Plunkitt, 'I seen my opportunities and I took 'em' (Riordon, 1963, p. 3). 'Honest graft' is there to be had – and so you take it! That is the American way.[24]

Veblen took this aggressive, amoral aspect of the culture more seriously than any other social scientist of his time, or today, for that matter. In their cynical opportunism, Veblen suggests, Americans forged a doubling of meaning that wrapped legality and extra-legality, morality and amorality, into complex webs of behavior that sully the prevailing norms even as they reinforce them. In effect, Americans sacrifice the progressive implications of insubordination when they adopt wily and aggressive forms of it, that feed off, rather than challenge, competitive emulation. People accept that fair play, equal opportunity and rule of law are less than real, that 'life is not fair'. They see through the illusions, or think they do. Hardened insight can often then become a justification for conduct at the obscure, blurry margins of legality and morality. Emulation of the successful embraces a willingness to play as hard as the powerful. Americans can cope with the pressures of living in a highly competitive, emulative culture by letting its very unfairness and injustice become tacit justification for their own playing fast and loose with rules whose legitimacy they accept, but whose fairness they question.[25] But ugly moral implications also permeate this opportunistic atmosphere of American hopes, for embedded in the opportunism of seizure is a learned tolerance for habits of predation that affected moral sensibilities in ways that would pay dividends of support for imperial ventures (Veblen, 1923 [1997], pp. 170–71).

WAR, THE STATE AND DEMOCRACY

Given the above, it is easy to see why many critics have insisted that Veblen's theory of politics pays too much attention to business influence and not enough to the state and politics in themselves. But such complaints do insufficient justice to the breadth of Veblen's thinking about the state, particularly about its warlike proclivities.

While Veblen gave ample credit to business power in foreign and defense policy, he also recognized that executive and military establishments had their own vested interests in maintaining warlike postures. He saw how they could very well generate their own political motivations for war, reasons centered on quests for demonstrating executive power and military ascendancy in international relations. These political forces were so strong, in fact, that they held the potential to generate an accelerating rate of military expansion and political ambition, one that could well bankrupt the economy, as the Soviet Union discovered when it could not keep up with US military spending in the 1980s (Veblen, 1904 [1978], pp. 292–301).

Most important, Veblen warned, when democratic leaders pursue militarily aggressive policies, underlying populations would be slow to resist. Leaders could count on the loyal sentiments of their underlying populations, who would, Veblen expected, be all too generous in sending ample numbers of their young people to kill or be killed on the state's behalf. *The Nature of Peace* offers a remarkably clear set of political theorems concerning the relation of war and democratic sentiment. Before we look at his theory of the warfare state, it may be useful to list several of Veblen's theorems as an introduction to the main thrust of his thinking on the state. These include the following predictions:

1. 'Once a warlike enterprise has been entered upon ... it will have the cordial support of popular sentiment even if it is a patently aggressive war.'
2. 'Any politician who succeeds in embroiling his country in a war, however nefarious, becomes a popular hero and is reputed to be a wise and righteous statesman, at least for the time being.'
3. 'Since the ethical values in any given international contest are substantially of the nature of after-thought or accessory, they may be safely left on one side in any endeavor to understand or account for any given outbreak of hostilities.'
4. 'Any warlike enterprise ... must have the moral sanction of the community, or of an effective majority of the community. It consequently becomes the first concern of the warlike statesman to put his moral force in train for the adventure on which he is bent' (Veblen, 1917, pp. 22–3).

These theorems indicate how predatory inclinations and imputations of heroic formidability can engulf popular democracy with pretensions to justice and righteousness in war. That underlying populations will rally to leaders who wave the bloody shirt underlined Veblen's gravest doubts for the future of democracy. In effect, democracy had trouble shedding its sentimental affections for the militaristic state, the violent patriotic loyalties it engendered and the state's proclivities for war.

As we have seen, aggression, exploit and predation were the hallmarks of barbarism, the sources of honor for military and soldierly virtues once 'the fight' had 'become the dominant note in the current theory of life' (Veblen, 1899b [1979], p. 19). For centuries, men fought wars for their villages and clans, for their city-states and for imperial powers; they fought as warriors in feudal armies and as crusaders for God. War manifested itself in all the various political institutions that preceded the first stirrings of the modern state, in the late Middle Ages. The modern state did not by any means create the problem of war, but Veblen recognized that its wider geographic scope, larger population, increased economic wealth and growing technical prowess decisively changed its conditions and consequences.[26]

The same handicraft era patterns of work that engendered the masterless man and his liberal values also endowed the jealous monarchs of early modern Europe with enormously greater powers of administration and destruction than any previous generation of warlords had been able to marshal. These changes allowed the evolving states 'to extend an effectual coercion over larger distances and over larger aggregations of population and wealth; it became practicable, mechanically, to swing a larger political aggregation and to hold it together in closer coordination than before'. Indeed, technical progress in human powers of destruction now exceeded 'in boldness of conception all the traceable improvements' in military power 'by all the warlike peoples of classical antiquity and all the fighting aggregations of Asia and Africa, from the beginning of the bronze age down to modern times' (Veblen, 1914 [1990], pp. 269–70). If the modern state did not invent war, it dramatically aggravated its consequences for the human race.

From its beginnings in the waning days of medieval society, the newly evolving states were characteristically dynastic, developed and ruled in the interests of royal families, whose competitive sensibilities were sharp, personal and well formed. Veblen is clear about the driving dynamic of state formation, and it was not fundamentally an economic one. 'State-making was a competitive enterprise of war and politics, in which the rival princely or dynastic establishments, all and several, each sought its own advantage at the cost of any whom it might concern.' Admittedly, these advantages included 'unearned incomes' for the civil, military and religious hierarchies that coalesced with the king. But the main 'aim of it all' was not wealth, it was 'princely dominion and prestige', the power and status ambitions of kings and princes (Veblen, 1923 [1997], p. 22).

With this observation, Veblen stakes a claim to one of his most important political themes. Political leaders of states tend to emulate and compete with their political rivals in other states, not primarily with the holders of domestic economic power within their own state. In the late nineteenth century, for example, dynastic states, such as Germany and Japan, stimulated domestic capitalist development as a way of strengthening their industrial base for military reasons. At the same time, the ostensible democracies, such as England and the US, fused their economic and military powers for imperial ends. But the collective penchant for war in this situation reflected first of all the political relations of these states in the international state system. Political emulation was a main motor of international grievances and imperial conflicts. When today's neo-conservative thinkers, Paul Wolfowitz and William Kristol, for example, speak of how the US must show its power at all points on the globe; when they urge the invasion of Iraq to show how the US can export democracy the way it exports movies; they evidence just the kind of ambition, the expansive expressiveness of power, that Veblen saw at the heart of exploit (Kagan and Kristol, 2000; Halper and Clarke, 2004).

Business interests surely have interests in imperial expansion, interests in access to markets, resources, cheap labor, not to mention profitable defense contracts (Veblen, 1904 [1978], pp. 292–300). But Veblen emphasized that the 'Concert of nations is a Concert of Powers, and it is only as a Power that any nation plays its part in the concert, all the while that "power" here means eventual warlike force.'[27] In short, nation-states have their own political reasons for war making, such as 'national jealousy', or, more specifically, the 'dynastic ambition of warlike statesmen' (Veblen, 1917, pp. 4, 25). And once warlike conditions take hold, these ancient political and military motivations and interests can assume a life of their own, with the result that political forces overtake even the restraint of economic rationality and business power. Once this happens, 'the objective end of warlike endeavor necessarily shifts from business advantage to dynastic ascendancy and courtly honor' (Veblen, 1904 [1978], p. 300), that is, to interests in the power claims of the state itself, especially those of its chief executive and the higher ranks of the military (Mills, 1956).[28]

In this respect and despite whatever other differences might distinguish democratic from dynastic or authoritarian states, Veblen held that democratic and dynastic states represented 'divergent variants rather than opposites', systems whose warlike character was their unifying or common feature (Veblen, 1917, p. 10). As Veblen's political theorems suggest, democracy may have repudiated the forms of absolute monarchy, but its loyalties to chief executives resonate with imperial habits. Thus, if democracies continue to claim the sovereign powers to make war and to demand the allegiance of their citizens, loyalty is a claim 'on which argument is not tolerated'. And on account of this 'civic duty – which still has much of the color of feudal allegiance', democratic states may coerce, control and direct 'the actions of the citizen or subject', including, of course, conscription of individuals for military service, taxation of their wealth to finance military preparation and denial of democratic access to information ostensibly relevant to national security, the very information essential to popular evaluation of defense and war policy. In all these respects, the ostensible democracies claim an 'eminent domain' over the lives and property of their populations, 'an undivided usufruct of their underlying populations and all their ways and works' (Veblen, 1923 [1997], p. 23). It is in these fundamentally common war-related respects that democratic states share a political genus with dynastic states and a comparable willingness to follow their leaders.

Nor is the impact of war politics restricted to foreign relations. The internal political relations of democracy will tend to function within the hostile terms and conditions of the international system. The more political leaders aim to secure their nation's status in that system, the more likely it is that the demands of 'external politics (war and diplomacy)' will 'take precedence' over 'its domestic concerns'. Through the behavior of their commanders-in-chief, emulative and military aspects of the state will impose themselves, more or less directly, on the conduct, character and even the ethics of domestic politics (ibid., p. 29). Those aspects of political behavior that breed success in inter-state competition (guile, deception and secrecy) will gradually bleed back into the practices and expectations of domestic politics, especially perhaps in such opportunistic cultures as America's, where playing by business rules already includes a wide berth for 'sharp practice'. In fact, as different forms of exploit, business and politics mirror each other's moral agnosticism. The amoral aspects of business exploit reflect nothing so much as the hard-headed dispositions of international politics and vice versa. Like corporate capitalism, but even more so, 'the administration of external politics, being an enterprise in chicane and coercion, is necessarily furtive, runs forever on sharp practice, carefully withholds "information that might be useful to the enemy", and habitually gives out information with intent to deceive' (ibid.).

The demands of such politics will thus tend to call forth political leaders notably gifted with abilities to play by these rules and who, by habit and experience, will find it increasingly difficult to draw firm distinctions between the proprieties of behavior suited to domestic as opposed to global politics. As a result, codes of acceptable political conduct in the two domains will tend to coalesce, with the result that 'any effectual difference between honest politics and corrupt politics' will, like that between democratic and dynastic states, come to a 'difference of degree, not a difference of kind' (ibid., p. 30).

That successful business executives will have displayed such skills makes them an excellent source of candidates for national leadership in foreign and defense policy, a role that they have indeed frequently played; although their preoccupations with profits and corporate politics make it useful for democracy to cultivate a more or less distinct pool of leaders habituated to the demands of politics (Block, 1984; Draper, 1977, pp. 321–6). Political conduct being what it is, those unfitted by temperament or morals to its amoral imperatives will most likely fail to reach the heights of executive power in the first place. Thus 'By selective elimination of artless persons the personnel of official life comes to be made up, in the main, of such persons as will feel at home in the spiritual twilight of official life, by native gift or by spiritual training' (Veblen, 1923 [1997], p. 30).

Veblen's prediction is plain enough. American democracy will embrace leaders who stand hard and fast for God, country, freedom and business enterprise, except insofar as they must abandon scruples in order to win. Patriotic and religious loyalties will assure democratic tolerance for what must be done, at least for a time. The underlying population, trained to suffer the costs of patriotic loyalty with religious grace, will indeed suffer much. But as war hurts, there are limits, albeit indistinct, to the leaders' ability to convert popular energies to warlike ends. Suffering the weight of war and exploit, the underlying population might well come to remember that insubordination, rather than loyalty, is the vital principle of free institutions. As Veblen once observed, 'conditions of life' under the rule of warlike leaders and absentee owners 'will necessarily be an agency of unrest as touches the frame of mind' of the insubstantial citizens, on whom the burdens of empire chiefly fall (ibid., p. 5).

CONCLUSIONS

Politically speaking, it would be far from an understatement to say that Veblen is pessimistic about American democratic prospects. But his work is not hopeless. He acknowledges that the public might come to revalue peace and productiveness; it might yet learn to reject rationales and institutions of exploit, emulation and war. In *The Engineers and the Price System*, and in *The Theory of Business Enterprise* even earlier, Veblen speculated that technicians might lead a popular political movement to change the system. In *The Nature of Peace,* however, a book steeped in Veblen's surer sense of the political realities, he anticipated that such a movement, whether or not led by technicians, would have to take a firm stand, for ruling groups would doubtless use 'all the coercive agencies of law and order to uphold the ancient rights of ownership'. At that critical point, a 'recourse to forcible measures is ... scarcely open to question. History teaches that in such a quarrel the recourse has always been to force' (Veblen, 1917, pp. 363–5).

Veblen abhorred violence, but he was not naïve about the dynamics of social change either. Ultimately, his hope was that human beings would come to see the benefits of a humble industrial republic, one with little need for legitimation or apology to justify its violence, for 'it would be nothing to bluster or give off fumes about', just 'an unsanctified workday arrangement for the common use of industrial ways and means' (Veblen,

1923 [1997], p. 28). As we have seen throughout, Veblen looked to matter-of-fact sobriety, never to sentiment, as the source of democratic possibility. But it is hard not to conclude from his work that he believed sentiment was the more powerful force at work in politics.

Thus the central point cannot be avoided. Veblen's critique of American democracy cuts deep. As currently organized, understood and practiced, democracy adds up to a political system that pacifies the population, except to the extent that it activates the population for ruling-class purposes of emulative competition and patriotic loyalty. It plainly does not encourage citizens to identify themselves as an economic majority with interests in a peaceable industrial republic. With the underlying population more or less content in their roles as insubstantial citizens, loyal patriots and eager competitors, absentee owners and state officials can all the more efficiently convert popular energies to their own predatory purposes. In this sense, the American political system provides more for emulation than it does for representation. It encourages the people to identify much more with their political leaders than it compels those leaders to fight for popular interests against those of power and wealth.

In the end, for Veblen, American democracy is more a system of exploit than a system of self-government. Its basic ideological underpinnings are the deep-seated patterns of emulation, loyalty and opportunism that lead the ruled to identify with their rulers in defiance of their more sober interests in workmanship and peace, in a tranquil political economy of live and let live.

Emulation functions to keep citizens and workers dedicated to habits of mind and action that allow rulers to convert the fruits of their work into the profits and taxes that finance absentee ownership and war. Emulation, the people's identification with their rulers' canons of value, keeps them from recognizing themselves as an economic majority, one whose material interests diverge from those of their rulers. People who closely identify with the emulative values and patterns of behavior of their rulers will find it difficult to decipher clues to their independent political identity, clues that lie within their own generic needs as human beings, clues well-masked by the politics and rewards of emulation.

Veblen's exploration of the politics of emulation, the incipient compatibilities between capitalism, democracy, cynicism and war may well constitute his most valuable contribution to the study of American ideology and institutions. Challenging Lincoln's famous quip about the limits of popular manipulation – 'you can not fool all the people all the time' – Veblen observed that 'in a case where the people in question are sedulously fooling themselves all the time the politicians can come near achieving that ideal result' (ibid., p. 34).[29]

Here Veblen's view of democracy turns darkest, most ominous. It leads him to question the most fundamental premise of democracy itself: the self-knowledge of citizens and their capacity for insight into their own most basic human needs and relationships, not the least of which is peace. Closely identifying with the opportunistic sentiments of absentee ownership and the militant patriotism of the state, ordinary people lose a sober sense of themselves and their class. They learn to distrust possibilities for alternative forms of life, community, work and politics. Like that battered class of nineteenth-century America, the small farmers, many of today's workers end up being 'good losers ... gracefully accepting the turn of things', all the while continuing 'to count on meeting with better luck or making a shrewder play next time' (ibid., pp. 140–41).

For such reasons, Veblen concluded, 'The common man does not know himself.' In this alienation from self-knowledge, the chance for people to make democratic common cause withers. 'The American tradition stands in the way' (Veblen, 1919, pp. 174–5)

NOTES

1. Cited in Meier (1995), p. 68.
2. For example, voters with incomes between $30 000 and $50 000 split nearly evenly, 49 per cent for Bush, 50 per cent Kerry. Bush also pulled substantial votes, 42 per cent, from those with incomes between $15 000 and $30 000 as well as 40 per cent of the union vote. Bush won handily, if not surprisingly, among voters who attend church weekly (61 per cent), own guns (63 per cent) and among veterans (57 per cent). Finally, Bush won overwhelmingly among voters who were looking for a 'strong leader' (87 per cent) and who strongly approved of the war in Iraq (94 per cent). Clearly, George W. Bush won support from substantial numbers of conservative, religious, working-class people, who chose not to make economic interest or class identification a central focus of their vote. (For a summary of relevant data, see http://www.cnn.com/ELECTION/2004/pages/results/states/US/P/00/epolls.0.html.)
3. 'Dementia Praecox', an essay Veblen wrote in 1922, shows how close he thought American society had come to being a 'psychiatrical clinic'. Amidst the post-World War I witch-hunt for radicals, immigrants, socialists and pacifists, 'The logical faculty appears to have suffered a notable degree of prostration throughout the American community ... There is a visible lack of composure and logical coherence, both in what they believe and in what they are ready to do about it' (Veblen, 1899a [1964], pp. 429–30).
4. For Veblen's critique of Marxian conceptions of class struggle and class interest, see the essays on socialism and Marx in *The Place of Science in Modern Civilization* (1898 [1969], pp. 387–456).
5. Veblen especially emphasized purposefulness as a distinguishing quality of human beings, a sense of purpose that is intimately related to the instinct of workmanship, 'by force of which all futility of life or of action is distasteful to him' (Veblen, 1899a [1964], p. 80). That exploiters strive to control, through force and fraud, the purposes and energies of others, suggests how, for Veblen, this both subverts the fundamental humanity of the other and obstructs the chances for self-knowledge. If people do not control their own purposes, how can they control those of society? Veblen's theory of exploit points directly at a critique of democracy.

6. It is illuminating to recall in this context that the great realist political thinker, Hans Morgenthau, defined politics precisely in terms of the intensity of political conflict. See Scheuerman (1999, pp. 231–2). The American realist, E.E. Schattschneider, put it this way: 'The excitement of conflict communicates itself to the crowd. *This is the basic pattern of all conflict'* (1960, p. 2, original emphasis).

7. Such mastery may include capacities to invoke the aid and comfort of powerful divinities, spirits and gods. Thus Veblen believed that the earliest leisure and ruling classes were likely to have been priestly or clerical in character: religion, make-believe and power formed an early connection in the make-up of human institutions (see Veblen, 1914 [1990], pp. 155–9, Veblen, 1899b [1979], ch. 12).

8. Among the 'many impulses' and motives that shape human behavior, Veblen counted 'a strong bent to admire and defer to persons of achievement and distinction, as well as a workmanlike disposition to find merit in any work that serves the common good'. Over time, as ruling groups perpetuated their power, 'the distinction which is admired and deferred to' by underlying populations 'may often be nothing more to the point than a conventional investiture of rank attained by the routine of descent, as, e.g., a king, or by the routine of seniority, as, e.g., a prelate'. In other words, institutions, rituals and regalia can turn the imputation of prowess into a generalized property of class domination (Veblen, 1923 [1997], pp. 115–18, Veblen, 1899a [1964], pp. 90–91).

9. That powerful men still seek 'trophy wives' suggests something of the way such barbaric habits endure.

10. To be sure, an economic 'desire for added comfort and security from want is present as a motive at every stage of the process of accumulation'. But if the chief purpose of accumulation is to overcome want of 'subsistence or ... physical comfort', it is not clear why the rich keep on accumulating (Veblen, 1899b [1979], p. 32). After all, it is the absentee owners who ceaselessly push for more; who continue to exploit others' labor, even though their own needs for heightened comfort have long since been met. People who have accumulated vastly more than anyone can possibly need or use, who keep driving others to produce more for them, must have something other than comfort or economic values in mind. Indeed, Veblen concluded, the economic incentive 'of subsistence or ... physical comfort never plays a considerable part' in the race among the wealthy for more (Veblen, 1899b [1979], p. 26).

11. The great baseball pitcher Satchel Paige put Veblen's basic idea this way: 'Don't look back – something might be gaining on you.' Veblen understood what Paige was getting at, and it was emulation. Veblen argued that power has no choice but 'to look back'. The powerful must constantly 'look back', because they want others to covet their power, to reach for it themselves, to try and outdo the powerful at their own game. In this sense, competition, conflict and uncertainty are intrinsic features of emulation, just as they are of politics. The powerful wish above all to be emulated and envied by the less powerful, by competitors in the ruling class even more than by those of lesser rank. The point is not the things accumulated, but the imputed power signified by things. Or as the saying goes on Wall Street, money is just a way of keeping score – keeping score of what? – mastery of the market, the 'smart money', the competition!

12. In fact, in one of his earliest essays Veblen speculated that the potential scope of political democracy was so broad that it could become a model for the evolution of democratic socialism down the road (Veblen, 1898 [1969], pp. 387–408).

13. One well-connected Washington lobbyist closely echoes Huntington's point. Speaking of the interest groups that infuse Washington with their claims and with their money, he observed, 'A lobby is like a night flower: it thrives in the dark and dies in the sun' (Goldberg, 2005, p. 34).

14. As it is, estimates of the monetary costs of corporate crime run as high as a trillion dollars annually, but the overwhelming media focus on violence perpetrated by and against poor people helps greatly to minimize public sensitivities to business abuses (Winslow, 1999).

15. 'Government secrecy has reached a historic high by several measures, with federal departments classifying documents at the rate of 125 a minute as they create new

categories of semi-secrets bearing vague labels like "sensitive security information"' (*New York Times*, 3 July 2005).

16. Tony Kushner's play, *Angels in America*, includes a powerfully apt expression of this point. There, a fictionalized Roy Cohen, who in fact was among the most well-connected lawyers in American politics, having just been diagnosed with AIDS, rejects his doctor's claim that he is homosexual. Homosexuality, Cohen insists, is a label, that like all 'labels tells you one thing and one thing only: where does an individual so identified fit in the food chain, in the pecking order. Not ideology, or sexual taste, but something much simpler, clout ... Homosexuals are not men who sleep with other men. Homosexuals are men who in fifteen years of trying cannot get a puissant antidiscrimination bill through City Council. Homosexuals are men who know nobody and who nobody knows. Who have zero clout. Does this sound like me, Henry?' (Kushner, 1993–94, p. 45).

17. Veblen suggests that it is mainly through the budget process, heavily influenced by corporate and upper class resistance to taxation and rising levels of government spending, that the state is 'is kept within constitutional bounds'. 'The expediency of business enterprise is not questioned, whereas the expediency of an increase of princely power and dignity, with the incidental costs, may be questioned' (Veblen, 1904 [1978], p 285; Plotkin and Scheuerman, 1994). In short, rising levels of profit are widely regarded as an index of social health; increased levels of taxation and public spending are treated as warning signs of imminent economic stagnation. Were Veblen alive today, he would doubtless add that business surveillance of the regulatory process has become equally important to the restraint of unbusinesslike public policy. A major exception to this tendency concerns military spending, however, whose claims may even exceed the limits of business rationality. I will discuss this theme in the section on the warfare state below.

18. It is especially noteworthy that Veblen uses the term 'ostensible' in reference both to democracy and to the pro-business cast of public policy. Democracy is ostensibly democratic to the extent that it appears to express the will of the people as revealed in free elections. The state's commitment to the growth of business enterprise is no less ostensible, but there is little sense of fraud about it. For there is nothing duplicitous about democracy's 'solicitude' for business interests, because this 'solicitude is borne out by current public sentiment', as it reflects 'a naïve, unquestioning persuasion abroad among the people to the effect that, in some occult way, the material interests of the populace coincide with the pecuniary interests of those business men who live within the scope of the same set of governmental contrivances' (Veblen, 1904 [1978], p. 286). So, 'barring a slight and intermittent mutter of discontent, this arrangement has ... the cordial approval of popular sentiment' (Veblen, 1917, pp. 154–5).

19. The Constitution does give Congress the power to regulate inter-state commerce, of course, but it does not provide any criteria that indicate how 'commerce' must function to meet terms of social responsibility. In fact, the Constitution mainly sweeps issues of work and industry under the rug (Veblen, 1904 [1978], p. 275). In this way, it resembles what Veblen considered one of the hallmarks of barbarism. Just as leisure class barbarians shoved industry and workers into the obscure background of their aristocratic culture, the Constitution reduces industry and labor to secondary details of law.

20. The irony is even more striking when we remember that the source of the law's personifica- tion of the corporation was the very same amendment (the fourteenth) that was designed ostensibly to secure 'the equal protection of the laws' to the newly freed slaves (Foner, 1998, chs 5–6, Samuels and Miller, 1987, Horwitz, 1992).

21. As Veblen adds, the 'claims and circumstances' of workers 'do not fit into the legal framework of business-as-usual; which is their misfortune, if not their fault. The legal validity of any of those demands and perquisites for which they contend is of slight and dubious nature', that is to say in comparison with those of corporate persons and their absentee owners. All of which helps to explain why a 'few hundred or a few thousand absentee owners acting in collusion as stockholders' could act without fear of conspiracy charges, such as those that were regularly brought against early twentieth-century workers who dared take the 'concerted action' of a strike (Veblen, 1923 [1997], p. 433).

22. Indeed, 'nowhere else,' Veblen observed, 'has the sacredness of pecuniary obligations so permeated the common sense of the community, and nowhere else does pecuniary obligation come so near to being the only form of obligation that has the unqualified sanction of current common sense. Here, as nowhere else, do obligations and claims of the most diverse kinds, domestic, social and civil, tend to take the pecuniary form and admit of being fully discharged on a monetary valuation' (Veblen, 1904 [1978], p. 272).

23. Peter Sloterdijk's *Critique of Cynical Reason* (1987) is an important work that bears consideration in this context. Sloterdijk's conception of cynicism as 'enlightened false consciousness' (deriving from his study of Weimar-era Germany) bears a different historical stamp and a different orientation to political enlightenment than Veblen's. As 'that state of consciousness that follows after naïve ideologies and their enlightenment' (p. 5) have been exhausted, its reference point is the dissolution of radical hopes in the twentieth century. Veblen's conception, rooted in a distinctive American brand of barely regulated nineteenth-century capitalism, situates its cynicism in a petty bourgeois culture of opportunism, one endemic to a society whose faith in the main chance enables an opportunistic cynicism that reflects faith in the future, a hard-bitten faith oftentimes, but one that continues to see its opportunities. For a study of Sloterdijk's theme as it worked out in a depleted American industrial town, see Dandaneau (1996). In the instance of Flint, Michigan, worker acceptance of the new 'reality' of global competition and 'dependent de-industrialization' displayed a harsh, grim edge, with considerably less of Veblen's belief in luck as a possible way out. Also in contrast with Veblen, Samuel P. Huntington's (1981) perspective on cynicism in American political culture claims that it grows out of a deep-seated liberal aversion to power in a society that cannot dispense with power. For Huntington, cynicism has political foundations, becoming a way by which Americans learn to tolerate the gap between the imperatives of power and the romance of liberty. Veblen's view is quite different. For him, far from shunning power, Americans embrace it as the ulterior motive of their economic liberties. Cynicism, for him, reflects the pressure of living under a system of economic opportunities that is interwoven with economic inequalities and coercions.

24. 'They are sitting out there waiting to give you their money,' shouts the star real estate salesman to an inept sales crew in David Mamet's film, *Glengarry Glen Ross* (1992), a work pervaded by the theme of pecuniary pressure in America. 'Are you man enough to take it?' Or, in Veblen's version of the same dictum: why not 'take a chance with the legalities and moralities ... when there is easy money in sight and no one is looking' (Veblen, 1923 [1997], p. 158).

25. Such conduct has its own psychic satisfactions; at least there is the knowing sense that one is not a sucker, that one will not be had. That 'self-preservation knows no moral law' is one of Veblen's working principles of everyday life in fiercely competitive America. It is not that all Americans are crooks, Veblen suggests, but a little crookedness is part of the price of success, a reasonable price to be paid for reaping whatever advantages can be grabbed at each niche of the social order. Because aspirations to 'gain in wealth or in rank' are 'imperative and ubiquitous', taking liberties is part of what it takes to succeed. As Veblen captures the conventional wisdom, 'It will not do for an honest man to let the rogues get away with the best.' 'A sound principle' for people intoxicated by the sweet smell of success is to take the main chance 'and, if worse comes to worse, let the courts determine tomorrow, under protest, just what the law allows, and therefore what the moral code exacts'. Besides, 'the courts will be wise enough to see that the law is not allowed to ... impede ... business-as-usual' (Veblen, 1923 [1997], pp. 157–8). For instance, a newspaper advertisement recently placed by a litigation consulting firm speaks directly to the kind of strategic cynicism Veblen has in mind, not to mention the aggressiveness of salesmanship, and the confusion of ownership and power. Beneath the photograph of a stern looking judge appears the following promise: 'The judge may rule the courtroom. But you'll own it.' Further below, in smaller print, the promise is amplified: 'Dominate opposing counsel. Be persuasive. Secure the verdict. We uncover key strategies, craft compelling arguments and develop convincing visual presentations. DOAR helps the nation's most prominent law firms and their clients achieve success in

their critical high-stakes cases. DOAR. Because winning matters most.' Adding to the ad's punch is the fact that it appeared on the same page as news stories detailing the recent acquittal of Michael Jackson and other celebrities in a series of highly publicized trials (*The New York Times*, 15 June, 2005, p. A14).

26. For more recent discussions of this subject, see McNeill (1982), O'Connor (1989), Creveld (1991).

27. Although I cannot explore here the implications of a Veblenian approach to the current situation, clearly the early twenty-first century no longer features what Veblen meant by the 'concert of powers'. No current state, after all, with the possible longer-term exception of China, seems remotely prepared to compete with the US in military spending and development, although the potential nuclear prowess of such states as Iran and North Korea suggests that state rivalry has not gone completely into abeyance. Still, most industrial states have become civilianized in the sense that their military budgets are dwarfed by their social budgets, indeed, the same is true for the US. Principal threats to global capital and its US headquarters now stem from state-less groups, especially, in recent years, from radical Islamic sects. Suffice it to say, the current moment can be defined in Veblenian terms as a conflict between two essentially atavistic movements: on the one hand, religious zealots, who advocate return to a radicalized, fundamentalist pre-modernism, and demand removal of the US and its western allies, including Israel, from Islamic lands; on the other, a militarized US state, whose policies have been conceived by neo-conservative policy intellectuals, unabashed in their confidence in the uses of US military and state power to re-order the world. One side wishes to organize its version of society on the basis of religious sentiment and coercion, the other celebrates state military power as the foundation of global democracy. (See Castells, 1997; Creveld, 1991, 1999, Harvey, 2003, 2005; Halper and Clark, 2004; Anonymous, 2004.)

28. For an illuminating discussion of the way leading US military officers have tried to rein in the ambitions of militant chief executives, see Bacevich (2005).

29. As John Diggins notes, 'In treating cultural ideas as the unconscious foundations of social life', Veblen anticipated the Gramscian notion of 'hegemony ... a phenomenon made all the more perplexing because it involves man's subjugation to ideas rather than to power and coercion'. I would disagree with Diggins' formulation to this extent: for Veblen, 'subjugation to ideas' is precisely a form of power (Diggins, 2000, p. 105).

REFERENCES

Anonymous (2004), *Imperial Hubris, Why the West is Losing the War on Terror*, Washington, DC: Brassey's Inc.

Bacevich, Andrew J. (2005), *The New American Militarism, How Americans Are Seduced by War*, New York: Oxford University Press.

Baran, Paul (1957), 'The theory of the leisure class', *Monthly Review*, 9(3–4), 83–91.

Bennett, W. Lance (2001), *News, The Politics of Illusion*, 4th edn, New York: Addison, Wesley, Longman.

Block, Fred (1984), 'The ruling class does not rule: notes on the Marxist theory of the state', in Thomas Ferguson and Joel Rogers (eds), *The Political Economy: Readings in the Politics and Economics of American Public Policy*, Armonk, NY: M.E. Sharpe, pp. 32–46.

Castells, Manuel (1997), *The Information Age: Economy, Society and Culture, Vol. 2: The Power of Identity*, Malden, MA: Blackwell.

Commons, John R. (1924), *The Legal Foundations of Capitalism*, reprinted 1968, Madison: University of Wisconsin Press.

Creveld, Martin Van (1991), *The Transformation of War*, New York: Free Press.

Creveld, Martin Van (1999), *The Rise and Decline of the State*, New York: Cambridge University Press.

Dandaneau, Steven P. (1996), *A Town Abandoned: Flint, Michigan Confronts De-Industrialization*, Albany: State University of New York.

Diggins, John P. (2000), *Thorstein Veblen, Theorist of the Leisure Class*, Princeton: Princeton University Press. Originally published (1978) as *The Bard of Savagery*, New York: The Seabury Press.

Draper, Hal (1977), *Karl Marx's Theory of Revolution, Volume I: State and Bureaucracy*, New York: Monthly Review Press.

Dobrianksi, Lev E. (1957), *Veblenism, A New Critique*, Introduction by James Burnham, Washington, DC: Public Affairs Press.

Dugger, William M. (1984), 'Veblen and Kropotkin on human evolution', *Journal of Economic Issues*, **18**(4), 971–85.

Edelman, Murray J. (1964), *The Symbolic Uses of Politics*, Urbana, IL.: University of Illinois Press.

Edsall, Thomas (1984), *The New Politics of Inequality*, New York: Norton.

Edsall, Thomas with Mary D. Edsall, (1991), *Chain Reaction, The Impact of Race, Rights and Taxes on American Politics*, New York: Norton.

Ferguson, Thomas and Joel Rogers (1986), *Right Turn: the Decline of the Democrats and the Future of American Politics*, New York: Hill and Wang.

Foner, Eric (1998), *The Story of American Freedom*, New York: Norton.

Frank, Thomas (2004), *What's the Matter With Kansas? How Conservatives Won the Heart of America*, New York: Metropolitan Books.

Friedman, Milton with the assistance of Rose D. Friedman (1962), *Capitalism and Freedom*, Chicago: University of Chicago Press.

Gilder, George F. (1981), *Wealth and Poverty*, New York: Basic Books.

Goldberg, Jeffery (2005), 'Real insiders', *The New Yorker*, **34**(4), 34–40.

Halper, Stefan and Jonathan Clarke (2004), *America Alone, The Neo-Conservatives and the Global Order*, Cambridge: Cambridge University Press.

Harvey, David (2003), *The New Imperialism*, New York: Oxford University Press.

Harvey, David (2005), *A Brief History of Neoliberalism*, New York: Oxford University Press.

Hayek, Friedrich A. (1945), *The Road to Serfdom*, Introduction by John Chamberlin, Chicago: University of Chicago Press.

Hodder, H.J. (1956), 'The political ideas of Thorstein Veblen', *Canadian Journal of Economics and Political Science*, **27**(3), 347–57.

Horwitz, Morton J. (1992), *The Transformation of American Law, 1870–1960: The Crisis of Legal Orthodoxy*, New York: Oxford University Press.

Huntington, Samuel P. (1981), *American Politics: The Promise of Disharmony*, Cambridge, MA: Harvard University Press.

Kagan, Robert and William Kristol (eds) (2000), *Present Dangers, Crisis and Opportunity in American Foreign and Defense Policy*, San Francisco: Encounter Books.

Kristol, Irving (1978), *Two Cheers for Capitalism*, New York: Basic Books.

Kushner, Tony (1993–94), *Angels in America, a Gay Fantasia on National Themes, Part One*, New York: Theatre Communications Group.

Lerner, Max (1948), *The Portable Veblen*, edited and Introduction by Max Lerner, New York: Viking.

Lindblom, Charles E. (1977), *Politics and Markets: The World's Political Economic Systems*, New York: Basic Books.

Lindblom, Charles E. (1984), 'The market as prison', in Thomas Ferguson and Joel Rogers (eds), *The Political Economy: Readings in the Politics and Economics of American Public Policy*, Armonk, NY: M.E. Sharpe, pp. 3–11.

Lynd, Robert S. (1956), 'Power in American society as resource and problem', in Arthur Kornhauser (ed.), *Problems of Power in American Democracy*, Detroit: Wayne State University Press, pp. 1–45.

Mamet, David (1992), *Glengarry Glen Ross*, film, James Foley, Director, New Line Cinema.

McNeill, William (1982), *The Pursuit of Power: Technology, Armed Force and Society Since AD 1000*, Chicago: University of Chicago Press.

Meier, Heinrich (1995), *Carl Schmitt and Leo Strauss: The Hidden Dialogue; including Strauss' Notes on Schmitt's Concept of the Political and Three Letters from Strauss to Schmitt*, trans. J. Harvey Lomax, Foreword by Joseph Cropsey, Chicago: University of Chicago Press.

Mills, C. Wright (1956), *The Power Elite*, New York: Oxford University Press.

Moynihan, Daniel Patrick (1998), *Secrecy, The American Experience*, Introduction by Richard Gid Powers, New Haven, CT: Yale University Press.

O'Connor, Robert L. (1989), *Of Arms and Men, a History of War, Aggression, and Weapons*, New York: Oxford University Press.

Patsouras, Louis (2004), *Thorstein Veblen and the American Way of Life*, Montreal: Black Rose Books.

Plotkin, Sidney and William E. Scheuerman (1994), *Balanced-Budget Conservatism and the Fiscal Crisis*, Boston: South End.

Riordon, William L. (1963), *Plunkitt of Tammany Hall, a Series of Very Plain Talks on Very Practical Politics*, Introduction by Arthur Mann, New York: E.P. Dutton.

Samuels, Warren J. and Arthur S. Miller (eds) (1987), *Corporations and Society, Power and Responsibility*, New York: Greenwood.

Schattschneider, E.E. (1960), *The Semisovereign People, A Realist's View of Democracy in America*, New York: Holt, Rinehart and Winston.

Scheuerman, William E. (1999), *Carl Schmitt, The End of Law*, Lanham, MD: Rowman & Littlefield.

Sloterdijk, Peter (1987), *Critique of Cynical Reason*, trans. Michael Eldred, Foreword by Andreas Huyssen, Minneapolis: University of Minnesota Press.

Tribe, Lawrence H. (1978), *American Constitutional Law*, New York: Foundation Press.

Tribe, Lawrence H. (1990), *Abortion, The Clash of Absolutes*, New York: Norton.

Veblen, Thorstein (1898), *The Place of Science in Modern Civilization and Other Essays*, reprinted 1969, New York: Capricorn Books.

Veblen, Thorstein (1899a), *Essays in our Changing Order*, reprinted in L. Ardzrooni (ed.) (1964), New York: Augustus Kelley.

Veblen, Thorstein (1899b), *The Theory of the Leisure Class*, reprinted 1979, Introduction by Robert Lekachman, New York: Penguin Books.

Veblen, Thorstein (1904), *The Theory of Business Enterprise*, reprinted 1978, Introduction by Douglas Dowd, New Brunswick, NJ: Transaction Books.

Veblen, Thorstein (1914), *The Instinct of Workmanship and the State of the Industrial Arts*, reprinted 1990, Introduction by Murray G. Murphey, New Brunswick, NJ: Transaction Publishers.

Veblen, Thorstein (1915a), *Imperial Germany and the Industrial Revolution*, reprinted 1954, Introduction by Joseph Dorfman, New York: Viking.
Veblen, Thorstein (1915b), *The Laxdaela Saga*, trans. and Introduction by Thorstein Veblen, New York: B.W. Huebsch.
Veblen, Thorstein (1917), *An Inquiry Into the Nature of Peace and the Terms of its Perpetuation*, New York: Macmillan.
Veblen, Thorstein (1918), *The Higher Learning in America: A Memorandum on the Conduct of Universities by Business Men*, reprinted 1957, Introduction by Louis Hacker, New York: Hill and Wang.
Veblen, Thorstein (1919), *The Vested Interests and the Common Man*, New York: Viking Press.
Veblen, Thorstein (1921), *The Engineers and the Price System*, reprinted 1983, Introduction by Daniel Bell, New Brunswick, NJ: Transaction Publishers.
Veblen, Thorstein (1923), *Absentee Ownership, Business Enterprise in Recent Times: The Case of America*, reprinted 1997, Introduction by Marion Levy, Jr., New Brunswick, NJ: Transaction.
Webster's New World Dictionary of the American Language (1968), Cleveland and New York: The World Publishing Company.
Wills, Garry (2003), *Negro President, Jefferson and the Slave Power*, Boston, MA: Houghton Mifflin.
Winslow, George (1999), *Capital Crimes,* New York: Monthly Review.
Wolin, Sheldon (1996), 'Fugitive democracy', in Selya Benhabib (ed.), *Democracy and Difference*, Princeton, NJ: Princeton University Press, pp. 31–45.

10. Getting to the good life: agents of change

Janet T. Knoedler

Thorstein Veblen articulated a vision of the good life as a rational society organized so that the institutions that guided both production and distribution could provision all of its members with the necessary means of material and intellectual sustenance.[1] In his most famous statement of this vision, *The Engineers and the Price System*, Veblen came close to laying out a plan for the creation of this good society. In his many other works, he also described elements of the political economy necessary to bring about the good life for the many rather than for the few. Yet many have criticized Veblen's vision of a good society as being in error on several counts: the feasibility of industrial democracy, the engineers as a revolutionary force, and the path of social change when entrenched vested interests were set in opposition.[2]

In this chapter, we will first examine the good life lived within this industrial democracy as envisioned by Veblen. We will next consider Veblen's argument that the engineers were the most likely architects of the positive social change that could bring about this ideal society, given their predilection for the use of knowledge, rather than custom and wasteful business principles, to shape society and economy. We will also discuss Veblen's recognition that the engineers who were, after all, benefiting from the existing economic order, might thus be dissuaded from filling this revolutionary role. We will finally investigate some other obstacles to progressive change, as seen by Veblen, in particular the business interests who shaped the economy to serve pecuniary rather than industrial aims, and the leisure class who shaped the larger culture by inspiring the rest of society to emulate their wastefulness and status seeking. We will conclude by looking briefly at modern interpretations of Veblen's vision for positive change and considering whether the prospects for the good life are any brighter in this twenty-first century.

THE GOOD LIFE, ACCORDING TO VEBLEN

While the version of industrial democracy in *The Engineers and the Price System* is usually cited as Veblen's definitive statement on the good life, one can find discussions about Veblen's good society throughout his works. It was a good life lived in a good society, that is, a society that was industrial, in Veblen's sense of that word, cooperative, non-wasteful, prosperous and democratic, organized as a modern and intelligent democracy governed collectively by modern values of rationality, industry and efficiency, to provision all of its members. To quote Rick Tilman, Veblen's ideal political economy would 'maximize the economic welfare of the common man' (Tilman, 1972, p. 314). Despite these clear precepts, however, Veblen did not describe the institutional apparatus that would run this industrial society in much detail. Therefore, his specific views about what is the good life and how it is to be attained must be inferred from his various writings.[3]

In *The Engineers and the Price System*, Veblen set forth his most detailed statement of the good life. In his famous 'Memorandum on the practicability of a soviet of technicians' (1921 [1990]), Veblen asserted that an incoming 'directorate' of engineers, if they freed themselves from control by the vested interests of the 'old order,' could

> . . . accordingly converge on those points in the administration of industry where the old order has most significantly fallen short; that is to say, on the due allocation of resources and a consequent full and reasonably proportioned employment of the available equipment and man power; on the avoidance of waste and duplication of work; and on an equitable and sufficient supply of goods and services to consumers. (Veblen, 1904 [1978], p. 134)

This failure of business enterprise to operate at full efficiency and to use its productive apparatus to provision all is a constant theme throughout Veblen's works. He hoped, therefore, that this 'incoming industrial order . . . would correct the shortcomings of the old' (ibid.) by using their collective expertise to decide matters of resource allocation and distribution of output, to solve the vexing problems of unemployment and scarcity, and to produce at maximum levels of output and technical efficiency; in short, to create a new economic order. Technical principles of efficiency would replace the outdated business principles that sought profit for the few over production for the many, and prioritized business sabotage and output restriction over technical efficiency and social provisioning.

In these essays written for the *Dial* and later published as *Engineers and the Price System*, Veblen sought to discuss, for a popular audience, his view that society's material welfare could be improved by collective, efficient and unimpaired operation of the increasingly complex industrial systems. This view of collective welfare brought about by efficient management of the machine process is not new to these later essays of Veblen, but can be found throughout his earlier works.[4] In his *Theory of Business Enterprise* (1904), in an extended discussion of the advantages of the modern machine process, he stressed the need for coordination, standardization and concatenation of the machine processes to achieve 'an efficient working of the industrial processes at large' (Veblen, 1904 [1978], p. 16). Veblen similarly argued for collective control of the industrial process in his *Instinct of Workmanship* (1914), where he stated that 'technological knowledge is of the nature of a common stock, held and carried forward by the community. . . . an affair of the collectivity, not a creative achievement of individuals working self-sufficiently in severalty or in isolation' (Veblen, 1914 [1990], p. 103). For Veblen, advances in technology came about as a result of the combined and untrammeled effects of the instinct of workmanship and the parental bent, that is, the innate inclinations of humans to explore new and better ways of doing things for the betterment of humanity, and the importance of communal efforts in that effort. He firmly believed that those trained in technology and science should be given free rein in the management of industrial enterprise. As he stated in one of his last essays in *Absentee Ownership*:

> The later advances in the industrial arts have taken such a turn as to throw the technicians more and more into a position of immediate and unremitting responsibility, in all this mechanical organization of work. So that the industrial system, drawn on this mechanical plan, will do its work in a competent fashion only on condition that competent technical men are placed in charge of it, at large and in detail, unhampered by other than technical considerations. (Veblen, 1923 [1964], p. 254)

However, it was not merely to enable maximum production and technological advancement that a system of management grounded in other than pecuniary values was required. For Veblen, the community welfare depended as well on distributive efficiency. As early as his *Theory of Business Enterprise*, Veblen argued that increases in output alone would not increase the community welfare if the net increase in community output were wasted on consumer superfluities, or if actual output were kept below potential capacity to ensure larger profits for business persons. According to Veblen, under the domination of business principles, prosperity had come to be defined in terms of rising prices and rising profits, not in terms of an improved standard of living for the average person. Veblen's point was that the ultimate purpose of a good economy is 'the provisioning of all members of society and not merely the enrichment of a few' (Champlin and Knoedler, 2002, p. 84). In contrast, the activities of businessmen were geared toward salesmanship and ownership rather than production (Veblen, 1919a [1990], p. 296), with an eye toward increased profits rather than improved provisioning. Thus the good society required a different mechanism for distribution from the existing price system.

Veblen applauded the prevalent industrial trends toward economic rationalization and consolidation, but doubted that business control of these consolidated industrial enterprises would permit either productive or distributive efficiency. Thus he outlined, albeit in imprecise terms, a centralized economic organization under collective control that would promote the maximum economic welfare. A key role for broad centralized planning was assigned to the engineers (cf. Rutherford, 1992; Knoedler and Mayhew, 1999; Stabile, 1987, 1988), who had the necessary training and thus the inclination to support maximum production. This important role of the engineers will be discussed in more detail in the next section.

Moreover, Veblen believed that the good society should be efficient in respect to consumption and not engage in such invidious practices as conspicuous consumption and wasteful emulation. In *The Theory of the Leisure Class*, Veblen discussed at length his concept of waste in respect to consumption, indicating that members of a good society should consume, neither to instill envy in their fellows nor to emulate the wealthy, but rather for reasons of serviceability (Veblen, 1899b [1994], p. 61). Given Veblen's scorn for the wasteful practices of salesmanship and other business practices aimed primarily at vendibility rather than serviceability of product, he hoped for these practices to be stripped from the economy. In his 1892 essay, 'Some neglected points in the theory of socialism', Veblen contended that the system of private property was the root of this problem, and that abolition of this institution would spur the betterment of society:

> Modern industry has developed to such a degree of efficiency as to make the struggle of subsistence alone, under average conditions, relatively easy as compared with the state of the case a few generations ago. . . . the modern competitive system has at the same time given the spirit of emulation such a direction that the attainment of subsistence and comfort no longer fixes, even approximately, the limit of the required aggregate labor on the part of the community. Under modern conditions the struggle for existence has, in a very appreciable degree, been transformed into a struggle to keep up appearances. The ultimate ground of this struggle to keep up appearance by otherwise unnecessary expenditure, is the institution of private property. . . . With the abolition of private property, the characteristic of human nature which now finds its exercise in this form of emulation should logically find exercise in other, perhaps nobler and socially more serviceable, activities; it is at any rate not easy to imagine it running into any line of action more futile or less worthy of human effort. (Veblen, 1892 [1990], p. 399)

Moreover, Veblen argued, with this need to 'keep up appearances' removed from the economy, 'common labor would no longer be a mark of peculiar economic necessity and consequent low economic rank on part of the laborer' (ibid., p. 401). Awarding dignity to the average working man would bring about important psychic benefits for most of the population in the good society.

Veblen does not offer more detail about this planned economy in his writings. Many Veblen colleagues and scholars have argued that this vagueness was intentional. His most famous student, Wesley Clair Mitchell, argued that Veblen's lack of specificity was due to his adherence to an evolutionary theory of change. To quote Mitchell at length on this point:

> Veblen has no definite specifications for the new structure of institutions that will grow up in place of the present one, beyond an expectation that technically qualified engineers will have a larger share in managing industry. His evolutionary theory forbids him to anticipate a cataclysm, or to forecast a millennium. What will happen in the inscrutable future is what has been happening since the origin of man. As ways of working shift, they will engender new habits of thinking, which will crystallize into new institutions, which will form the cultural setting for further cumulative changes in ways of working, world without end. (Mitchell, 2002, p. 61)

Moreover, given that Veblen was essentially calling for the triumph of 'industrial' values over 'pecuniary' values, the path of change was uncertain. Certain key elements would nonetheless be required, as Morris Copeland argued:

> Veblen's broad economic policy would entail avoiding 'virtually all unemployment of serviceable equipment and manpower on the one hand, and all local and seasonal scarcity on the other.' It would mean eliminating all sorts of wasteful and obstructive practices inherent 'in the businesslike control of industry' (competitive sales effort is cited by way of illustration). And it would involve the abolition of absentee ownership, i.e., the abolition of intangible properties and of business proprietorship net worths as sources of individual income and as a basis for the 'businesslike control of industry'. (Copeland, 1958, p. 69)

Similarly, according to Rick Tilman, Veblen's 'utopia is largely based on the long-term incompatibility of science and technology with the institutions and values of business enterprise. The machine process and the spirit of science cannot be reconciled with individualist values and modes of behavior that are rapidly becoming archaic' (Tilman, 1996, p. 189). As Tilman argued, for this reason, Veblen's lack of specificity was deliberate:

> Veblen's concern was not with the structural forms and procedural basis of representative government but with a political economy that would maximize

the economic welfare of the common man. He placed far more emphasis on maximizing the production and distribution of goods than on the traditional institutional and procedural mechanisms of representative government. . . . This was not due to his ignorance of these facets of representative government but to his conviction that a basic test of any system is the way it utilizes the state of its industrial arts and its productive apparatus. (Tilman 1996, p. 188)

Many others have argued that the bare outline provided by Veblen is not intended as a detailed blueprint, but rather put forward as a suggestion for an idealized future direction for all of society to attain the good life.[5] In that regard, Patsouras has concluded, 'No matter, Veblen presented a socialism of economic democracy which was dynamic and vibrant, details to be worked out by its practitioners; in this sense he was not a utopian sketching preordained pictures' (Patsouras, 2004, p. 108).

To quote Stephen Edgell's excellent summary of Veblen's utopian ideal:

In sum, Veblen's utopianism is readily apparent in terms of: *content*, ideal commonwealth based on workmanship; *form*, political vision of a new order in which full production is shared by all and limited only by the state of the industrial arts, knowledge of which is also available freely; *function of constructive criticism*, directed at support for the price system, which is increasingly 'incompatible with the common good'; and *catalyst for change*, skilled workers led by the engineers who are 'experienced in the ways and means of technology' and are therefore 'entrusted' to take control of the industrial system. In Veblen's ideal of an industrial republic, there is no place for competition; it is all about 'team-work between the constituent processes' since, without this, 'the system will not work'. (Edgell, 2001, p. 156)

Moreover, the bare sketches of the good life offered by Veblen have provided a sufficient basis for us to understand the nature of the planning that he envisioned and the benefits that would accrue to the ordinary citizen. Significant institutional change would be required in both the public and private sectors. Allan Gruchy detected three new institutional arrangements being advocated by Veblen: transfer of the means of production to public ownership; the establishment of a national economic planning council; and construction of national economic budgets for the co-ordination and guidance of economic activities (Gruchy, 1958, p. 169). Stabile has described this ideal Veblen society as a form of scientific collectivism, because of its heavy reliance on industrial expertise in the planning process (Stabile, 1987). Rutherford has argued that Veblen emphasized industrial or technical organization rather than political because 'industrial democracy [had to] be conducted within the constraints imposed by the "mechanical exigencies"' (Rutherford, 1992, p. 143). Yet, according to Hodder, Veblen believed that 'not only industrial institutions but the whole of society can be reorganized according to principles of scientific management' (Hodder, 1956, p. 348).

However, given Veblen's recognition in his early *Theory of Business Enterprise* that 'constitutional government is a business government' (Veblen, 1904 [1978], p. 295), it seems clear that Veblen always envisioned some form of collective management of government and other social institutions beyond the engineering directorate's control of industrial enterprise as the ideal arrangement. The main question to be addressed by these technocratic managers of the good society would be whether the material product serves directly to enhance human life on the whole. Efficiency in provisioning and consuming would be the standard by which industrial and distributive activities were to be assessed. As Gruchy summarized the situation, 'material welfare, having a foundation in science and technology, is for Veblen fundamentally a matter of technological efficiency' (Gruchy, 1958, p. 170). To quote Lawrence Nabers on this same point, the proper measure of value, for Veblen, 'is the degree to which a commodity contributes to the ability of the economy seen as an interrelated and inseparable concatentation of industrial processes, to produce required goods and services' (Nabers, 1958, p. 97).

As Rick Tilman interprets Veblen's good society, its ideal political economy required 'a division of labor that places the engineer, the technician, the skilled workman, and the economist in positions where they can wield power and influence over the rest of the labor force' (Tilman, 1996, p. 172). Beyond these key decision makers, Tilman argues that Veblen referred obliquely at times to the desirability of 'an ungraded commonwealth of masterless men' (ibid., p. 189). Control of the industrial plant would be held collectively rather than by the privileged class of business persons (Tilman, 1973, p. 164). In addition, Veblen looked forward to a different set of values that prized 'human solidarity and brotherhood' over 'pecuniary values and status emulation' (ibid.). This broader industrial republic as envisioned by Veblen would represent 'the large scale realization of the values and ethos of science, community, and craftsmanship' (Tilman, 1996, p. 189) via 'the mass fostering and achievement of "idle curiosity" (critical intelligence), the "parental bent" (altruism), and the "instinct of workmanship" (industrial proficiency)' (ibid.).

Arguably the good society described by Veblen – if attainable – would represent a series of progressive human achievements: a more productive economy that would employ the most advanced apparatus of modern industry to provide meaningful work and a high standard of living for all members of society, a more collaborative economy where all workers would work together intelligently and imaginatively, and a less invidious economy where consumers would choose freely to consume based on need and serviceability. Yet Veblen understood that this good society, however desirable to the population at large, would only emerge if the agents of change were stronger than the impeding forces. And the emergence of the good society also entailed elimination of the property rights held by the captains of industry and a tamping down of other vested interests. We will turn to consideration of these elements in our next two sections.

INDUSTRIAL ACTIVITIES AND THE ENGINEERS

The engineers were key agents of economic change, according to Veblen, those persons already installed in corporate hierarchies, trusted by their corporate employers and yet, perhaps, who possessed the training and the inclination to alter both internal production processes and the economic system at large in order to bring about the good life for all. We now turn to a closer look at the engineers and their role in the economy at the time Veblen wrote.

To understand why Veblen assigned the engineers the role of guiding society to the good life, it is necessary first to review briefly his famous distinction between industrial and pecuniary employments. Industrial activities, as first laid out in his essay, 'Industrial and pecuniary employments', were the activities that produced material wealth: they were those activities concerned with 'the shaping and guiding of material things and processes . . . with the phenomena of material serviceability' (Veblen, 1919a [1990], p. 293). In contrast, pecuniary activities belonged not with production but with distribution because they 'begin and end within what may broadly be called "the haggling of the market"' (Veblen, 1919a [1990], p. 294).

The key for Veblen was that industrial activities as advanced by the technicians were in conflict with the pecuniary interests of the business entrepreneurs. When he penned his analyses of the emerging modern industrial economy during the turn of the twentieth century, Veblen recognized that modern business enterprise was then controlled by businessmen – the 'captains of industry', and, later, the 'captains of finance', as he dubbed them (Veblen, 1904 [1978], p. 30), with pecuniary aims as their priority over maximum production. As he stated in 'Industrial and pecuniary employments', 'industry must be conducted to suit the business man in his quest for gain' (Veblen, 1919a [1990], p. 298). The implications of this pecuniary control of the industrial apparatus for preventing positive social change will be taken up in greater depth in the next section of this chapter. For now, we will simply note that Veblen saw those engaged in pecuniary activities as, at best, permitting, at worst, inhibiting the workings of modern industry.

Thus, instead of the heroic entrepreneur celebrated by orthodox economists, Veblen focused on the engineer as the key agent in promoting the important industrial activities that would lead to a growing economy. While the collection of essays written for *Dial* later published as *Engineers and the Price System* represents Veblen's most obvious discussion of the engineers, Veblen had always placed the engineers in a position of prominence in the industrial activities of modern business firms. In his earliest writings on business enterprise, his essay 'Industrial and pecuniary employments', written in 1901, and his second major theoretical volume, *Theory of Business Enterprise*, written in 1904, Veblen argued that the technology of modern industry had reached an advanced state by the end of the nineteenth century. The 'machine process', the term he used to describe the high degree of mechanization of modern industry and the 'concatenation' or inter-related workings of the various industrial processes, was a 'reasoned procedure on the basis of a systematic knowledge of the forces employed' (Veblen, 1904 [1978], p. 6). The high degree of technological complexity of modern industry, accordingly, required a cadre of highly trained workers and industrial technicians for firms to function at their highest level of efficiency.

These industrial workers (mechanics, production workers, and especially engineers) differed from the other workers on the shop floor or from the owner–managers engaged in pecuniary activities because they were 'on the whole, occupied with the production of goods' (Veblen, 1919a [1990], p. 299). As Veblen described their functions in *Instinct of Workmanship*, engineers and technicians were engaged in 'that general category of human material through which the community's technological proficiency functions directly to an industrial effect . . . their interest as well as their discipline of their workday life converges, in effect, on a technologically competent apprehension of material facts' (Veblen, 1914 [1990], p. 188).

Veblen singled out the engineers in particular because they could apply their scientific knowledge to the technological apparatus of the firm: 'the engineer or inventor who designs processes, appliances, and expedients within these premises is required to apprehend and appreciate the working facts after that dispassionate, opaque, unteleological fashion in which the phenomena of brute matter occur' (Veblen, 1914, p. 303).

Modern industry required both standardization and precision to function at a high level of efficiency, and the job of the engineers was to 'concatenate' the various industrial processes (Veblen, 1904 [1978], pp. 8, 13). Veblen's late nineteenth-century view of modern industry as a technologically advanced, highly interrelated, and highly efficient mass production system has been validated through the work of Alfred Chandler and other business historians (cf. Chandler, 1977, 1990; Lamoreaux, 1985; Lazonick, 1991). The notion of an industrial *system* was crucial: it was not simply individual firms that achieved a high degree of plant efficiency, but rather Veblen's description of modern industry as an interrelated industrial *system* of firms, all working smoothly together to process materials into finished products and to deliver these products to the final consumer.[6] Crucial to industrial efficiency of this system as a whole was prompt delivery of needed industrial inputs via reliable transportation and communication systems, and in turn quick distribution of industrial output to wholesalers and retailers to deliver the output to its ultimate consumers (Knoedler, 1997). To quote Veblen at length on this point:

> This industrial system runs on as an inclusive organization of many and diverse interlocking mechanical processes, interdependent and balanced among themselves in such a way that the due working of any part of it is conditioned on the due working of all the rest. Therefore it will work at its best only on condition that these industrial experts, production engineers, will work together on a common understanding; and more particularly on condition that they must not work at cross purposes. (Veblen, 1921 [1990], p. 72)

Veblen correctly recognized that the different constituent parts of the modern industrial system had to be synchronized at the interstices between the various processes in order to eliminate any idleness and industrial waste that might come about owing to business mismanagement of the industrial processes. This work of industrial coordination fell largely to the engineers, who found ways to improve, not only the production technology, but also the flow of the production process, from testing and improvement of raw materials, to the production floor, to rapid distribution of the final product to wholesalers and retailers. In *Vested Interests*, Veblen described the task of engineers in maintaining that efficiency:

> . . . the control of the system had best be entrusted to men skilled in these matters of technology. The industrial system does its work in terms of mechanical efficiency, not in terms of price. . . . The material welfare of the community is bound up with the due working of this industrial system, which depends on the expert knowledge, insight, and disinterested judgment with which it is administered. (Veblen, 1919d [2002], p. 89)

The engineers were, in short, the 'indispensable General Staff of the industrial system; and without their immediate and unremitting guidance and correction, the industrial system will not work' (Veblen, 1921, p. 82).

To summarize the argument thus far, engineers and other technical workers were the agents of economic change within industry, in Veblen's view. The engineers were directly involved in creating and implementing technologies for use in their firms and, by dint of their training, were also interested in putting these skills to work to make continuous improvements in the technological processes that they supervised and maintained, thus expanding production and promoting economic growth rather than pecuniary gain for the businesspersons they served. As Veblen stated in *Absentee Ownership* (1923), the skills required for industrial activities are 'of the nature of opaque fact. Pecuniary gain is not one of these impersonal facts' (Veblen, 1923 [1964], p. 262). Therefore, in his view, the engineers would be guided by the dictates of the industrial process and their own scientific training and not by pecuniary directives. More broadly, Veblen saw technology and the associated matter-of-fact thinking as the key progressive force in human society. Moreover, a central theme running through Veblen's analysis is that changes to the institutional structure of the larger society always lagged behind technological changes. In short, Veblen believed, or at least hoped, that engineers would not confine their analytical and matter-of-fact thinking to industrial processes, but would look more broadly at the pecuniary organization of the whole of modern society.

Therefore Veblen believed that engineers would eventually come around to criticize the pecuniary institutions of their economy and society. As he argued in 'Industrial and pecuniary employments', engineers were 'relatively free from the constraint of [the] conventional norm of truth and validity [regarding property and ownership]' (Veblen, 1919a [1990], p. 317). By the time of his later writings on the engineers, Veblen had observed the role of the engineers in mobilizing resources for World War I, and believed that they could utilize these same skills to create a better economic order for society (Veblen, 1923 [1964]; Stabile, 1988, pp. 222–3).[7] As he stated in a 1919 essay for the *Dial*,

> . . . the training given by the mechanical industries and strengthened by the experience of daily life in a mechanically organized community lends no support to prescriptive rights of ownership, class perquisites, and free income. This training bends the mental attitude of the common man at cross-purposes with the established system of rights, and makes it easy for him to deny their validity so soon as there is sufficient provocation. (Veblen, 1919c, p. 176)

Therefore, in Veblen's vision of the good society, the leaders and decision makers for the new industrial order would comprise a suitable group of engineers and economists, drawn together 'on the basis of a common interest in productive efficiency, economical use of resources, and an equitable distribution of the consumable output' (Veblen, 1904 [1978], p. 141). The key for this new group of decision makers would be training in 'the ways and means of productive industry' (ibid., p. 137) rather than in salesmanship and business enterprise.[8] Assuming that the technical inclinations of engineers could lead them to recognize their broader role in society, Veblen argued in the *Engineers and the Price System* that a directorate of engineers be responsible, not only for managing the production facilities but also for making allocative and distributive decisions.[9]

Given that engineers had a different mindset by virtue of their scientific training, Veblen hoped that they might also have the desire to undertake the rebellion needed to reject business practices. In his early essays, Veblen predicted that, among 'the industrial population, and especially among the more intelligent and skillful men employed in the mechanical industries . . . the socialistic disaffection spreads' (Veblen, 1919a [1990], p. 321). In his later *Engineers and the Price System*, Veblen stated that the engineers had recently become 'uneasily "class-conscious" . . . with their class consciousness having taken the immediate form of a growing sense of waste and confusion in the management of industry by the financial agents of the absentee owners' (1921 [1990], p. 84). Obviously, Veblen hoped that engineers would recognize that industry was being mismanaged for pecuniary gains. The younger engineers in particular, according to Veblen, less enthralled to the pecuniary system, were 'beginning to understand that commercial expediency has nothing better to contribute to the engineer's work than so much lag, leak, and friction' (1921, p. 86). This realization by engineers 'brings home a realization of their own shame and of damage to the common good. So the engineers are beginning to draw together and ask themselves, "what about it?"' (ibid., p. 84).

An examination of the work of some progressive engineers during the early part of the twentieth century does indicate that some radical engineers were indeed pursuing the same questions that Veblen had raised about industrial versus pecuniary efficiency and the gap between industrial capacity and industrial output. A few of these engineers, most notably Henry Gantt and Morris Cooke, even endeavored to bring these ideas to bear on the industrial and business practices of American industry (cf. Jordan, 1994; Knoedler, 1997; Knoedler and Mayhew, 1999; Stabile, 1984, 1988; Rutherford, 1992).[10] And many of these ideas were represented by thinkers during the Progressive Era and the New Deal (Barber, 1985).

In short, Veblen therefore saw the engineers as the most likely group to challenge the existing pecuniary order of society and the pecuniary mismanagement of modern industry. As he stated in *Engineers and the Price System*, 'it is a question whether the discretion and responsibility in the management of the country's industry shall pass from the financiers, who speak for the Vested Interests, to the technicians, who speak for the industrial system as a going concern. There is no third party to make a colorable bid' (Veblen, 1921 [1990], p. 127).[11] A key point made by Tilman is that Veblen believed that engineers would first have to interpret the 'technological laws for the rest of society' (Tilman, 1996, p. 171). If, in the long-term, the majority of the population came to have the technological–instrumental values, as Veblen hoped, they would not always require guidance by the engineers but, rather, the entire population would be governing itself.

But, as Veblen also recognized, engineers were also susceptible to be drawn into the management side of industry and to abandon any progressive views. The dominance of pecuniary values in our modern capitalistic system led all participants, most especially the captains of industry and finance, but even the engineers – those most likely, in Veblen's view, to reconstruct society along rationalistic and efficiency lines – to gravitate toward pecuniary ways of thinking. And it is to these obstacles to progressive change that we now turn.

OBSTACLES TO POSITIVE CHANGE

The obstacles to positive change were many, according to Veblen, and included those with vested interests in the existing system, especially the captains of finance and captains of industry who earned their profits from exploiting the interstices of the industrial system. It also included those other members of the leisure class whose vested interests resided in maintaining their higher status than the average working persons of their day. Veblen was also skeptical of the revolutionary capacity of the average working person: even though this group was also intimately involved in production and thus more likely than their business employers to support an economic system organized on the basis of greater industrial efficiency, they were often members of unions that had themselves become vested interests, in Veblen's view. Workers were also caught up in an economic system where they were driven to emulate, not to rebel against, the leisured and moneyed classes. Engineers themselves, despite their inclination for greater production efficiency, were not yet part of management, not yet positioned to undertake major social or economic changes, and as susceptible as the workers to the blandishments of emulation and conspicuous consumption. Finally, Veblen's own understanding of the evolutionary nature of change takes all of these obstacles into account in making any prediction.

Most prominent among the vested interests were the businessmen, the great captains of finance who controlled the large pools of capital, and the captains of industry, who brought together, by means of merger and acquisition, large business enterprises. As discussed above, Veblen greatly admired the technologies employed in modern industry and their immense productive capacity (Veblen, 1904 [1978], p. 7). However, the industrial processes were controlled, not by the engineers who designed the mechanical works, but by businesspersons. In an earlier era, these businesspersons, in Veblen's evolutionary scheme, had been producer–owners, working side-by-side with their technicians, with the primary goal being to produce serviceable products for the needs of humankind. But as their firms grew, both in size and in technical sophistication, technical management of their firms was handed over to the technicians and engineers, and the businessmen focused on the business management of their expanding enterprises. And, in the aggregate, as the productivity of industry expanded, a social surplus was created that made it worthwhile for some to 'own the material means of industry, and ownership of the material means in such a situation carries with it the usufruct of the community's immaterial equipment of technological proficiency' (Veblen, 1914 [1990], p. 151). Hence evolved what Veblen called 'the pecuniary regulation of industry' (ibid.).

As a consequence, Veblen recognized that business persons had come to be concerned only secondarily, and sometimes quite remotely, with the material welfare of the community, in contrast to the engineers. Veblen characteristically summarized the problem thus: 'the vital point of production with [the business man] is the vendibility of the output, its convertibility into money values, not its serviceability for the needs of mankind' (Veblen, 1904 [1978], p. 51). Moreover, if it proved to be more profitable to withhold output than to produce it, so be it, in Veblen's view. As he saw it, the large business owners of his day made their profits, not by facilitating but, rather, by upsetting the smooth workings of the industrial system. He referred to this 'conscientious withdrawal of efficiency' (Veblen, 1921 [1990], p. 1) as sabotage. Thus, in contrast to the work of the engineers, which was to effect an ever greater efficiency and interconnection between the constituent parts of the industrial economy, business persons aimed at causing disruptions to the smooth flow of goods from producer to consumer with the aim of inflicting 'pecuniary damage' (Veblen, 1904 [1978], p. 32) on their rivals.[12]

The effect of pecuniary management on the industrial productivity of the system, in Veblen's view, was 'pecuniary damage', that is, 'a set-back to the industrial plants concerned, and a derangement, more or less extensive, of the industrial system at large' (Veblen, ibid.). The great merger wave that was proceeding apace during the time that Veblen wrote *Theory of Business Enterprise* was intended, in his view, not to make the industrial system function more efficiently, as is often argued by modern merger proponents, but instead to make profits (Veblen, 1904 [1978], p. 39).[13] In other words, the normal work of the business persons was more often than not set in opposition to achievement of the technical efficiency that was the purview of the engineers.

By defining prosperity in business terms and on account of their dominance in the economic system, the measure of business success came to be an excess of business profits rather than serviceability to the material welfare of the community. This entrenched business class presented the most significant obstacle to the good life. In his last work, *Absentee Ownership*, Veblen discussed the continued intransigence of business principles and their extension to all aspects of modern life, declaring that

> ... no where else does the captain of big business rule the affairs of the nation, civil and political, and control the conditions of life so unreservedly as in democratic America; as should also be the case, inasmuch as the acquisition of absentee ownership is, after all, in the popular apprehension, the most meritorious and the most necessary work to be done in this country. (Veblen, 1923 [1964], p. 118)

As Sidney Plotkin discusses at length in his excellent chapter in this volume, the dominance of business interests over the institutions of government further hinders progressive change by assigning primacy in the influential circles that determine government policies to the 'substantial citizens' among the captains of industry and finance.

However, the dominance of the business class in both industry and government, in Veblen's evolutionary approach, is only one element of the vested and entrenched interests that prevented positive change. Veblen's theory of the leisure class also explains, as Douglas Dowd has argued, 'how and why the vested interests gain, hold, and use power; and through his concept of "emulation", . . . how and why the "common man" seeks to be like, rather than to overthrow, the vested interests' (Dowd, 1958a, p. 27).[14] The modern leisure class emerged from the ancient warriors and hunters who gained prestige through their demonstrated power and the evidence of their fierce exploits in battle.[15] The higher honor accorded those engaged in these 'predatory' pursuits has persisted; thus the values and practices of the modern leisure class continue to dominate modern society: individualism, competition, predatory behavior, and warfare, all, for Veblen, evidence of immaturity and wastefulness, and all values that detracted from the greater material benefit of the community (Veblen, 1904 [1978], pp. 374ff.). Rather than sustaining the workmanship and cooperation inherent to human beings, our modern economy instead sustains these immature and inefficient values. The dominance of leisure class values inherited from centuries earlier served to inhibit the emergence of the good society.

Another obstacle created by the dominance of the leisure class was its holding of wealth and, more importantly, the social status attached to the conspicuous and wasteful display of wealth. Possession and display of wealth came to be equated with social status: in Veblen's words, 'possession of wealth confers honor' (Veblen, 1899a [1973], p. 35). Over time, mere possession of wealth came to bestow status on its possessor. In Veblen's era, the wealthy captains of industry were considered both successful *and* honorable because they were wealthy, because they had accumulated great wealth through the new leisure class pursuits of business. Success, in short, required accumulation: as Veblen stated, 'it becomes indispensable to accumulate, to acquire property, in order to retain one's good name' (ibid., p. 37).

Of course, mere possession of wealth was not sufficient to bestow upon the possessor an honorific position in society unless the rest of society can observe the wealth on display. Therefore, the wealthy had to engage in 'conspicuous consumption' to demonstrate their wealth and, thus, their success in war or in business. The conspicuous consumption of the wealthy consequently promoted wasteful spending throughout the rest of society. Emulation was for Veblen the most powerful economic motive, given that we are social creatures; we yearn for social status on the basis of consumption and ownership rather than on the basis of workmanship and cooperation (ibid., pp. 37–8). The recent examples of Dennis Koslowski's thousand dollar shower curtain and Donald Trump's extravagant homes indicate that this kind of conspicuous display of wealth remains extremely important.

According to Veblen, then, these two leisure-class institutions, pecuniary emulation and industrial exemption, have 'been erected into canons of life, and have become coercive factors of some importance in the situation to which men have to adapt themselves' (Veblen, 1899b [1994], p. 131). In other words, human nature itself has become altered through the institutions of emulation of the wealthy and disparagement of the ordinary worker to support emulation and industrial exemption, values at odds with the good society envisioned by Veblen. Moreover, as William Dugger has recently argued, the desire to emulate the wealthier classes keeps the lower classes from rebelling against the existing order because they hope to join the leisure class themselves or at least to emulate their lifestyles insofar as they can: 'Emulation keeps the underlying population thinking in terms of younger sex, older whiskey, and faster horses, not in terms of liberty, equality, and fraternity' (Dugger, 2000, p. 39). Moreover, dominance of society by the leisure class has kept other key institutions and economic players in thrall. According to Dowd, the 'kept creatures' of the business class include the media, schools, government, and labor (Dowd, 1958a, p. 28).[16]

Given these significant obstacles, the important question is how constructive social and economic change might come about. Perhaps the general strike that Veblen suggests in *Engineers and the Price System* will sweep away the predatory institutions associated with business enterprise in one large rebellion, or perhaps change will come about only slowly through the growing incompatibility of industrial values with the existing pecuniary system,[17] with the latter case more likely, in Veblen's view. Despite the revolutionary nature of these changes outlined by Veblen, in *Engineers and the Price System*, Veblen did not set forth a description of a Marxian revolution to bring about the good society, but rather suggested that the engineers would gradually realize that their own outlook and work experiences differed from their capitalist employers. As Veblen put it, the engineers were 'beginning to draw together and ask themselves, "what about it?"' (Veblen, 1921 [1990], p. 84). In his view, the rest of the society would be drawn along to support this change as they acquired industrial values. As Murray Murphrey has put it, if Veblen is correct about inherent human values, that is, 'if men really value the material welfare of the community at large, and efficiency, they will carry out the processes Veblen called industrial without there being any need for pecuniary values to be involved' (Murphrey, 1990, xxxv).

Yet Veblen's own analysis of institutions throughout his many writings indicates that he recognized that the scope and direction of this kind of change would be strongly resisted by long-established institutional structures of society. Arrayed against the dominant business class within their workplaces and the leisure class within the larger society, could the engineers and technicians prevail? Veblen outlined the necessary steps for the engineers to take if they expected to bring about this change:

> [T]here will be at least two main lines of subsidiary preparation to be taken care of before any overt move can reasonably be undertaken: (a) an extensive campaign of inquiry and publicity, such as will bring the underlying population to a reasonable understanding of what it is all about; and (b) the working out of a common understanding and a solidarity of sentiment between the technicians and the working force engaged in transportation and in the greater underlying industries of the system. (Veblen, 1921 [1990], p. 150)

Veblen's argument that an industrial republic *could* come about was premised on the notion that those in the industrial system, chiefly the engineers, but also the workers, who shared industrial values, would reject the old order of pecuniary values and absentee ownership as being at odds with technological progress and material well-being for all of society. Veblen, however, became skeptical that workers would help promote revolutionary change. This later view contrasts with Veblen's earlier writings, where he argued that workers, who were also engaged directly with the actual workings of industry and who thus might be inclined toward a reorganization of society, might be supportive of socialism. And in one of his *Dial* essays republished in 'The vested interests and the common man', Veblen argued that the 'habits of thought engendered by the machine system in industry and by the mechanically standardized organization of daily life under this new order, as well as by the material sciences' could bring about a society where economic decisions were made on a different basis than at present, with 'all men and things [rated] in terms of tangible performance rather than in terms of legal title and ancient usage' (Veblen, 1919d [2002],

p. 119). Over time, therefore, the new forms of distribution would come to make sense for the ordinary worker. As Veblen put it, the average person could come to 'consider any income unearned which exceeds a fair return for tangible performance in the way of productive work on the part of the person to whom the income goes' while 'income derived from property, simply on the basis of ownership, will be disallowed' (ibid.).

Yet, in his later *Engineers and the Price System*, he described the American Federation of Labor as itself a vested interest, 'as ready as any other to do battle for its own margin of privilege and profit' (Veblen, 1921 [1990], p. 7). Unions were organized, according to Veblen, '[not] for production but for bargaining' (Veblen, 1921 [1990]). To quote Veblen more directly on this point, '[the union] is, in effect, an organization for the strategic defeat of employers and rival organizations, by recourse to enforced unemployment and obstruction, not for the production of goods and services' (ibid., p. 97). Don Stabile has examined at length Veblen's writings about the role of workers in socialistic movements, and has concluded that Veblen overestimated these socialistic tendencies in his earlier work. According to Stabile, Veblen recognized that such countervailing forces as education, the press and patriotism all inveighed against socialistic tendencies among American workers (Stabile, 1988, pp. 218–19).

Was it possible that engineers could radicalize the rest of society? Louis Patsouras has observed the following:

> Veblen's schema for a successful socialist revolution was predicated on an alliance between workers, the potentially most revolutionary class, and the engineers who would lead it not only on the basis of their 'instinct of workmanship, increasing class consciousness,' and utilitarian rejection of 'waste and confusion in the management of industry by the financial agents of the owners,' but belief of being indispensable in production. The workers themselves, for Veblen, becoming ever more skilled with the passage of time, would have a greater role in management. This class alliance would thus be as based on shared cultural values as on broad socioeconomic interests. (Patsouras, 2004, p. 105)

However, in Patsouras's view, Veblen ignored 'the sharp class dichotomy at this time between manual and mental labor in a society of general economic scarcity basically devoid of a broad socialist culture' (ibid.). If that were the case, then an alliance between workers and engineers was unlikely. Moreover, given Veblen's skepticism about radical elements in any unions but the Industrial Workers of the World (IWW), he was unconvinced that they would be the source of any constructive change.

Veblen also recognized that engineers were themselves susceptible to the same conservative tendencies that protected these other vested interests. Veblen recognized that the engineers were also afflicted by 'settled habit' and 'somewhat placidly content with the "full dinner pail" which the lieutenants of the Vested Interests habitually allow them' (Veblen, 1921 [1990], p. 128). Moreover, some engineers were themselves comfortable with the existing system, 'pretty well commercialized, particularly the older generation, who speak with authority and conviction' (ibid., p. 130).[18]

Thus, even in *Engineers and the Price System*, Veblen himself concluded that the prospect of a revolution by a soviet of technicians is unlikely, 'just yet' (ibid., p. 151).[19] Veblen outlined the conflict of interest faced by engineers in *Engineers and the Price System*. Engineers had achieved greater importance inside the business firms that constituted modern industry, but they remained 'employees of the captains of industry, that is to say, of the captains of finance, whose work it has been to commercialize the knowledge and abilities of the industrial experts and turn them to account for their own gain' (ibid., p. 77). And, as documented by several historical accounts of these early engineers, the allure of pecuniary values combined with a backlash against the progressive aims of the radical engineers led engineers to affiliate themselves to greater and greater degrees with the business persons (Jordan, 1994; Layton, 1971; Tilman, 1996; Knoedler and Mayhew, 1999; Edgell, 2001).

More broadly, it is useful to consider how Veblen's theory of evolutionary change informed his general skepticism that positive change would occur. Douglas Dowd has explained Veblen's theory of change thus: '... cumulative causation and blind drift – not reason – is for Veblen the force behind social change. . . . the ideological emphasis and the institutional situation in the United States have been, and seem likely to remain, pointed in almost precisely the opposite direction from that which is most likely to support our, and the world's, life interests' (Dowd, 1958a, p. 301). Therefore, while Veblen described a theory of positive social change that would come about thanks to the expansion of knowledge and the erosion of customary privileges and institutions, he remained cautious about predicting such change. Clarence Ayres also recognized that Veblen's theory of evolutionary change made him wary of predicting the triumph of industrial values.[20] Veblen himself commented in 1919 that, even though

> . . . twentieth-century technology has outgrown the eighteenth-century system of vested rights . . . so that it is perhaps not reasonably to be questioned that the Vested Interests in business are riding for a fall. But the end is not yet; . . . There seems no reason to apprehend any substantial disallowance of the vested rights of property to follow from such an essentially ephemeral interlude of dissension. In fact, the tenure of the Vested Interests in America should seem to be reasonably secure, just yet. (Veblen, 1919d [2002], p. 301)

In other words, in a society dominated by pecuniary values, in which even the lower classes were more inclined to emulate than to reject the values of the dominant class, and in which all groups were gradually more and more conditioned to accept pecuniary values, change became less and less likely the longer these values adhered. To quote Rick Tilman at length on this point:

> . . . the long-range perspective that Veblen held in his more optimistic moods was that of movement toward the industrial republic as a consequence of the progression of science and technology and the value system this process generates among the masses. But the triumph of the New Order would long remain in doubt due to the power of the vested interests, the rigidity of established institutions, and the ambivalence of human nature. These kept open the possibility of a reversion to barbarism, or to an era of conservative stagnation. . . . In short, Veblen's ideal society, the industrial republic, was one possibility but so was the reversion to authoritarian militarism and barbarism that Veblen predicted might occur in totalitarian Germany and Japan long before it actually did. (Tilman, 1996, p. 188)[21]

The one certainty in Veblen's analysis was that change would occur. It was the nature of human society to experience constant evolutionary change. But would the institutional structures of society consciously adapt to progressive and technological values or would the prevalent institutions act to reshape and submerge these progressive values within their existing structures? In other words, one of the reasons that change was unlikely was the tight grip held by the dominant groups in society on the key economic institutions. As Veblen stated in his 1919 essay on the Bolshevik revolution,

> . . . On scant reflection it should seem that, since the common man has substantially no vested rights to lose, he should come off indifferently well in such an event. But such a hasty view overlooks the great lesson of history that, when anything goes askew in the national economy, or anything is to be set to rights, the common man eventually pays the cost and he pays it eventually in lost labor, anxiety, privation, blood, and wounds. The Bolshevik is the common man who has faced the question: What do I stand to lose? and has come away with the answer: Nothing. And the elder statesmen are busy with arrangements for disappointing that indifferent hope. (Veblen, 1919c, p. 179)

CONCLUSION

How feasible is it in the twenty-first century to achieve the good life as described by Veblen? On the one hand, one might assume that a century of technological advance and expansion of higher education would make an industrial republic even more feasible today. On the other hand, if we simply take Veblen's own template as the model for the good society, we would have to conclude that we are farther than ever from that ideal. The engineers have not become the revolutionary force in society that Veblen may have envisioned them to be, but have become instead, for the most part, staunch corporate citizens or even well-heeled CEOs of their own financially lucrative firms.[22] Among the underlying population, status emulation and conspicuous consumption appear stronger than ever, and have spread, through the reach of global media, to the wealthy and middle classes in countries across the globe.[23] Finally, the vested interests in the business class appear to be unchallenged in their global dominance of the economy and more influential than ever in imparting their cultural values of pecuniary success and rampant individualism to the rest of us.

Moreover, we seem now to live in an era when these pecuniary values have infected the few potential corrective institutions: our universities increasingly serve as sports franchises or as corporate research labs, our media serve up infotainment and ubiquitous advertising rather than information, and our government serves the powerful lobbyists and their well-heeled clients rather than the citizenry at large. And if these institutions, however tainted by pecuniary interests, nonetheless prove insufficient to keep the underlying population from contemplating broad social and economic change, the first decade of this twenty-first century has witnessed a rise of militarism and enforced patriotism that have helped to suppress any criticism of the American system and to reinforce the notion of American exceptionalism.[24] Thus the good society seems farther than ever from our reach.

Why do the obstacles to progressive change remain so strong? We turn first to Douglas Dowd's excellent reflection from the vantage point of the mid-twentieth century before offering our own views:

> [We are the] business society par excellence; our outlook is dominated by emulation and by an invidious, competitive materialism. Our basic optimism – provided with second thoughts only intermittently by economic crises – has led us to adopt a naïve individualism. . . . We have built an almost unbelievably productive economy; but its health is now crucially dependent upon what Veblen termed unproductive consumption and unproductive public expenditure – upon what he might today have termed 'inspired waste'. The largest percentage of Americans have easy access to economic plenty, but our social outlook is ill suited to the problems presently confronting us and the rest of the world. We are enthralled, in a word, by what Veblen called 'imbecile institutions'. (Dowd, 1958a, p. 300)

At the time Dowd wrote these words, the American society – indeed at the time the 'business society par excellence' – dominated the world economy. These dominant American business values of success, measured primarily in pecuniary terms, at times, forcibly, have been nourished and sustained by American business enterprise for decades and spread throughout the global economy. In a Veblenian understanding of the difficulty of social and economic change in the face of the vested interests, it makes sense that these habits of thinking have thus become ever more entrenched across the entire population. Yet we wonder if the twenty-first century, the century that will see the emergence of new industrial and business giants (India, for example) will also see an emergence of a new set of values that are set in opposition to the pecuniary values that have so dominated the past century. At the same time, we also wonder if the global energy usage, considered by any reasonable analysis, to be unsustainable beyond the next two decades, forces us to reconsider both the technological apparatus needed for provisioning of basic needs and our consumption habits. And we wonder if the underlying population will continue to be quiescent and compliant citizens as they come to recognize the pecuniary corruption of their basic governing institutions. We are even more wary than was Veblen of making predictions, but we wonder if the harsh realities of this age may finally force some reconsideration of our long-established institutions of provisioning and governing. To quote Bernard Rosenberg, 'Modern man in the technological age could enjoy untold freedom and bounty if only he divested himself of intractable habits' (Rosenberg, 1953, p. 186). To which we add, slyly, 'not just yet'.

NOTES

1. See Edgell (2001, p. 121) and Tilman (1972, p. 314).
2. See Stephen Edgell's discussion of the critics of Veblen's argument (Edgell, 2001, pp. 138–47).
3. In his 'Veblen's ideal political economy and its critics', Rick Tilman argues that Veblen's analysis of the social structures of his ideal political economy is deliberately vague (1972, p. 312).
4. We note that there has always been some controversy about whether Veblen's argument in *Engineers and the Price System* differs substantively from his earlier arguments. See, for example, Knoedler and Mayhew (1999).
5. See, for example, Stabile (1987), Tilman (1972) and Rutherford (1992). Louis Patsouras has noted in particular that such questions as allocation of the gains from technological change and economic growth or the division of spoils were not considered by Veblen, nor did he address the potential power imbalances in the workplace (Patouras, 2004, p. 108).
6. See, for example, Anne Mayhew and Sidney Carroll (1993), 'Alfred Chandler's speed: monetary transformation', *Business and Economic History*, **22**(1), Fall, 105–113.
7. As Don Stabile has argued, Veblen's analysis of the engineers is useful 'as one of the first studies of what has come to be known these days as "The New Class"' (Stabile, 1988, p. 222). Crucial for this new group of decision makers would be training in 'the ways and means of productive industry' (Veblen, 1904 [1978], p. 137) rather than in salesmanship and business enterprise, as Veblen defined those terms.
8. Tilman has argued that Veblen is ambiguous in regard to the division of labor between economists, workers, technicians and engineers in organizing and making decisions about

the industrial economy. As Tilman states, whatever decision-making body is put into place would likely be done with the consent of the rest of the labor force, although 'Veblen does not tell us what mechanisms of representation will be used to determine the views of the labor force' (Tilman, 1972, p. 312).

9. Veblen's argument that those engaged in the technical side of production would be disinclined to support pecuniary forms of management was not new in *The Engineers and the Price System*. He had made this argument early on in his writing career, most notably in his 1901 essay, 'Industrial and pecuniary employments', where he noted that those 'habitually employed in the specialized industrial occupations . . . by the circumstances of their daily life are brought to do their serious and habitual thinking in other than pecuniary terms' (Veblen, 1919a [1990], p. 321). Technical workers are also prominent in his *Theory of Business Enterprise* (1904), where he states that the 'higher degree of training in such matter-of-fact habits of thought is . . . to be looked for among the higher ranks of skilled mechanics, and perhaps still more decisively among those who stand in an engineering or supervisory relation to the processes' (Veblen, 1904 [1978], p. 312). Hence he consistently expressed concern in *Theory of Business Enterprise* and elsewhere that pecuniary activities merely disturbed the machine process rather than aiding its smooth operation.

10. See also Stephen Edgell's useful summary of the literature concerning Veblen's view of the engineers as a potential revolutionary force (Edgell, 2001, pp. 137 ff).

11. Why was there no other third party available to push positive economic change? According to Morris Copeland, '[Veblen] thought of the prevalence of mechanical processes as affecting everyone's thinking and so leading to broad institutional changes. But he thought also that for some classes of the population the influence was particularly strong – for manual workers, engineers, and physical scientists' (Copeland, 1958, p. 68).

12. To the degree that the business man contributed to efficiency, that is, to reducing costs of operation by carrying out efficiency-enhancing business mergers, as Veblen saw it, the savings were derived simply by curtailing the amount of business to be done: 'The heroic role of the captain of industry is that of a deliverer from an excess of business management' (Veblen, 1904 [1978], p. 48).

13. Cf. Lamoreaux (1985), Chandler (1990).

14. The root of Veblen's difference with Marx lies in Veblen's having added 'prestige' to 'power' (Dowd, 2002, p. 27).

15. This short discussion of the leisure class appears in extended form in 'The predatory economy of Thorstein Veblen', Janet T. Knoedler, in *Introduction to Political Economy*, edited Geoffrey Schneider and Charles Sackrey.

16. As Lawrence Nabers asserted, Veblen analyzed those aspects of the economic system which were disserviceable owing to their immersion in pecuniary culture: invidious uses of leisure and conspicuous consumption, activities which interfere with industrial processes including those which involve certain 'customary forms of waste, which are unavoidable so long as an industry is managed for businesslike methods and for businesslike ends' (Nabers, 1958, p. 98). Waste for Veblen included the unemployment of labor and resources, the use of salesmanship rather than technical proficiency to sell goods, excess capacity that was used for profit rather than production, and production of spurious goods, as well as those institutions 'whose value lies in their turning the technological inheritance to the injury of mankind'; that is, the military establishment and the constabulary insofar as the function of the latter is to protect the predatory rights of the leisure class' (Nabers, 1958, p. 98).

17. Cf. Rick Tilman (1973), especially pp. 156ff.

18. Tilman has also argued, 'there is little evidence, however, that Veblen believed that engineers and technicians were about to seize power with popular support in the immediate future and make themselves into a ruling elite, since he expressed extreme skepticism about this potential occurrence in Veblen [1921] 1990' (Tilman, 1996 p. 171).

19. Cf. Edwin Layton (1971).

20. According to Ayres, as Veblen conceived them, workmanship and sportsmanship are at cross purposes with one another. . . . As Veblen interpreted the record, all human cultures have been the scenes of struggles between conflicting forces, the outcome of which is far

from certain' (Ayres, 1958, p. 33). Ayres goes on to state: 'Indeed, no words of his have been more often quoted than the sentence in *The Instinct of Workmanship* in which he says: "History records more frequent and more spectacular instances of the triumph of imbecile institutions over life and culture than of peoples who by force of instinctive insight saved themselves alive out of a desperately precarious institutional situation, such, for instance, as now faces the peoples of Christendom'" (ibid.).

21. According to Tilman, there is 'a strong vein of what might be called "utopian realism"' (Tilman, 1996, p. 179) in Veblen's policy prescriptions, but on terms that 'usually called for sweeping changes in the institutional fabric of society' (ibid.).

22. See Knoedler and Mayhew (1999). It is also the case that unions represent fewer workers, in relative terms, than at any time in the last century and continue to focus on securing full 'dinner pails' for their members rather than on effecting the broader social and economic change that might guarantee them greater economic security over the long run. See, for example, George DeMartino (various), Zweig and others.

23. See, for example, Juliet Schor (1999), *The Overspent America*, New York: Harper Perennial and Robert Frank (1999), *Luxury Fever*, New York: Free Press.

24. See, for example, Rick Tilman (1996) and Plotkin in this volume.

BIBLIOGRAPHY

Akin, William E. (1977), *Technocracy and the American Dream,* Berkeley: University of California Press.

Ayres, Clarence E. (1958), 'Veblen's theory of instincts reconsidered', in Douglas Dowd (ed.), *Thorstein Veblen: A Critical Reappraisal,* Ithaca, New York: Cornell University Press, pp. 25–37.

Barber, William J. (1985), *From New Era to New Deal: Herbert Hoover, the Economists and American Economic Policy, 1921–1933*, New York: Cambridge University Press.

Champlin, Dell and Janet Knoedler (2002), 'Wages in the public interest: insights from Thorstein Veblen and J.M. Clark', *Journal of Economic Issues,* **36**(4), 877–91.

Champlin, Dell and Janet Knoedler (eds) (2004), *The Institutionalist Tradition in Labor Economics*, Armonk, New York: M.E. Sharpe.

Chandler, Alfred D., Jr (1977), *The Visible Hand*, Cambridge, Massachusetts: The Belkap Press of Harvard University Press.

Chandler, Alfred D., Jr (1990), *Scale and Scope*, Cambridge, Massachusetts: The Belkap Press of Harvard University Press.

Copeland, Morris (1958), 'On the scope and method of economics', in Douglas Dowd (ed.), *Thorstein Veblen: A Critical Reappraisal,* Ithaca, New York: Cornell University Press, pp. 57–75.

Dowd, Douglas (1958a), 'Technology and social change: Japan and the Soviet Union', in Douglas Dowd, (ed.), *Thorstein Veblen: A Critical Reappraisal*, Ithaca, New York: Cornell University Press, pp. 283–301.

Dowd, Douglas (ed.), (1958b), *Thorstein Veblen: A Critical Reappraisal*, Ithaca, New York: Cornell University Press.

Dowd, Douglas (2002a), 'The strengths and weaknesses of Veblen', in Irving Horowitz (ed.), *Veblen's Century: A Collective Portrait,* New Brunswick, New Jersey: Transaction Publishers, pp. 17–39.

Dowd, Douglas (2002b), 'The theory of business enterprise', in Irving Horowitz (ed.), *Veblen's Century: A Collective Portrait*, New Brunswick, New Jersey: Transaction Publishers, pp. 195–202.

Dugger, William (2000), 'Class and evolution: an institutionalist view', in Ron Baiman, Heather Boushey and Dawn Saunders (eds), *Political Economy and Contemporary Capitalism*, Armonk, New York: M.E. Sharpe, pp. 36–41.

Edgell, Stephen (1975), 'Veblen's theory of evolutionary change', *American Journal of Economics and Sociology*, **34**(3), 267–80.

Edgell, Stephen (2001), *Veblen in Perspective: His Life and Thought*, Armonk, New York: M.E. Sharpe.

Fishman, Leslie (1958), 'Veblen, Hoxie, and American Labor', in Douglas Dowd (ed.), *Thorstein Veblen: A Critical Reappraisal*, Ithaca, New York: Cornell University Press, pp. 221–36.

Gruchy, Allan (1958), 'Veblen's theory of economic growth', in Douglas Dowd (ed.), *Thorstein Veblen: A Critical Reappraisal*, Ithaca, New York: Cornell University Press, pp. 151–78.

Hill, Forest (1958), 'Veblen and Marx', in Douglas Dowd (ed.), *Thorstein Veblen: A Critical Reappraisal*, Ithaca, New York: Cornell University Press, pp. 129–49.

Hodder, H.J. (1956), 'The political ideas of Thorstein Veblen', *The Canadian Journal of Economics and Political Science*, **22**(3), 347–57.

Jordan, John (1994), *Machine-Age Ideology*, Chapel Hill, NC: University of North Carolina Press.

Kaplan, Norman (1958), 'Idle curiosity', in Douglas Dowd (ed.), *Thorstein Veblen: A Critical Reappraisal*, Ithaca, New York: Cornell University Press, pp. 39–55.

Knoedler, Janet (1997), 'Veblen and technical efficiency', *Journal of Economic Issues*, **31**(4), 1011–26.

Knoedler, Janet T. (2002), 'The predatory economy of Thorstein Veblen', in Charles Sackrey and Geoffrey Schneider (eds), with Janet Knoedler, *Introduction to Political Economy*, Cambridge, Massachusetts: Dollars and Sense.

Knoedler, Janet and Anne Mayhew (1999), 'Thorstein Veblen and the engineers: a reinterpretation', *History of Political Economy*, **31**(2), 255–72.

Lamoreaux, Naomi (1985), *The Great Merger Movement in American Business, 1895–1904*, New York: Cambridge University Press.

Layton, Edwin (1971), *The Revolt of the Engineers*, Cleveland, Ohio: The Press of Case Western Reserve University.

Lazonick, William (1991), *Business Organization and the Myth of the Market Economy*, Cambridge: Cambridge University Press.

Mitchell, Wesley Clair (2002), 'The place of Veblen in the history of ideas', in Irving Horowitz (ed.), *Veblen's Century: A Collective Portrait*, New Brunswick, New Jersey: Transaction Publishers, pp. 41–63.

Morrison, Philip (1958), 'The ideology of the engineers', in Douglas Dowd (ed.), *Thorstein Veblen: A Critical Reappraisal*, Ithaca, New York: Cornell University Press, pp. 237–48.

Murphrey, Murray (1990), 'Introduction', *Thorstein Veblen, Instinct of Workmanship*, New Brunswick, New Jersey: Transaction Publishers.

Nabers, Lawrence (1958), 'Veblen's critique of the orthodox economic tradition', in Douglas Dowd (ed.), *Thorstein Veblen: A Critical Reappraisal*, Ithaca, New York: Cornell University Press, pp. 77–111.

Patsouras, Louis (2004), *Thorstein Veblen and the American Way of Life*, Montreal: Black Rose Books.

Rosenberg, Bernard (1953), 'Clarification of some Veblenian concepts', *The American Journal of Economics and Sociology*, **12**(2), 179–87.

Rutherford, Malcolm (1992), 'Thorstein Veblen and the problem of the engineers', *Revue Internationale de Sociologie*, Nouvelle Serie, **3**, 125–50.

Spindler, Michael (2002), *Veblen and Modern America,* London: Pluto Press.

Stabile, Donald R. (1982), 'Thorstein Veblen and his socialist contemporaries: a critical comparison', *Journal of Economic Issues*, **16**(1), 1–28.

Stabile, Donald R. (1984), *Prophets of Order*, Boston, MA: South End Press.

Stabile, Donald R. (1986), 'Veblen and the political economy of the engineer', *American Journal of Economics and Sociology*, **45**(1), 41–52.

Stabile, Donald R. (1987), 'Veblen and the political economy of technocracy', *American Journal of Economics and Sociology*, **46**, 35–48.

Stabile, Donald R. (1988), 'Veblen's analysis of social movements: Bellamyites, workers, and engineers', *Journal of Economic Issues*, **22**(1), 211–26.

Sweezy, Paul M. (1958), 'Veblen on American capitalism', in Douglas Dowd (ed.), *Thorstein Veblen: A Critical Reappraisal*, Ithaca, New York: Cornell University Press, pp. 177–97.

Tilman, Rick (1972), 'Veblen's ideal political economy and its critics', *American Journal of Economics and Sociology*, **31**, 307–17.

Tilman, Rick (1973), 'Thorstein Veblen: incrementalist and utopian', *American Journal of Economics and Sociology*, **32**, 154–69.

Tilman, Rick (1985), 'The utopian vision of Edward Bellamy and Thorstein Veblen', *Journal of Economic Issues*, **19**(4), 879–98.

Tilman, Rick (1996), *The Intellectual Legacy of Thorstein Veblen: Unresolved Issues*, Westport, Connecticut: Greenwood Press.

Tilman, Rick (2003), *Thorstein Veblen, John Dewey, C. Wright Mills, and the Generic Ends of Life*, Lanham, Maryland: Rowman and Littlefield Publishers.

Veblen, Thorstein (1892), 'Some neglected points in the theory of socialism', in *The Place of Science in Modern Civilization*, reprinted 1990, New Brunswick, NJ: Transaction Publishers.

Veblen, Thorstein (1899a), *The Theory of the Leisure Class*, reprinted 1973, Boston, MA: Houghton Mifflin Company.

Veblen, Thorstein (1899b), *The Theory of the Leisure Class*, reprinted 1994, New York: Dover Publications.

Veblen, Thorstein (1901), 'Industrial and pecuniary employments', in *The Place of Science in Modern Civilization*, reprinted 1990, New Brunswick, NJ: Transaction Publishers.

Veblen, Thorstein (1904), *The Theory of Business Enterprise*, reprinted 1978, New Brunswick, New Jersey: Transaction Publishers.

Veblen, Thorstein (1914), *Instinct of Workmanship*, reprinted 1990, New Brunswick, New Jersey: Transaction Publishers.

Veblen, Thorstein (1919a), *The Place of Science in Modern Civilization*, reprinted 1990, New Brunswick, New Jersey: Transaction Publishers.

Veblen, Thorstein (1919b), 'Bolshevism and the vested interests in America', *The Dial*, **67**(800), pp. 896ff.

Veblen, Thorstein (1919c), 'Bolshevism is a menace – to whom?', *The Dial*.

Veblen, Thorstein (1919d), *The Vested Interests*, reprinted 2002, New Brunswick, New Jersey: Transaction Publishers.

Veblen, Thorstein (1921), *The Engineers and the Price System*, reprinted 1990, New Brunswick, New Jersey: Transaction Publishers.

Veblen, Thorstein (1923), *Absentee Ownership*, reprinted 1964, New York: Augustus M. Kelley, Bookseller.

Veblen, Thorstein (1934), *Essays in Our Changing Order*, reprinted 1964, New York: Augustus M. Kelley, Bookseller.

Index